The Magic of [Catholicism]
Real Magic for De[vout Catholics]

Brother A.D.A.

Thavma Publications
Columbus, Ohio.
http://facebook.com/OccultCatholicism

- Holy Water 124
- Blessing One's Implements 136
- The Use of Candles 141

6. Angels and Saints 154
   - The Tripartite Church 155
   - Latria and Dulia 158
   - Working with the Angels 159
   - The Nine Orders 161
   - Calling on the Angels 171
   - Working with the Saints 177
   - Making Contact with the Saints 178
   - A List of Commonly-Invoked Saints 179

7. Tying it All Together 209
   - The Pentagram 183
   - Circumambulation 214
   - Alternate Signs of the Cross 218
   - Techniques of Meditation 223
   - The Lesser Ritual of the Pentagram 227
   - In Conclusion 231

8. Epilogue: A Magician's Spiritual Journey 232
   - The Rosary as an Analogy 233
   - The Five Keys and Spirituality 250

Appendix A: Long Quotes from the Endnotes 252
Appendix B: How to Draw the Pentagrams 259
Index 260

FOREWORD:

A long time ago, I had retired this book and never again thought it would see the light of day, let alone a new edition. Yet here it is: the fruit of much re-reading and many nights of hard labor!

When I was approached about republishing this book, the first thing I did was shake my head. When I seriously considered it and then looked over what I'd written, I shook my head even more. Once I finished shaking my head, I jumped in and fixed everything I felt was wrong.

The volume now in your hands the result of that fixing, so much so that over 90% of the book has been completely re-written. So much so that it can rightly be called a brand new book.

Statements of bias have been removed, all untranslated quotations have been translated, and all claims have been vetted against primary sources where available. When I have not been able to track down a primary source, I disclose that in the footnotes; the one exception is in dealing with tangential subjects where detailed discussion lies outside the scope of this writing. Unorthodox content is labeled as such, if any claims cannot be reconciled to Catholic doctrine without tortuous leaps in logic, those assertions have either been clearly marked or discarded.

The original format of "part-theology textbook/part-practical manual" has been retained, and when I make a doctrinal or theological claim, I endeavor to cite pre-Vatican II sources and the *Catechism of the Catholic Church* in tandem. Since many primary sources are now on the internet, I provide weblinks for as many as I've found, and give the date when I visited that site.

I'd like, however, to apologize in advance for one possible inconvenience. I often cut a lot out of my quotes because of space constraints, and in return I give the reader a way to check my sources quickly and see firsthand whether the source exists and/or is being quoted in context.

It is also hoped that by adding charts for the pronunciation of Hebrew, Greek, and Latin, the reader will be more able to engage the content of this book in particular and his or her faith in general. I firmly believe that a believer who doesn't critically engage their faith is no true believer, but merely parroting the beliefs of others. Even if the reader doesn't agree with my premises or conclusions, if this book moves them toward a more critical engagement, then my job is done.

I'd like to add that I make no claim to be 100% "faithful to the magisterium," because accepting any hierarchy's pronouncements with docility (CCC 87) is not in my nature. I will say that to the best of my knowledge and ability, I have striven to keep this book within the realm of Catholic orthodoxy. If such is not the case, I trust my readers will let me know soon enough!

Unless otherwise noted, all Biblical quotations are from the *New Revised Standard Version-Catholic Edition* (NRSV-CE), and I have used the most commonly-known translation for the *Catechism of the Council of Trent* (McHugh and Callan, 1923) and the standard translation of the *Catechism of the Catholic Church*. The majority of quotations from the Early Fathers and St. Thomas are from the translations found at the New Advent website. It is hoped that a common pool of texts may lead to a better mutual understanding, no matter how alike or different people's conclusions may be.

INTRODUCTION:

Upon seeing the title for this book, I'm sure many of you are probably jumping out of your seats, either with ecstasy over finding an orthodox treatment of the subject matter at hand, or with indignation over what you believe to be a "perversion of the True Faith." I'm sure that either way, the reader will more than likely find ample fuel for his or her respective position, especially if their mind was made up long before opening the pages of this volume. Yet for a reader who knows not to judge a book by its cover, it is hoped that there might be an opportunity for learning – or perhaps even for refreshing one's insights – into the spiritual and magical world at the heart of that institution which God, when He came down to earth, left unto us as His legacy under the care and feeding of St. Peter and his successors: the One, Holy, Catholic, and Apostolic Church.

Shrouded in ritual and steeped in two thousand years of tradition, the Catholic Church is probably the largest mystical Order in the world. She is the mother and nurturer of great men and women known for holiness of life – St. Augustine of Hippo, St. Francis of Assisi, St. Teresa of Avila, St. Therese of the Child Jesus, and thousands upon thousands of others – and her arsenal is replete with powerful rituals, spiritual helps, meditation techniques, and a rich treasury of spirituality explored by barely a fraction of those who identify as "practicing Catholics."

But that, precisely, is where the problem lies. Only a fraction of practicing Catholics dare to explore this spiritual treasury, perhaps because only a tiny fraction of the Church's population is aware this treasury exists! Rest assured that there is no cover-up, because Canon Law states that all Catholics have a right to learn the Faith's deeper teachings,[1] yet people in the pews aren't commonly made aware of these deeper things. Catechism classes barely teach a minimal knowledge of the Faith, with emphasis on "pay, pray, and obey." So even though the people have a right to learn, the people who wish to learn have a responsibility to seek out the knowledge and find it. This is as it should be; discipline is necessary to any spirituality, and the quest itself is an exercise in the value of discipline and determination.

With this in mind, we venture forward with this book.

Marktkirche ("Market Church") in Hanover, Germany. Consecrated 1360, and became a Lutheran church after the Reformation. Notice the inverted pentagram on the side of the tower. (see Chapter 7)

---

[1] 1983 Code of Canon Law, Canon 229, ss. 1 and 2. Laypersons have the right and responsibility to acquire knowledge of Christian doctrine according to their capacity to understand, and limits their right to deeper knowledge to what is taught in official Catholic institutions.

PRONUNCIATION OF HEBREW

Hebrew is read from right to left, and each consonant has a numerical value.

There are two main forms of pronunciation, the *Sephardi* and the *Ashkenazi*. This chart reflects the latter, which is used by the author.

CONSONANTS WITH NUMERICAL VALUES

א Alef (silent), 1
ב Ves (V), 2
בּ Bes (B), 2
ג Gimel (G), 3
גּ Gimel (G), 3
ד Dales (D), 4
דּ Dales (D), 4
ה Heh (H), 5
ו Vav (V), 6
וֹ Vav (O), 6
וּ Vav (U), 6
ז Zayin (Z), 7
ח Ches (CH, gutteral), 8
ט Tes (T), 9
י Yod (Y), 10
כ Khaf (CH, gutteral), 20
ך Khaf (at the end of a word), 20
כּ Kaf (K), 20
ל Lamed (L), 30
מ Mem (M), 40
ם Mem (at the end of a word), 40
נ Nun (N), 50
ן Nun (at the end of a word), 50
ס Samekh (S), 60
ע Ayin (silent), 70
פ Fe (F), 80
ף Fe (at the end of a word), 80
פּ Pe (P), 80
צ Tsade (TS), 90
ץ Tsade (at the end of a word), 90
ק Qof (K, Q), 100
ר Resh (R), 200
שׁ Shin (SH), 300
שׂ Sin (S), 300
ת Sav (S), 400
תּ Tav (T), 400

VOWELS (Under consonants. Alef used as an example)

אַ Patach (a in f*a*ther)
אָ Qamats (aw as in s*aw*)
אֵ or אֵי Tsere (ey as in th*ey*)
אֶ Segol (e as in m*e*t)
אִ or אִי Hiriq (i as in mach*i*ne)
וֹ or אֹ Holam (o as in al*o*ne)
אֻ Qubuts (oo as in m*oo*n)
וּ Mapiq (oo as in m*oo*n)
אְ Sheva (end of syllable or schwa)
אֲ Hataf Patach (quick "a" sound)
אֳ Hataf Qamats (quick "aw")
אֱ Hataf Segol (quick "eh")

PRONUNCIATION OF GREEK

The pronunciation given here is Modern Greek, used in conversation as well as the liturgy of the Greek Orthodox Church.

LETTERS

A, α Alpha (a as in f*a*ther)
B, β Beta (v as in *v*ictor)
Γ, γ Gamma (g as in *g*o)
    (Before e, e, i, y, y as in year)
Δ, δ Delta (th as in *th*at)
E, ε Epsilon (e as in m*e*t)
Z, ζ Zeta (z as in *z*ebra)
H, η Eta (i as in mach*i*ne)
Θ, θ Theta (th as in *th*eater)
I, ι Iota (i as in mach*i*ne)
K, κ Kapa (k as in *k*eep)
Λ, λ Lambda (l as in *l*ake)
M, μ Mi (m as in *m*usic)

N, ν Ni (n as in *n*ew)
Ξ, ξ Xi (x as in e*x*cellent)
O, o Omicron (o as in al*o*ne)
Π, π Pi (p as in *p*lastic)
P, ρ Rho (r as in *r*hyme)
Σ, σ Sigma (s as in *s*ail)
    (written ς at the end of a word)
T, τ Tav (t as in *t*alk)
Y, υ Ypsilon (i as in mach*i*ne)
Φ, φ Phi (f as in *f*un)
X, χ Chi (guttural ch or h sound)
Ψ, ψ Psi (ps as in oo*ps*)
Ω, ω Omega (o as in al*o*ne)

DIPTHONGS

αι (ey in th*ey*)
ει (i in mach*i*ne)
ηι (i in mach*i*ne)
οι (i in mach*i*ne)

υι (i in mach*i*ne)
αυ (like ov in "mazzel t*ov*")
ευ (like ev in *ev*erlasting)
ου (like oo in m*oo*n)

CONSONANT GROUPS

νδ (nd as in sa*nd*wich)
    (beginning of word, d as in *d*ata)
μπ (mb as in thi*mb*le)
    (beginning of word, b as in *b*oy)

γγ (ng as in a*ng*le)
    (beginning of word, g as in *g*o)
γκ (ng as in a*nk*le)
    (beginning of word, g as in *g*o)
τζ (dz as in a*dz*e)

When a diaresis mark occurs, it means two vowels should be pronounced individually. For example, *aï* should be pronounced "ah-ee" instead of "ay."

PRONUNCIATION OF LATIN

There are three major forms of Latin Pronunciation: the *Classical*, taught in classrooms; the *Continental*, most often heard in German-produced classical music recordings; and the *Italianate*, used in Church services, horror movies, and most occasions when one hears Latin. We give the Italianate, because it's the most commonly used outside the classroom.

VOWELS:
a as in f*a*ther
e *as* in th*ey* or m*e*t
i as in mach*i*ne

o as in al*o*ne
u as *oo* in m*oo*n
y as *i* in mach*i*ne

DIPTHONGS
ae like ey in th*ey*
oe like ey in th*ey*
au like ou in o*u*t

When a diaresis mark occurs, it means two vowels should be pronounced individually. For example, *aë* should be pronounced "ah-ay" instead of "ay."

Consonants are pronounced just like in English, with the exception of the following:
c before e, i, y, ae, or oe: like *ch* in *ch*air
ch always hard as in a*ch*e
g before e, i, y, ae, or oe: like *j* in *j*ar (or *su* in trea*su*re)
h is silent
j like y in *y*es
sc before e, i, y, ae, or oe: like *sh* in *sh*all
th always like *t* in *t*alk
ti before vowels, like *tsee*

Missale Romanum 2002 (*MR 2002*)
http://www.clerus.org/bibliaclerusonline/en/vf.htm
This is the official Latin text behind the "Novus Ordo" or "English Mass" celebrated in parishes today. The English translation is the 2011 *Roman Missal, Third Edition*, which replaced the *Sacramentary* of 1985 and 1974.

It should be noted that all these links are to official documents of the Church, or documents written by Saints of the Church and given official sanction. The reason for this is to give a starting ground that is common to all Catholics, and to give the reader directions to find the riches that we, as members of the Church, all share in common.

CHAPTER ONE: MAGIC AS DEFINED IN CATHOLICISM

THE IDEA OF MAGIC FOR A CATHOLIC

To the average Catholic, the term "magic" would be greeted with considerable antipathy, and the very idea of its practice is proscribed by Church law, written up as a violation of the First Commandment. Now if you understand, by the term "magic," the Church's definition of *"the art of performing actions beyond the power of man with the aid of powers other than the Divine,"*[2] then such an act would indeed be sinful.

If that were all there is to magic, then we could clearly end the discussion here and now; there would be no need for writing this book, would there? So – and just as obviously – there has to be more to the idea of magic not only in general, but also of import to a Catholic mentality.

To do this, let's start by looking at where the word "magic" comes from, and what caused the Church to react against it so strongly during the course of history.

HISTORY: PART I

Again referring to the Catholic Encyclopedia, the word "magic" comes to us from the Sumerian or Turanian word *imga*, which means 'deep' or "profound," and was used to refer to a class of Proto-Chaldean wizard-priests. In ancient Persia, this word became *magu* and was used for the priests of the Zoroastrian religion. From the Zoroastrians, the word passed to the Greeks and became μάγος (*mágos*), meaning a

---

[2] Arendzen, John. "Occult Art, Occultism." The Catholic Encyclopedia. Vol. 11. New York: Robert Appleton Company, 1911. http://www.newadvent.org/cathen/11197b.htm. (December 3, 2014).

magician (a practitioner of μαγεία – *mageía* – or "a person endowed with secret knowledge and power like a Persian magus.")[3]

This brings us to the Greek language of the New Testament. There are about six verses where magic is mentioned in the NT, and three separate words are used: μαγεία (*mageía*), φαρμακεία (*pharmakeía*), and περίεργα (*períerga*). Regarding the latter, it's only found once, in reference to the book burning in Acts 19:19. The word itself means "curiosities" and can be taken to mean "magical curiosities," but to say anything beyond that is mere speculation on the part of the translator.

On the word *mageía*, there is more we can say. The "wise men" that came to see Jesus are described as *mágoi* in the original Greek,[4] and it was by their art (presumably astrology) that they came to find Him. The New Testament also refers to two other individuals as *mágoi* – Simon Magus[5] and Elymas Bar-Jesus[6] – and although both are portrayed in a bad light, nowhere in the New Testament is the practice of *mageía* explicitly condemned.

What is condemned is *pharmakeía*, which refers to drugging, poisoning, or witchcraft, and is the root for our modern word "pharmacy." It is this word, describing a separate type of practice, that occurs in all verses where magical activity is explicitly proscribed.[7]

---

[3] Ibid.
[4] Matthew 2:1.
[5] Acts 8:9-13
[6] Acts 13:6-11
[7] Galatians 5:20; Revelation 9:21, 18:23, 21:8, 22:15

- Chapter One: Magic as Defined in Catholicism -

So the New Testament distinguishes between two separate types of magic, right? If this were all that's to it, we could happily go about our merry way. Yet we see that before the end of the first century, it is no defense to split hairs over what word the New Testament writers chose to ignore or condemn. In both the *Didache* and the *Epistle of Barnabas*, likely written before the end of the first century, *mageía* is condemned by name.[8]

Why is this? The answer lies in three factors: the change in the Greek language over the centuries, the type of magical formulae extant at the time, and the laws against magic in the Pagan-ruled society where the early Christians lived. For a change in language, we can again look to the Bible. In particular Psalm 96:5. The original Hebrew tells us:

כִּי, כָּל-אֱלֹהֵי הָעַמִּים אֱלִילִים; וַיהוָה, שָׁמַיִם עָשָׂה.

"For all the Gods of the peoples are as works of nought, but the LORD made the heavens."[9]

The Hebrew word אֱלִילִים, *elilim*, means "idols" or "worthless things" or "things of no value." The translation "works of nought" perfectly captures these senses of the word.

When the Hebrew Bible was translated into Greek in the 3rd century B.C. (the "Septuagint" or LXX version), the translators chose to word this verse differently:
ὅτι πάντες οἱ θεοὶ τῶν ἐθνῶν **δαιμόνια**, ὁ δὲ Κύριος τοὺς οὐρανοὺς ἐποίησεν.
"For all the Gods of the nations are spiritual beings, but the Lord made the skies."[10]

---

[8] *Didache* 2:2. *Epistle of Barnabas* 20:1
[9] Translation by the Jewish Publication Society (JPS), 1917
[10] My translation

Do you see what happened here? The verse was mistranslated from *elilim*, "works of nought," to *daimónia*, "spiritual beings." At the time, this new translation had a polemical meaning, as *daimónia* referred to a class of spiritual beings who were beneath the *theoí*, the gods. In this case, the intent was likely to say that Pagan gods were all inferior to the one true God. As the Greek language changed over the next few hundred years, the word *daimónia* came to take on the meaning of an evil spirit (the root of the English "demon"), which sets the stage for the next development.

The next development is seen in the types of magical texts extant at the time, collectively called the "Greek magical papyri."[11] The papyri date from roughly 200 B.C. to 400 A.D., and contain spells for summoning deities and commanding them as if they were *daimónia*, forcing them to bring women or kill the operator's enemies.[12] Another involves killing a cat and commanding the *daimónion* of that place to do the operator's bidding.[13] These papyri freely mingled Greek, Jewish, and Egyptian religious elements and often promised (or pursued) things that would be criminal even if magic weren't involved: theft of money, forcing women to have sex with the operator, and so forth.

This brings us to the third factor, the laws regarding magic that were already in place in Pagan societies. No religion starts in a vacuum, and no culture starts without imbibing at least some portion of the culture that preceded it; Catholicism is no exception.

---

[11] Many of the Greek magical papyri can be found online. An archive can be found here: http://hermetic.com/pgm/ (December 3, 2014)
[12] Papyrus "Acquiring a Supernatural Assistant." At the above website.
[13] Papyrus I.54.

Amongst the Pagans, the practice of magic had long been made illegal. As early as 2000 B.C., the Code of Hammurabi opens with a death penalty for anyone who casts a spell upon another (or death to the accuser, if the accusation is false).

> "If a man charge a man with sorcery, and cannot prove it, he who is charged with sorcery shall go to the river, into the river he shall throw himself and if the river overcome him, his accuser shall take to himself his house (estate). If the river show that man to be innocent and he come forth unharmed, he who charged him with sorcery shall be put to death. He who threw himself into the river shall take to himself the house of his accuser."[14]

In the Roman period, magic was deemed illegal almost from the start. In the Laws of the Twelve Tables, we find the following:

> "Whoever enchants by singing an evil incantation ... If anyone sings or composes an incantation that can cause dishonor or disgrace to another ... he shall suffer a capital penalty."[15]

Around 82 B.C. we encounter the *Leges Corneliae de Sicariis et Veneficiis* (Cornelian Laws against Assassins and Sorcerors), passed in the time of Lucius Cornelius Sulla and named after him. This section of the Cornelian Laws is lost to us in the original, but we know it through

---

[14] Translation by Robert Francis Harper, 1904. Available at: http://en.wikisource.org/wiki/The_Code_of_Hammurabi_%28Harper_translation%29. (Retrieved December 4, 2014).

[15] *Laws of the Twelve Tables*. Table VIII, laws 1a and 1b. The *Laws* were established circa 450 B.C., and are at the foundation of ancient Roman society. http://avalon.law.yale.edu/ancient/twelve_tables.asp. (Retrieved December 4, 2014).

way of quotation, particularly that of the 3rd-century author Julius Paulus:

> "15. Persons who celebrate, or cause to be celebrated impious or nocturnal rites, so as to enchant, bewitch, or bind anyone, shall be crucified, or thrown to wild beasts.
>
> "16. Anyone who sacrifices a man, or attempts to obtain auspices by means of his blood, or pollutes a shrine or a temple, shall be thrown to wild beasts, or, if he is of superior rank, shall be punished with death.
>
> "17. It has been decided that persons who are addicted to the art of magic, shall suffer extreme punishment; that is to say they shall be thrown to wild beasts, or crucified. Magicians themselves shall be burned alive.
>
> "18. No one shall be permitted to have books on the art of magic in his possession, and when they are found with anyone, they shall be publicly burnt, and those who have them, after being deprived of their property, if they are of superior rank shall be deported to an island, and if they are of inferior station shall be put to death; for not only is the practice of this art prohibited, but also the knowledge of the same."[16]

Around 16 B.C., once Augustus assumed the office of Pontifex Maximus, he gathered more than two thousand

---

[16] Julius Paulus. *Sententiae ad Filium*. Book V, Title 23, Sentences 15-18. http://droitromain.upmf-grenoble.fr/Anglica/Paul5_Scott.htm. (Retrieved December 24, 2014).

- Chapter One: Magic as Defined in Catholicism -

Greek and Latin writings on the subject of prophecy and had them burned, "retaining only the Sybilline books and making a choice even among those."[17]

It is from here that we pass into the Christian era, which merely saw the enforcement of already-existing laws.[18] In the face of such laws, the prevalence of magical writings explicitly invoking demons, the change in language to the word "demon" now meaning "an evil spirit," and the fact these texts promised results that Christians would consider sinful even if magic weren't involved – set against this background, is it any wonder why the Church was so dead-set against magic from the beginning?

This is why in 397 A.D., we have St. Augustine of Hippo attacking magic in his *De Doctrina Christiana* ("On Christian Doctrine"), in which he attacks magic as idolatry, superstition, and fellowship with demons,[19] that God turns His back on them and allows them to sink deeper into their sins, and that people must fear and shun "this fellowship with demons," barring the door against their return.[20]

---

[17] Suetonius. *The Life of Augustus*. 31:1. (Retrieved December 4, 2014).
http://penelope.uchicago.edu/Thayer/E/Roman/Texts/Suetonius/12Caesars/Augustus*.html.
[18] The *Codex of Justinian*, for example, records pronouncement of Constantius II in 357: "No one shall consult an haruspex, a diviner, or a soothsayer, and wicked confessions made to augurs and prophets must cease. Chaldeans, magicians, and others who are commonly called malefactors ... shall be put to death, and laid low with the avenging sword." Book IX, Title xviii, n. 5.
http://www.constitution.org/sps/sps15.htm. (December 5, 2014).
[19] *De Doctrina Christiana*. Book II, Chapter 20. (December 3, 2014)
http://faculty.georgetown.edu/jod/augustine/ddc2.html.
[20] *De Doctrina*, Bk II, ch 23.

During the Middle Ages, literature on magic didn't become any less demonic. If anything, it became explicitly more so. The names of God and Jesus were used to summon demons (now firmly seen as evil beings), in order to find hidden treasure or command women to being themselves to the operator in the nude. An example of such a book is a fifteenth-century manuscript known only as *Codex Latinus Monacensis 849* (or CLM 849), found at the Bavarian State Library in Munich, which contains spells explicitly demonic in nature.[21] Other magic books belonged to the "Solomonic Cycle," claiming that King Solomon trapped demons and used them to become rich and build his public works. Still others claimed to be written by Popes and sought to use the Mass to constrain the powers of hell for whatever the operator wanted.[22] In addition, we encounter forms of "low magic" based on superstition, involving actions such as urinating in a ditch in order to cause rain or sticking pins in a wax image in order to cause pain.[23]

This leaves us with small wonder that St. Thomas Aquinas took it upon himself to devote several chapters to magic in his *Summa Contra Gentiles* and the *Summa Theologiae*. In Book III of the *Summa Contra Gentiles*, St. Thomas spends several chapters analyzing the subject of magic, pointing out that magic can only be brought about by communication with spiritual intelligences,[24] that the intelligence in question cannot be naturally good because it

---

[21] The entire text of CLM 849 can be found in *Forbidden Rites: A Necromancer's Manual of the 15th Century* by Richard Kieckhefer. 1998. Pennsylvania State University Press. University Park, PA.
[22] For a study of various grimoires, see Waite, Arthur Edward. *Book of Ceremonial Magic*. 1913. The entire book can be found online at: http://www.sacred-texts.com/grim/bcm/index.htm. (December 3, 2014)
[23] Russell, Jeffrey Burton. *Witchcraft in the Middle Ages*. 1972. Cornell University Press.
[24] *Contra Gentiles*. Book III, chapter 105.

assists in acts of a sinful nature,[25] neither can the intelligence be naturally evil because all God's creation is good (though they can have an evil affect – "accident" – about them).[26]

In the *Summa Theologiae*, St. Thomas relies heavily on Augustine in declaring magic "unlawful and futile," that magic consists of "empty signs, a kind of covenant made with demons," and that "never did anyone acquire knowledge by means of the demons."[27] He seems to keep a level head when adjudicating whether an act is magical, though:

> "I answer that, in things done for the purpose of producing some bodily effect we must consider whether they seem able to produce that effect naturally: for if so it will not be unlawful to do so, since it is lawful to employ natural causes in order to produce their proper effects. But, if they seem unable to produce those effects naturally, it follows that they are employed for the purpose of producing those effects, not as causes but only as signs, so that they come under the head of "'compact by tokens entered into with the demons.'"[28]

So what's a devout Catholic to do? The proscriptions against magic are firm and go all the way back to the earliest centuries. Merely relying on the word choices found in Scripture is not a valid defense, as those word choices stand condemned elsewhere. I think it's more important to look to what the Church has historically called

---

[25] *Contra Gentiles*. Book III, 106.
[26] *Contra Gentiles*. Book III, 107.
[27] *Summa Theologiae*. Part II, II, Question 96. Article 1.
[28] *Summa Theologiae*. Part II, II, Q. 96, Art. 2 .

"magic" – that is, vain superstitions and fellowship with demons – and ask: "Is this the kind of thing I'm doing?" Only you will know the answer, but I can tell you that's not the stuff you'll find in this book.

Perhaps it'll help to continue our tour.

HISTORY: PART II

During the Renaissance, scholars such as Giovanni Pico della Mirandola attempted to rehabilitate magic through studying the classical texts with which the West had become re-acquainted. In 1486 Pico wrote in his manifesto, *Oration on the Dignity of Man*, that magic is "worship of the divine"[29] and elsewhere that "Nothing certifies us of the divinity of Christ more than magic and Kabbalah."[30] The heresy of that statement is obvious – he seemed to place Kabbalah and magic on the level of Tradition and the Gospels – but one can find a grain of truth in the statement: generally that as one continues to see his prayers answered and his needs met, so too does his faith in the divine become strengthened, and so too does he find himself more and more thankful to God.

It may help to look into Pico a little further. In his *Oration on the Dignity of Man*, he goes on to say that the ancients made note of two different and mutually exclusive kinds of magic, one which he called μαγεία (*mageía*) and the other which he called γοητεία (*goeteía*). The first kind he describes as lofty and noble, and the other as base and

---

[29] Pico, *Oratio quaedam elegantissima sive de hominis dignitate*, n. 231. (Retrieved December 3, 2014).
http://vserver1.cscs.lsa.umich.edu/~crshalizi/Mirandola/.
[30] *Conclusiones philosophicae, cabalisticae et theologicae sive theses DCCCC*, conclusion 9, section 38: «*nulla est scientia quae nos magis certificet de divinitate Christi quam magia et Cabala.*»

- Chapter One: Magic as Defined in Catholicism -

profane. *Mageía* uplifts man and glorifies God, while *goeteía* drags a man down, trafficking with evil spirits and is a petty perversion of divine and natural law.[31]

During this time we also see the infamous witch-hunting manual, the *Malleus Maleficarum* of Sprenger and Kramer, which discusses the possibility of a "lawful enchantment," and then has this to say:

> "And even if he uses adjurations, through the virtue of the Divine Name, and by the virtue of the works of Christ, His Birth, Passion and Precious Death, by which the devil was conquered and cast out; **such benedictions and charms and exorcisms shall be called lawful, and they who practise them are exorcists or lawful enchanters.**"[32]

After this, the *Malleus* continues to give conditions by which to determine whether the enchantment is lawful or not. In their essence they state that the operator must understand all the words being used, no untrue or superstitious statements may be used (the text cites an example that refers to Mary walking on the water), no demons may be invoked, and the result must rest in the hands of almighty God. From this, it is plain as day that

---

[31] *Oratio.* nn. 228-230.

[32] Part II, Quest. 2, Chap. 6. (*Quoted in full in Appendix A*) The reader would be well advised to use caution when dealing with the *Malleus;* its theology is suspect, and the book seems to be more of a forum for Kramer's sexual hang-ups than anything else. Fortunately, however, this is one of the more orthodox points of the book, and thus worth being quoted here. For more information about the history and actual use of the Malleus, please see Jenny Gibbons' online review of the *Malleus* at:
http://www.summerlands.com/crossroads/remembrance/_remembrance/malleus_maleficarum.htm. (Retrieved December 3, 2014)

the writers of this treatise clearly knew there was a magic usable by a devout Catholic, and provided that such Catholic magicians can be protected under the umbrella term of "lawful enchanter."

Closer to the modern period, in the mid-nineteenth century, we find Eliphas Levi (a defrocked Catholic Deacon whose real name was Alphonse Constat) saying roughly the same things about the distinction between the magician and the sorcerer. In his *Le Grand Arcane*, he cites the Church as a magical Order, writing that the Roman Church "alone possesses the monopoly of Transcendental Magic and its efficacious ceremonies. It charms demons with water and salt; with bread and wine it invokes God and constrains Him to become visible and palpable on earth; it imparts health and pardon with oil. It does yet more, for it creates priests and kings."[33]

On this subject, we even see Aliester Crowley, the deranged anti-Catholic genius (whose anti-Catholicism is strange when contrasted against his friendship with Fr. Montague Summers), recognized the distinction between magic and sorcery, referring to the latter as "witchcraft," and he stated quite clearly that witchcraft is illusory and denies the Holy Ghost the right to indwell His temple.[34]

So again we should ask, what's a devout Catholic to do? Only you will know the answer for yourself, but I will tell you this: the principles found in this book have no truck with demons, no truck with evil intentions, and no truck

---

[33] Levi, *Le Grand Arcane*, p. 52, translation by A.E. Waite.
[34] Crowley, Aliester. *Magick in Theory and Practice*, Book III, Ch. 4. "Witchcraft consists in treating it as the exclusive preoccupation of Magick, and especially in denying to the Holy Spirit his right to indwell His Temple."

- Chapter One: Magic as Defined in Catholicism -

with alien theologies. The intention is to fall within the *Malleus'* definition of a "lawful enchanter," and the work revolves around God as our true source and true end. The magic found in this book can thus be called "applied theology,"[35] because that's exactly what we'll be pursuing.

If this is what you've come looking for, then you're in the right place!

BASIC MAGICAL THEORY
Thus far, we have talked about the idea of the word "magic" in the minds of the Catholic faithful, as well as its conceptions and/or misconceptions. So now let's take a brief detour and discuss the more important aspects of magical theory.

Magical theory can pretty much be summed up by a fairly small number of "laws," many of which are hinted at (if not directly expressed) in Church teaching or in the Liturgy. These laws are, by name: the Law of Knowledge, the Law of Imitation, the Law of Mentalism, the Law of Correspondence, and the Law of Contagion. There are other laws as well, most of which are subsets of those here listed, but these are the ones which most hold our attention.

1. The Law of Knowledge
The Law of Knowledge is perhaps one of the most obvious, as it holds that the more a person knows about himself, the world, and the supernatural hierarchies, the more effective he will be as a magician. The magician is required to know himself, so that he truly knows his limitations, strengths,

---
[35] By "applied theology," I mean that we begin with theology, which Anselm defines as "faith seeking understanding" (i.e. a systematic understanding of the contents of our faith). The next step, the step of application, is to take that understanding and apply it to all aspects of our lives.

and weaknesses; likewise he must know as much as he can about the world around him and the spiritual hierarchies, so that he may better interact with them. While not much seen in practice, in theory the Church encourages people to know themselves, their world, and their faith.[36] Thus, the application of this law within Catholicism should be painfully obvious.

2. The Law of Imitation

Directly related to the Law of Knowledge is the Law of Imitation. This states that the more one acts like a given person, animal, or spirit, the more that person will become like that person, animal, or spirit. The two may be different at their root essence, but will become more and more alike in their similarities. Again, this should be obvious as to how we apply this Law in Catholicism, as from the cradle we are told to behave like Christ or Mary, to imitate them in virtue and in disposition, so that we may ever become more and more like them.

3. The Law of Mentalism

With the Law of Mentalism, however, we take our first steps into the realm of practical magic, for it is here that we are taught that the first source of everything we do is in our minds. "All energy follows thought, the universe is mental," is how this is often worded, and in practice it says

---

[36] In English-speaking countries, much of the problem with knowledge not being encouraged stems from the mid-nineteenth century "Devotional Revolution" that took place amongst Irish and Irish-American Catholics. Simultaneously organized on both sides of the Atlantic, it is directly responsible for the attitude of "pay, pray, and obey" prevalent amongst rank-and-file American Catholics today. This article at *The Irish Echo* provides a concise overview of the major players and how the "revolution" was implemented.
http://irishecho.com/2011/02/hibernian-chronicle-the-devotional-revolution-2/. (Retrieved December 5, 2014).

that when we can imagine something in our minds, without a doubt that it is done, then we shall have whatever we have imagined. This law has its place in Church teaching by way of the Scriptures, in which Our Lord says:

> "Truly I tell you, if you say to this mountain, 'Be taken up and thrown into the sea,' and if you do not doubt in your heart, but believe that what you say will come to pass, it will be done for you. So I tell you, whatever you ask for in prayer, believe that you have received it, and it will be yours."[37]

4. The Law of Correspondence

The Law of Correspondence is also important to the practicing magician, for it speaks of the correspondence between the various planes of existence. It is most commonly stated as the maxim: "As above, so below; as below, so above," or in its longer form: "That which is above is like unto that which is below; that which is below is like unto that which is above." By this, it means that the spiritual, mental, emotional, and physical planes each have an effect upon one another, and are brought into line so as to be a mirror image of each other. Thus, so as the higher planes may influence the lower by way of decree, so the lower planes influence the higher by way of petition.

This law is described In the Epistle to the Hebrews, where we read:

> "Thus it was necessary for the **sketches of the heavenly things** to be purified with these rites, but **the heavenly things themselves** need better sacrifices than these. For Christ did not enter a sanctuary made by human hands, a mere copy of the true one, but he entered into heaven itself,

---

[37] Mark 11:23-24

now to appear in the presence of God on our behalf."[38]

What's interesting here is that where the English gives us "sketches," the Greek and Vulgate texts both give us "copy." The Greek says ὑποδείγματα (*hypodeigmata*) and the Vulgate gives *exemplar*, both of which refer to a copy, model, or example. Thus the things of earth (in particular, the temple) are depicted as merely the copies – mirror images – of what is in heaven. On a similar note, it should be noted that the Church's liturgical worship is based on a model of worshipping God in heaven as closely as possible to how the Angels in heaven do, which worship is extracted from the descriptions given in Scripture. Both of these examples are applications of the Law of Correspondence, and shows how it applies both in the early and modern Church.

5. The Law of Contagion
Now lastly, we move on to what is called the "Law of Contagion." This law simply states that when one object comes into contact with another object, then the first object will continue to have an influence upon the second one. For example, in the Roman Ritual,[39] there are times when Holy or Baptismal Water becomes frozen, and thus may be mixed with a smaller quantity of unblessed water. By the law of contagion, the blessing from the Holy Water will influence the unblessed water, and thus the blessing will transfer.

---

[38] Hebrews 9:23-24

[39] The *Roman Ritual* (Latin: *Rituale Romanum*) is the book containing the official rites for Sacraments and blessings in the pre-Vatican II Church.

- Chapter One: Magic as Defined in Catholicism -

The same can be said for touching a person or object with a consecrated Host, and this is why in the Traditional Latin Mass, the priest keeps thumb and forefinger, the fingers that touch the Host, together after the Consecration and is careful never to touch anything else with those fingers until after he was washed his hands after Communion.[40] This is the Law of Contagion in action, perhaps in its highest and finest application.

So much for basic magical theory, but a quick introduction to the Laws of magic will prove helpful in later chapters, as well as in understanding the concepts and theories encountered there.

---

[40] *Ritus Servandus in Celebratione Missae.* Title VIII, n. 5. "… and soon, by the right hand only, he places the Host on the Corporal in the same place whence he lifted it, and from thence he keeps his thumbs and forefingers together (lit. – he does not disjoin thumbs and foregingers) – unless he must touch or pick up the Host – until the washing of fingers after Communion." (My translation). In 1967 this practice was made optional (*Inter Oecumenici*, n. 12).

Η Αγια Τρια, by Andre Rublev

CHAPTER TWO: CATHOLICISM AS AN INITIATORY MAGICAL SYSTEM

THE SACRAMENTS AS MAGICAL OPERATIONS
If we're going to refer to magic as "applied theology," we need to realize this: that application has to start by building a bridge between the heaven in which we believe and the earth on which we live. The image of this bridge is itself nothing new, as we find the word *pontifex* ("high priest," literally means "bridge-builder") being used in reference to bishops throughout Latin literature.[41] In fact, all validly consecrated bishops living today can trace themselves back to the bishops who consecrated them, and the ones who consecrated them, and so on, in a line that goes all the way back to one or other of the Twelve Apostles, who in turn were consecrated by Jesus Christ himself. The technical term for this is "apostolic succession," and this means that every bishop living today is both the builder of a bridge, and is also a brick in that bridge connecting us directly with Christ himself; we can thus say that the episcopate forms a living bridge between heaven and earth.

In addition to the bishops, we have the priests, men who are ordained by the bishops to be their assistants in helping them spread the word of God as well as in imparting God's grace and power to the people by means of the Sacraments. Thus as the bishops serve as bricks on the bridge, the priests and deacons serve as that bridge's support system, while the diaconate, subdiaconate, and minor Orders[42] serve as additional supports to the priesthood.

---

[41] The word *pontifex* comes from *pons*, "bridge," and *-fex*, a suffix meaning "maker."
[42] The Minor Orders as such – Porter, Lector, Exorcist, and Acolyte – were abolished in 1968 (Paul VI, *Pontificalis Romani*), but traces live on in the ministries of Lector, Catechist, and so forth.

The bridge is a useful illustration, but what is it good for? This is where the laity comes in. Through that bridge in which the clergy become as bricks and stone, help is made available for the laity to traverse into heaven and where, conversely, the laity may become imbued and endowed with the Divine power which travels downwards across that bridge. Thus the Catholic Church is far more than a hierarchical political organization; the Church as a whole – clergy and laity together – becomes a massive conduit through which people are empowered on earth and souls obtain into heaven.

If we can visualize the Church as a bridge between heaven and earth, it should behoove us to look further into how this bridge works, and more importantly how this bridge is used for our temporal and spiritual benefit.

In the first place, that means exploring the Sacraments, "visible signs of invisible graces," which in and of themselves are focused on the devotee's initiation into a spiritual current, and then his continued purification and ever closer connection with Deity. In doing so, we transcend the limitations of this world, its necessities, and its hardships, and as we draw even nearer to God, so too may we, as a side effect, gain power over those things and circumstances which once restrained us.

These powers, known as "mystical gifts," "gifts of the Holy Ghost," or "charisms,"[43] are a small part of what the Saints had which made them special. St. Alphonsus, for example,

---

[43] Joseph Cardinal Ratzinger (later Pp. Benedict XVI), *Letter to the Bishops of the Catholic Church on Some Aspects of Christian Meditation*, issued by the Congregation for the Doctrine of the Faith on October 15, 1989, nn. 24-25.

was a telepath[44] and a bi-locator, and St. Peter could heal people who so much as walked in his shadow.[45] These kinds of miracles are the stuff and stories that our parents raised us on, and it's easy to become sidetracked and begin looking for them as an end-all and be-all in themselves. This seems to be a common error, and we would do well to remember Our Lord's own words about "signs and wonders."[46] Rather, we should simply focus our attention on God the Son, who is the source of our life, or redemption, and in whose power we have been initiated through the waters of baptism, and we should never deviate from Him as our intention. When our hearts and minds are fixated on the proper focus, the rest will follow.

BAPTISM, CONFIRMATION, AND HOLY ORDERS AS SPECIAL INITIATIONS
1. Baptism

To begin in the proper place, we must first look upon Baptism, as it is the first and most important Sacrament, the gateway to all the others. The Nicene Creed tells us: "I confess one baptism for the remission of sins" (*Confíteor unum baptísma in remissiónem peccatórum.*), and this is a good starting point. Baptism, as Scripture tells us,[47] is the means by which we are reborn of water and the Holy Ghost, and in which we become the sons and daughters of a most loving Father. This is also our initiation into the spiritual powerhouse which is the Church, and our first step on that bridge leading to heaven.

---

[44] *Catholic Encyclopedia*, 1910: "His intercession healed the sick, he read the secrets of hearts, and foretold the future. He fell into a clairvoyant trance at Arienzo on 21 September, 1774, and was present in spirit at the death-bed in Rome of Pope Clement XIV."
[45] Acts 5:15-16
[46] John 4:48
[47] John 3:5-7

a. Initiatory Traditions and their Claims.

In many initiatory traditions, the world is seen as being steeped in a sort of darkness or infested with a problem of evil, and the tradition offers initiation into its ranks as a solution. Without debating the truth or falsehood of any of these other traditions, the fact remains that the Catholic Church makes exactly these types of claims:

1. Adam and Eve ate the forbidden fruit.
2. The world is in the darkness of sin because they did.
3. Jesus came to deliver us from sin.
4. Jesus founded the Church to continue His work.
5. Only through joining us will you find salvation.

According to Catholic theology, the world is seen as being steeped in a darkness caused by Original Sin, committed by Adam and Eve with side effects passed on to all humanity.[48] Through initiation into the Catholic Church, i.e. the sacrament of Baptism, we are washed away from the stains of that sin.[49] This in turn makes us reborn – the theological term is "regenerated" – and gives us the first step towards regaining that innocence which our first

---

[48] Council of Trent, Session V, anathema 2: "If any one asserts, that the prevarication of Adam injured himself alone, and not his posterity; … or that he, … has only transfused death, … but not sin also, … let him be anathema: – whereas he contradicts the apostle who says; 'By one man sin entered into the world, and by sin death, and so death passed upon all men, in whom all have sinned.' (Romans 5:12)"
https://history.hanover.edu/texts/trent/ct05.html. (December 5, 2014).

[49] *Catechism of the Council of Trent*, Part II, Ch II, n. 42: "…such is the admirable efficacy of this Sacrament that it remits original sin and actual guilt, however unthinkable its enormity may seem."
http://www.cin.org/users/james/ebooks/master/trent/tsacr-b.htm.
(Retrieved December 5, 2014). Also **Catechism of the Catholic Church (CCC) 1263**: "By Baptism *all* sins are forgiven, original sin and personal sins, as well as all punishment for sin."

parents had lost.[50] While Protestants and Modernists may believe Baptism is merely a symbolic act or a welcome into the community, Catholics believe that baptismal regeneration and the washing away of sin are quite real.

b. Original Sin.
Now I know that was a little complicated, so perhaps we should backtrack a little. In Catholic dogmatic theology, God created Adam and Eve in a state of "original justice" (*justitia originalis*) meaning He imbued them with Sanctifying Grace and four gifts that came along with it, called the "gifts of integrity" (*dona integritatis*).[51]

By name, these gifts are known as the *donum immortalitatis*, or freedom from death; the *donum impassibilitatis*, or freedom from suffering; the *donum scientiae*, or knowledge of God's will and intentions; and finally the *donum rectitudinis*, or freedom from base and impure desires.[52] In Genesis 3, when Eve allowed herself to be tempted by the serpent and Adam allowed himself to be tempted by Eve, this act caused them to become stripped of that innocence, which is why they felt such a sudden shame at being naked. As Bishop Challoner's comment on Gen. 3:7 – the aftermath of eating the fruit – tells us:

---

[50] *Catechism of the Council of Trent*, Part II, Ch II, n. 5: "…Thus it follows that Baptism may be rightly and accurately defined: The Sacrament of regeneration by water in the word. By nature we are born from Adam children of wrath, but by Baptism we are regenerated in Christ, children of mercy." **Also** CCC 1265: "Baptism not only purifies from all sins, but also makes the neophyte a 'new creature,' an adopted son of God, who has become a 'partaker in the divine nature,' member of Christ and co-heir with him, and a temple of the Holy Spirit."
[51] Ott, Ludwig. *Fundamentals of Catholic Dogma*. 1955. Translated from the German by Patrick Lynch. B. Herder Book Company. St. Louis, Missouri. Book 2, §18, n. 2
[52] Ott. Book 2, §18, n. 2, a-d.

> "And the eyes, etc... Not that they were blind before, (for the woman saw that the tree was fair to the eyes, ver. 6.) nor yet that their eyes were opened to any more perfect knowledge of good; but only to the unhappy experience of having lost the good of original grace and innocence, and incurred the dreadful evil of sin. From whence followed a shame of their being naked; which they minded not before; because being now stripped of original grace, they quickly began to be subject to the shameful rebellions of the flesh."[53]

We now have the basic backdrop for the problem. Mankind lost its innocence by way of Original Sin, and our entire spiritual process – the "economy of salvation" – is all about obtaining a "state of restored nature" (*status naturae glorificatae*), in which the soul completes its destiny, obtains the perfection of Sanctifying Grace, and sees the Immediate Vision of God.[54]

So much for Adam and Eve and Sanctifying Grace and Original Sin. What about the rest of us? The question has already largely been answered, though a little clarification never hurt anybody.

Catholicism teaches that after Adam and Eve ate the fruit and were cast out of Garden of Eden, their descendants (read: you and me) were inheritors of Original Sin. The effects we inherit are the inevitability of physical death and

---

[53] *The Holy Bible, Douay-Rheims Version*, 1582-1610; edited and with commentary by Bp. Dr. Richard Challoner, 1749-1752.
[54] Ott. Book 2, §19, n. 1, c.

the inclination to commit sin. We retain our free will,[55] but of our own power we are simply unable to enter into heaven.[56]

c. Effects of Baptism. Why Baptism is an Initiation.

This is where the Sacrament of Baptism comes in. We are quite literally washed clean of both the stain of Original Sin and any guilt from actual sin,[57] given Sanctifying Grace (regeneration), and adopted as children of God the Father.[58]

Yet there's a catch: Baptism doesn't fix everything. Even if we are given Sanctifying Grace, we are still inclined to commit sin (technically called "concupiscence"). Even if the guilt of sin is gone, we can still die. This is because we've been given grace, but Baptism is only the beginning of the process, not the end.[59]

---

[55] Council of Trent, Session VI, Canon 5: "If any one saith, that, since Adam's sin, the free will of man is lost and extinguished; ... let him be anathema." See also CCC n. 405; nn. 1730-1748; n. 2002.

[56] Council of Trent, Session VI, Canon 1: "If any one saith, that man may be justified before God by his own works, ... without the grace of God through Jesus Christ; let him be anathema." **See also** CCC nn. 2006, 2010-2011.

[57] *Catechism of the Council of Trent*, Part II, Ch II, n. 42. See above.

[58] *Catechism of the Council of Trent*, Part II, Ch II, n. 50: "But to return to the effects of Baptism, ... Our souls are replenished with divine grace, by which we are rendered just and children of God and are made heirs to eternal salvation." **See also** CCC nn. 1265-1266: "Baptism not only purifies from all sins, but also makes the neophyte 'a new creature,' an adopted son of God ... The Most Holy Trinity gives the baptized sanctifying grace, the grace of justification ..."

[59] *Catechism of the Council of Trent*, Part II, Ch II, n. 48: "The second reason why bodily infirmity, disease, sense of pain and motions of concupiscence remain after Baptism is that in them we may have the seed and material of virtue from which we shall hereafter receive a more abundant harvest of glory ..." **See also** CCC n. 1264: "Yet certain temporal consequences of sin remain in the baptized, such as

We earlier said that rites of initiation are characterized by a theme of death and rebirth, and Baptism is no exception. Around 55 A.D., St. Paul writes to the Christians in Rome, saying:

> "Do you not know that all of us who have been baptized into Christ Jesus were baptized into his death? Therefore we have been buried with him by baptism into death, so that, just as Christ was raised from the dead by the glory of the Father, so we too might walk in newness of life."[60]

In the Epistle to the Colossians, we are told:

> "When you were buried with him in baptism, you were also raised with him through faith in the power of God, who raised him from the dead."[61]

This belief in death and rebirth (often called "regeneration") can be traced throughout the early Church. In roughly 156 A.D., St. Justin Martyr writes of Baptism to the Emperor of Rome, where he also calls it "illumination:"

> "As many as are persuaded and believe that what we teach and say is true, and undertake to be able to live accordingly, ... are brought by us where there is water, and are regenerated in the same manner in which we were ourselves regenerated ... and may obtain in the water the remission of sins formerly committed, ... And this washing is called illumination, because they

---

suffering, illness, death, and such frailties inherent in life as weaknesses of character, and so on, as well as an inclination to sin ..."

[60] Romans 6:3-4
[61] Colossians 2:12.

who learn these things are illuminated in their understandings."[62]

We could produce a long list of quotes from the Early Fathers on this subject, too long for the scope of this volume. For our purposes, what matters is that we come to see the importance of our Baptism, both in connection to our salvation and the spiritual powerhouse to which it connects us.

Before moving on, we should probably point out that the word "initiation" wasn't in general use before Vatican II, as the emphasis was on regeneration and the washing away of sins. The modern concept of initiation seems to have its roots in *Divinae Consortium Naturae*, an apostolic constitution written by Pope Paul VI in 1971.[63] The document speaks of "sacramental initiations" throughout its text, although its primary intent is to introduce the new rite for Confirmation (a subject we'll discuss in the next section).

2. Confirmation.

In the post-Vatican II church, Baptism, Confirmation, and the Eucharist are called "Sacraments of Initiation,"[64] and these, we could say, quite easily correspond to one or another person of the Trinity. In Baptism, we become children of God the Father; in the Eucharist, we become nourished with the Body, Blood, Soul, and Divinity of God the Son; and in Confirmation we are made soldiers of Christ, strengthened and given the gifts of the Holy Ghost. One can easily notice that postconciliar discourse on the

---

[62] St. Justin Martyr, *First Apology*. Ch 61. (December 6, 2014). http://www.newadvent.org/fathers/0126.htm.
[63] Official English translation. Link retrieved December 6, 2014: https://archive.org/details/paulvisapostolic00cath
[64] CCC n. 1212

sacraments makes a point to use the word "initiation" frequently.

Amongst Traditionalist Catholics, the word "initiation" is never used in regard to the Sacraments,[65] but the ideas and principles are still present. If a Traditionalist were to designate any three Sacraments as initiations, the list would most likely be: Baptism, Confirmation, and Ordination; the reason is that these three are said to imprint an "indelible character" on the soul.[66] The first, Baptism, has already been described in the above section, in that through this sacrament we become members of the Catholic Church. Through Confirmation, ordinarily received when the confirmand is in adolescence,[67] the recipient is called upon to renew his baptismal vows, the Holy Ghost is called upon to help him through the troubles of life (i.e. "make him a soldier of Christ"),[68] and in post-Vatican II Catholicism he is now considered to be made a full Catholic.[69]

---

[65] Amongst some Traditionalists, refusing to use the word "initiation" is held as a badge of honor.

[66] Council of Trent, Session VII, Canon 10: "If any one saith, that, in the three sacraments, Baptism, to wit, Confirmation, and Order, there is not imprinted in the soul a character, that is, a certain spiritual and indelible Sign, on account of which they cannot be repeated; let him be anathema." See also **CCC 1121** which also confirms the sacramental character.

[67] The custom of when to administer Confirmation can vary according to country. In the western Church, the minimum age for Confirmation is the "age of reason," and explicitly stated to be seven years old. (Canon 788, *1917 Code of Canon Law*). The *1983 Code* re-iterates this (Canon 889, 2) by saying "use of reason," with the age of reason having been defined in Canon 97, 2.

[68] *Catechism of the Council of Trent*, Part II, Ch III, nn. 17-19: "The Effects of Confirmation." Compare and contrast the parallel section in **CCC 1302-1305**.

[69] CCC 1303.

- Chapter Two: Catholicism as an Initiatory Magical System -

While mainline Protestant denominations tend to see Confirmation as the day when children renew their Baptismal vows and profess the faith of their own free will (radical Protestants do not practice Confirmation, but see adults-only Baptism as the time to profess one's faith),[70] Catholics look on Confirmation as one of the seven Sacraments established by Jesus Himself when he sent the Holy Ghost down on the apostles in tongues of fire:

> "When the day of Pentecost had come, they were all together in one place. And suddenly from heaven there came a sound like the rush of a violent wind, and it filled the entire house where they were sitting. Divided tongues, as of fire, appeared among them, and a tongue rested on each of them. All of them were filled with the Holy Spirit and began to speak in other languages, as the Spirit gave them ability."[71]

At this first Pentecost,[72] the Apostles were given the fullness of the Holy Ghost, and then proclaimed the Gospel to the crowds in their own language. The Book of Acts is filled with testimonies of what the Apostles did after being filled with the Holy Ghost's power; this is the basis for Catholic Church's beliefs concerning Confirmation.

Fair enough. But let's ask another question: what does Confirmation do for us? It's not strictly necessary for

---

[70] Instead of "mainline" and "radical," it may be better to distinguish between those who practice infant Baptism (pedobaptism) and those who practice "believers-only" Baptism (credobaptism).

[71] Acts 2:1-4

[72] Actually, the Jewish festival of Shavuos (שָׁבוּעוֹת), held 50 days after Passover and celebrating Moses' receiving the Law on Mount Sinai. Early Greek translations of the Bible rendered Shavuos as *Pentekoste* (Πεντηκοστή, "fiftieth"), whence we derive the name of the Christian feast-day (Latin *Pentecostes*) along with our English word "Pentecost."

salvation,[73] so what's the point? I would answer that the point depends on what you're looking for.

If you're only looking to get into heaven, then Baptism is the only Sacrament that's strictly necessary. Since Baptism cleans the soul, it stands to reason that if one dies immediately after being baptized, that person automatically gets into heaven. This means that if Confirmation wasn't instituted as necessary for salvation, then it must exist for some other reason.

a. Not a "Coming of Age" Ceremony.
Neither is Confirmation a "coming of age" ceremony, like a Bar Mitzvah or a Quinceañera, though it's often treated like one. In the Book of Acts, we read:

> "Now when the apostles at Jerusalem heard that Samaria had accepted the word of God, they sent Peter and John to them. The two went down and prayed for them that they might receive the Holy Spirit (for as yet the Spirit had not come upon any of them; they had only been baptized in the name of the Lord Jesus). Then Peter and John laid their hands on them, and they received the Holy Spirit."[74]

One could get the sense from this passage that Confirmation (reception of the Holy Ghost) is a completion

---

[73] *Catechism of the Council of Trent*, Part II, Ch III, n. 14: "First, it is necessary to teach that this Sacrament is not ... utterly essential to salvation." And n. 15: "Confirmation has not been instituted as necessary to salvation." **CCC n. 1129** quotes Trent (Sess. VII, 4) in a general statement that the Sacraments are necessary for salvation, but seems not to pronounce on the necessity of Confirmation for salvation one way or the other.

[74] Acts 8:14-17.

of what one received in Baptism. This sense is confirmed later in the Book of Acts:
> "While Apollos was in Corinth, Paul passed through the interior regions and came to Ephesus, where he found some disciples. He said to them, 'Did you receive the Holy Spirit when you became believers?'"[75]

Reading through the various accounts in Acts, the impression forms that Confirmation normally took place immediately after Baptism, and if we follow the course of Church history, we find that impression would be right. In the late second century, Tertullian tells us:
> "After this, when we have issued from the [baptismal] font, we are thoroughly anointed with a blessed unction,— (a practice derived) from the old discipline, wherein on entering the priesthood, men were wont to be anointed with oil from a horn, ever since Aaron was anointed by Moses. ... Thus, too, in our case, the unction runs carnally, (i.e. on the body,) but profits spiritually; in the same way as the act of baptism itself too is carnal, in that we are plunged in water, but the effect spiritual, in that we are freed from sins."[76]

In the early third century, Hippolytus likewise establishes that Confirmation (the anointing with the "Oil of Thanksgiving") takes place immediately after Baptism.[77]

---

[75] Acts 19:1-2
[76] Tertullian. *De Baptismo*. Chapter 8. (Retrieved December 6, 2014) http://www.newadvent.org/fathers/0321.htm.
[77] *Apostolic Tradition*. 21:19-25. (Retrieved December 6, 2014). http://www.bombaxo.com/hippolytus.html.

In the middle of the third century, Cyprian of Carthage speaks of Confirmation as a necessity:
> "It is also necessary that he should be anointed who is baptized; so that, having received the chrism, that is, the anointing, he may be anointed of God, and have in him the grace of Christ."[78]

Our final quote will come from the middle of the fourth century, written by Cyril of Jerusalem:
> "And to you in like manner, after you had come up from the pool of the sacred streams, there was given an Unction, the anti-type of that wherewith Christ was anointed; and this is the Holy Ghost;"[79]

As with our discussion of Baptism as a rite of rebirth, the list of quotations here could go on and on, but I think we've made our point that Confirmation can never have been conceived as a "coming of age" ceremony or a "rite of passage." Rites of passage routinely mark various stages in a person's life, which necessitates a certain amount of time to have passed between one rite and the next. When we consider that Confirmation was originally administered immediately following Baptism, the two could not have been intended as separate rites of passage. Doubly so when

---

[78] *Epistle 69*, 2. http://www.newadvent.org/fathers/050669.htm. (Retrieved December 6, 2014). Cyprian should be taken with a grain of salt, as he argued that Baptisms and other Sacraments conferred by heretics is invalid, giving rise to the belief in "Cyprianism" found in the Eastern Orthodox Churches to this day (i.e. the belief that non-Orthodox are not even baptized and their priests are not ordained). It's ironic that he should become a heretic while trying to defend the Church against heresy!

[79] *Catechetical Lectures*. 21:1. (retrieved December 6, 2014). http://www.newadvent.org/fathers/310121.htm.

we realize that most Baptisms and Confirmations in the first century were (of necessity!) adult converts, with infant Baptism only becoming the rule once those converts had children and, of course, their children's children. While infant Baptism can be dated to the early period,[80] it would be at least a century before the numbers would allow it to become the rule rather than the exception.

We can also infer that between the practice of infant Baptism and the above quotes, infants were confirmed immediately after they were baptized. This is the practice of the Eastern Churches even to this day (where it is called "Chrismation"),[81] and was also the custom in Spanish-speaking countries as recently as 1932,[82] when the Sacred

---

[80] Acts 16:15, 18:8; 1 Corinthians 1:16 describe the Baptism of entire households, and this is traditionally interpreted to favor infant Baptism because households typically number children amongst their members. This interpretation is supported by a number of Fathers when describing the practice of the Early Church. See Iranaeus, *Adversus Haereses*, II, 22; Origen, *Homily on Romans*, 5:9 and *Homilies on Leviticus*, 8:3; Hippolytus, *Apostolic Traditions*, 21:4; Cyprian's *Letter to Fidus*; Tertullian's *Against Marcion*, 1, 28. Generally the Church of the first centuries defended infant Baptism as a matter of course, and characterized the opposing view as anathema.

[81] *Orthodox Church in America*, official website: "It is also the Orthodox tradition that the mysteries of baptism and chrismation, called officially "holy illumination," are fulfilled in the immediate reception by the "newly-enlightened" of Holy Communion in the eucharistic liturgy of the Church. This is the case with infants as well as adults." http://oca.org/orthodoxy/the-orthodox-faith/worship/the-sacraments/chrismation. (Retrieved December 6, 2014).

[82] *Instruction of the Sacred Congregation of Rites*, May 24, 1934, n. 3: "Since there thrives in Spain and other places, especially South America, the custom of administering Confirmation to children before the use of reason, even immediately after Baptism . . . it had been asked (of the Sacred Congregation of Rites) whether such a custom may still be observed." The response, given on February 27, 1932, was: Whether the most ancient custom flourishing in Spain and other places

Congregation of Rites was asked to discuss whether the practice may be allowed to continue.

b. Separation of Confirmation from Baptism.
It was in the West that Confirmation came to be separated from Baptism, largely out of a desire to retain the earlier practice of bishops administering the Sacrament. Originally it was the bishop who baptized and confirmed, but as the Church grew it became impossible for bishops to be present at all baptismal celebrations. Therefore Baptism and Confirmation were split into two separate Sacraments: Baptisms were left to the priests, but in order to maintain the traditional practice, the bishops confirmed when they visited the local parish.[83] By the fifth century, we find the separation between Baptism and "Anointing" discussed by Pope Innocent I:

> "Priests, when baptizing, may anoint the baptized with chrism, previously consecrated by a bishop: but they must not sign the brow with the same oil; this belongs to the bishop alone, when he gives the Paraclete."[84]

In 439, the provincial Council of Riez (in modern-day southeastern France), in dealing with the illicit consecration of Armentarius as bishop of Embrun, specifically uses the word "Confirmation" and says that in whatever parish church he is placed, "it is conceded to him alone to confirm the neophytes (those newly baptized)" and again, "he has

---

of administering Confirmation before the use of reason can still be observed, the Fathers respond: Yes." (My Translation)
[83] The history of this split is summarized in CCC 1290.
[84] Innocent I, *Epistola ad Decentium*. Quoted in *Summa Theologiae*, III, 72, 3.

the right of consecrating virgins and confirming neophytes."[85] Since the "right of consecrating virgins" historically belongs to the bishop alone, we see the custom of the bishop administering confirmation is taking on the force of ecclesiastical law.

In the late sixth/early seventh century, Pope St. Gregory the Great writes to bishop Januarius of Caligari, saying:
> "… let the presbyters anoint those who are to be baptized on the breast, that the bishops may afterwards anoint them on the forehead."[86]

In the eighth century, the Gregorian-Hadrian Sacramentary contains a rubric restricting confirmation to the bishops:
> "And the infant is clothed in its garments. If a bishop is present, [the infant] must be confirmed at once with chrism, and receive communion afterwards. If the bishop is not present, then let him receive communion from the priest."[87]

This separation of Sacraments, further justified by the developing theology that Baptism "cleans" while Confirmation "completes and strengthens," paved the way for adolescent Confirmation. This was further enforced by rubrics in local rites such as Sarum either said Confirmation could take place if the child was "of age," or enjoined the parents or godparents to teach the child the

---

[85] Council of Riez. Canons 3 and 4. (my translation).
[86] Gregory the Great. *Registrum Epistolarum*. IV, 9. http://www.newadvent.org/fathers/360204009.htm. (December 6, 2014)
[87] Wilson, H.A. *The Gregorian Sacramentary*. Henry Bradshaw Society, Volume XLIX. 1915. p. 163. Full text available online at: https://archive.org/details/gregoriansacrame00cath. (December 6, 2014)

Our Father, Hail Mary, and Apostles' Creed before being confirmed:

> "If the Bishop is present he must confirm [the child], if he is of age, and then give him communion."[88]

And:

> "If [the child] is an infant, it falls to the father and mother to protect the child (or have the child protected) from fire and water and all other dangers until the age of seven years ... similarly the godfather and godmother are enjoined to teach the infant the Our Father, Hail Mary, and Apostles' Creed, or have them taught; for chrismation is deferred to the Church; because he may similarly be confirmed as soon as the Bishop arrives ..."[89]

c. Spiritual Effect of Confirmation.

So we know that Confirmation is neither necessary for salvation, nor is it merely a "coming of age" ceremony, and we've already rejected the Protestant understanding that Confirmation is a rite where the candidates profess the vows made for them as infants in baptism. This leaves only one option: *Confirmation has an actual spiritual effect.*

What this spiritual effect is, we've largely already discussed, and we see the thread develop from the Scriptural quotes we've shared, the writings of the Early Fathers, the *Catechism of the Council of Trent*, and the *Catechism of the Catholic Church*. Through Confirmation

---

[88] *Manuale et Processionale ad Usum Sarum*. The Surtees Society. Volume LXIII. 1875. p. 17. (my translation) Available online at: https://archive.org/details/manualeetproces01minsgoog. (12/6/2014).

[89] Ibid, my translation. The translation is a bit awkward, because the Latin of the passage is itself a bit awkward.

we receive yet another level of initiation, one that fulfills and adds greater grace to the one we received in Baptism, and one that puts us into deeper connection with divine power into which we've been initiated, and one which stands to give us more strength in our faith, in our practice, and in our lives.

d. Grace as Energy. A Segue into the East.
Perhaps we should pause here and say a word about the term "grace." In the western Church, we tend to see grace in static terms, as a "favor, free and undeserved help" that God gives us.[90] The Eastern Churches have a competing – yet not exactly incompatible – concept: grace is the very energies of God Himself,[91] a "direct manifestation of the living God Himself."[92]

Now think about that and let it sink in for a moment. It is not merely a gift of forgiveness that God's giving you, nor is it merely a gift of salvation, nor a gift of various helps to make it through your life. When God gives you His grace, *He is actually giving you Himself.*[93]

This understanding of grace, right here, is what should answer any questions about Confirmation: it opens the soul of the recipient for a greater participation in the life – in the

---

[90] CCC 1996.
[91] The idea of God's energies (often translated "operations") can be found in St. Basil the Great, *Letter 234*, 1. Also in Gregory of Nyssa, *Against Eunomius*. These can be found online at New Advent.
[92] A good introductory source for this is *Excerpts from The Orthodox Church*, which summarizes Abp. Ware's account of Orthodox history, and is found in the internet at: (Retrieved December 7, 2014). http://www.fatheralexander.org/booklets/english/history_timothy_ware _1.htm. This is covered in the section where Ware discusses Gregory Palamas and the Hesychast controversy.
[93] The CCC begins to engage the Eastern idea of grace=energy in n. 1997: "Grace is *a participation in the life of God.*"

very energies – of God Himself. Through this anointing, we are given the grace – in fact a *huge* bundle of energies – connected with the Holy Ghost and known as the "seven gifts," and brought into the maturity of Christian life.

e. What Confirmation Can Do.
Thus as in Baptism we are made babes in God the Father, and in Holy Communion we are nourished by God the Son, so in Confirmation are we lead to maturity by God the Holy Ghost, being given a wider direct interaction with God's energies so as even more to cooperate with sanctifying grace and be transformed from corruptible human nature, and back into the image of God.

Thus, as the Apostle asks us: "Have ye received the Holy Ghost, since ye have believed?"[94]

3. Holy Orders
In Baptism and Confirmation, the candidate is initiated into the Church and is then made a complete Catholic. In Holy Orders – also called "Order" or "Ordination" – the recipient takes a part in the Church's leadership and becomes part of the bridge we discussed earlier, that bridge by which the faithful traverse into heaven and receive God's grace – His energies – here on earth below.

a. The Sacramental Character.
Up to this point, the reader may have noticed that I used the word "character" in relation to these Sacraments. Since the doctrine of the "indelible sacramental character" is so important in regard to Holy Orders, it may be prudent to discuss this in more detail before proceeding.

---

[94] Acts 19:2 (KJV)

Chapter Two: Catholicism as an Initiatory Magical System

Traditionally, the three Sacraments of Baptism, Confirmation, and Order are referred to as *Character Sacraments*, because they imprint an indelible mark on the soul of the recipient. This mark is technically referred to as the *Sacramental Character*.

b. History: Persecutions, the Lapsed, Heresy, Schism.

The theology of the sacramental character finds its roots in Scripture[95] and its earliest best expression in St. Augustine, who in turn was responding to a controversy that extended back much earlier than his own time, and stems from two causes.

In the early Church, the situation for Christians could go from toleration to persecution at the drop of a hat. As with all things pertaining to human nature, there were those who would renounce their faith under persecution, while they quickly go back to calling themselves "Christians" again during the next period of toleration. This caused the Church to ask: "Should we let them back in?"

The second cause, also pertaining to human nature, pertains to heresy. Almost as soon as the Jesus Movement spread outside Jerusalem, people broke off into sects: some over a leadership dispute, and others professing one or another leader's personal take on Jesus' teachings. These sects are technically known as "schismatic" (when they break away but do not alter their doctrine) or "heretical" (when they do alter the doctrine).[96]

---

[95] 1 Timothy 4:14: "Do not neglect **the gift that is in you**, which was given to you through prophecy with the laying on of hands by the council of elders." (Emphasis mine). The "the gift that is in you" is what the Church came to interpret as the sacramental character.

[96] The difference between a *heretic*, an *apostate*, and a *schismatic* is defined thusly in the 1917 *Code of Canon Law*, Canon 1325 §2 (my translation): "A heretic is one who, after being baptized, retains the

The issue of people splintering off into sects is not unique to Christianity. For example, Josephus mentions four "Denominations" of Jews in his time: Pharisees, Saducees, and Essenes.[97] Within Christianity, the New Testament letters contain warnings about sects and heresy, and the beginning of St. Paul's First Letter to the Corinthians is perhaps the best example:

> "For it has been reported to me by Chloe's people that there are quarrels among you, my brothers and sisters. What I mean is that each of you says, 'I belong to Paul,' or 'I belong to Apollos,' or 'I belong to Cephas,' or 'I belong to Christ.' Has Christ been divided? Was Paul crucified for you? Or were you baptized in the name of Paul?"[98]

Of course, when a group splinters off into various sects or factions, there will be members who want to "jump ship" from one sect to another. Just like the issue of persecutions, this raised two questions: first, "Are they really Christians" and second, "Should we let them (back) in?"

---

name of 'Christian' while obstinately denying or doubting one or other of the truths to be believed with divine and catholic faith.

"If [he or she] leaves the Christian faith entirely, [he or she is] an apostate.

"Lastly, if [he or she] rejects submission to the Supreme Pontiff or refuses communion with the members of the Church subject to him, [he or she] is a schismatic."

These definitions are retained with slight re-wording in the 1983 *Code of Canon Law*, Canon 751 and re-iterated in CCC 2089

[97] Josephus, *The Wars of the Jews*, Book I, 8:2. (December 8, 2014). http://www.gutenberg.org/files/2850/2850-h/2850-h.htm.

[98] 1 Corinthians 1:11-13

Chapter Two: Catholicism as an Initiatory Magical System

In 250 A.D. the Roman emperor Decius sought to restore traditional Roman piety, and he issued an edict which had the result of a massive empire-wide persecution against Christians. We do not know if persecution against Christians was intended, but we do know it had massive consequences for the Church; many Christians either sacrificed to the Roman gods or renounced Christianity, later to join one or other heretical sect. Because of this, the question of whether to accept baptisms performed by heretics boiled over into a full-blown controversy.

The churches in Africa and Asia Minor, represented by Bishop Cyprian of Carthage, took the position that Baptism performed by heretics was invalid. When writing to Bishop Quintus of Mauritania on the subject, he says:

> "For I know not by what presumption some of our colleagues are led to think that they who have been dipped by heretics ought not to be baptized when they come to us, for the reason that they say that there is one baptism which indeed is therefore one, because the Church is one, and there cannot be any baptism out of the Church. ... But we say that those who come thence are not re-baptized among us, but are baptized. For indeed they do not receive anything there, where there is nothing; but they come to us, that here they may receive where there is both grace and all truth, because both grace and truth are one."[99]

Cyprian also wrote to Pope St. Stephen I in 255 A.D., regarding a local council that had taken place in Carthage, where he says:

---

[99] Cyprian of Carthage, *Epistle 70*, n. 1. (retrieved December 8, 2014). http://www.newadvent.org/fathers/050670.htm.

> "But that that is not baptism which the heretics use; and that none of those who oppose Christ can profit by the grace of Christ; has lately been set forth with care in the letter which was written on that subject to Quintus, our colleague, established in Mauritania."[100]

We do not have Stephen's response, but Cyprian quotes from it in a letter to Pompey:

> "... [Stephen] moreover added this saying: 'If any one, therefore, come to you from any heresy whatever, let nothing be innovated (or done) which has not been handed down, to wit, that hands be imposed on him for repentance; since the heretics themselves, in their own proper character, do not baptize such as come to them from one another, but only admit them to communion.' He forbade one coming from any heresy to be baptized in the Church; that is, he judged the baptism of all heretics to be just and lawful."[101]

In the fourth century, we come to the persecution under Diocletian, the most severe against Christians in Roman history. This caused a rift between those Christians who lapsed from their faith under pressure (called *traditores*, "traitors"), and those who remained "pure." The best-known of these "pure" groups, the Donatists, existed in North Africa from around 311 A.D. and until the Arab conquest of the region in the seventh and eighth centuries.

The Donatists were rigorists who believed that a sinful minister could not confer a valid sacrament, and "sin"

---

[100] *Epistle 71*, n. 1
[101] *Epistle 73*, nn. 1-2.

- Chapter Two: Catholicism as an Initiatory Magical System -

included both heretics and those they branded *traditores*. The Church was for the pure, while sin was something outside the door.[102] They followed Cyprian's lead in this line of thinking, and it was against them that Augustine articulated the doctrine of the indelible sacramental character.

In his *Three Books Against the Epistle of Parmenianus*, St. Augustine likens the sacramental character to the mark of military service, which cannot be removed from the soldier's flesh even if he deserted, was discharged, or if he offended the emperor; the man carries the mark permanently, and if he re-enters the military service, the old mark is simply recognized and approved.[103]

For Augustine, the Sacraments of Baptism (and by extension, Confirmation) and Holy Orders imprint a mark on the recipient's soul which can never be removed, nor can it be surrendered under any circumstances.

This theology had already become standard by the thirteenth century, when St. Thomas writes in the *Summa Theologiae* that the Sacraments of the New Law imprint a character, that the character cannot be blotted out, and that

---

[102] Our main surviving source for our knowledge of Donatist doctrine is Optatus of Milevis' *Against the Donatists*. (December 9, 2014). http://www.tertullian.org/fathers/optatus_01_book1.htm.

[103] St. Augustine, *Contra Epistolam Parmeniani Libri Tres*, ii, 29: "But if strong be the character on his body that the panicked [soldier], trembled, not performing his duty; and he flew to the emperor's mercy and by effusive prayer, having obtained favor, again started to take up military service, is the mark again re-impressed upon the man now freed and corrected, or is not the mark more ably recognized and approved? And do the Christian sacraments adhere any less strongly than these bodily things?" (Original Latin Retrieved December 9, 2014) http://www.augustinus.it/latino/contro_parmeniano/index2.htm.

the three Sacraments that impose a character are Baptism, Confirmation, and Order.[104]

We see the doctrine of the sacramental character spelled out in Eugene IV's Decree for the Armenians at the Council of Florence in 1439:

> "Among these sacraments there are three, baptism, confirmation, and orders, which imprint an indelible sign on the soul, that is, a certain character distinctive from the others. Hence they should not be repeated in the same person. The remaining four do not imprint a sign and admit of repetition."[105]

Finally we come to the Council of Trent, when the doctrine of the sacramental character was officially defined, which brings us full circle to the present day.[106] In spite of modernist-leaning post-Vatican II theologians' attempts to weaken or undermine the doctrine,[107] it is still very much a part of official Catholic teaching.[108]

---

[104] *Summa Theologiae.* III, 63.
[105] Eugene IV, *Exsultate Deo*. Found in the *Enchiridion Symbolorum*, known in English as Denziger's "Sources of Catholic Dogma." Cited in the 1954 edition as DZ 695. (Standard abbreviation for this book is "DZ"). Available online. (Retrieved December 9, 2014)
https://archive.org/details/TheSourcesOfCatholicDogma.
[106] Council of Trent, Session VII, can. 9: "If any one saith, that, in the three sacraments, to wit, Baptism, Confirmation, and Order, there is not imprinted in the soul a character, that is, a certain spiritual and indelible Sign, on account of which they cannot be repeated; let him be anathema."
[107] For an example, see McBrien, Richard, *Catholicism.* 2nd edition. 1994. Harper San Francisco. p. 795, "The term *character* does not refer to an indelible mark on the soul, as some catechisms had it. It is simply the word used to describe the permanent effect of three sacraments: Baptism, Confirmation, and Holy Order." This statement is self-contradictory in this author's opinion, since it's impossible to have a permanent effect without leaving some kind of a mark. **See also** Hill,

c. Effects of the Character.

As this applies to the Sacrament of Baptism, the mark on the soul is one that:

> "... has a twofold effect: it qualifies us to receive or perform something sacred, and distinguishes us by some mark one from another. In the character impressed by Baptism, both effects are exemplified. By it we are qualified to receive the other Sacraments, and the Christian is distinguished from those who do not profess the faith."[109]

If we place this description in an initiation paradigm, this means that, by "being qualified to receive the other sacraments" – or as CCC 1273 says consecrated "for Christian religious worship" – we see the character of Baptism walks the recipient through a proverbial door, a door of being put in contact with God's graces and the source of energy that created the world. The Baptized person has just put made his or her first step on the bridge that leads to heaven-ward.

In Confirmation, yet another character is imprinted, though as Confirmation completes the grace of Baptism,[110] it could be said its character is merely the second half of that imprinted in Baptism; I leave the reader to his or her own conclusions. As to the character of Confirmation:

Brennan R., *Exploring Catholic Theology*. 1993. Twenty-Third Publications. He mentions the sacramental character only once (pp. 268-269), and implies that it is a medieval creation displacing the original "ministry of service" model.

[108] CCC 1121, 1272, 1304, 1570.

[109] *Catechism of the Council of Trent*, Part II, Ch I, n. 31. See also CCC 1272-1274, which seem to say the same thing in a less clear and roundabout way.

[110] CCC 1288

"By Confirmation we are armed and arrayed as soldiers of Christ, publicly to profess and defend His name, to fight against our internal enemy and against the spiritual powers of wickedness in the high places; and at the same time we are distinguished from those who, being recently baptised, are, as it were, newborn infants."[111]

In the context of an initiatory paradigm, Confirmation can be seen as putting the recipient in greater contact with the source of power that feeds the Church, and an opportunity to receive greater strength for the sake of warding off sin, representing that power source (Christ) in the world, and attaining the self-discipline that leads to a healthy and effective spirituality.

As to the Sacrament of Holy Orders the character:
"... confers the power of consecrating and administering the Sacraments, and also distinguishes those who are invested with this power from the rest of the faithful."[112]

The character is also described this way:
"Another grace is clearly conferred by this Sacrament; namely, a special power with reference to the most Blessed Sacrament of the Eucharist. This power is full and perfect in the

---

[111] *Catechism of the Council of Trent*, Part II, Ch I, n. 31. See also CCC 1304-1305, which de-emphasizes the "soldier of Christ" aspect but instead speak of "clothing [the recipient] with power from on high so that he may be [Christ's] witness."

[112] *Catechism of the Council of Trent*, Part II, Ch I, n. 31. CCC 1570 says the character is imprinted upon ordination to the diaconate, and makes no attempt to describe the character beyond saying it "configures [the recipients] to Christ."

> priest, because he alone can consecrate the body and blood of our Lord; but it is greater or less in the inferior ministers in proportion as their ministry approaches the Sacrament of the Altar.
>
> This power is also called a spiritual character, because those who have been ordained are distinguished from the rest of the faithful by a certain interior mark impressed on the soul..."[113]

As an initiation, the Sacrament of Holy Orders needs to be considered as several grades of initiation – anywhere from three to eight – depending on whether we count by the pre- or post-Vatican II system of reckoning.

d. Number of Holy Orders.

Prior to Vatican II, the Catholic Church held that there were seven Orders – four "minor" and three "major" – that can be traced at least as far back as the mid-third century; Eusebius of Caesaria lists that, during the time of Pope Cornelius (reigned 251-253 A.D.), there were in the city of Rome:

> "...forty-six presbyters, seven deacons, seven sub-deacons, forty-two acolytes, fifty-two exorcists, readers, and door-keepers..."[114]

These were the seven orders known up to Vatican II: the "minor" Orders of porter (doorkeeper), lector (reader), exorcist, and acolyte; and the "major" Orders of subdeacon, deacon, and priest (presbyter). The priesthood was

---

[113] *Catechism of the Council of Trent*, Part II, Ch VII, n. 57.
[114] Eusebius of Caesaria. *Church History*. Book VI, Chapter 43, n. 11. http://www.newadvent.org/fathers/250106.htm. (December 9, 2014).

considered the final Order, with a bishop seen as being a "high-priest:"

> "Now although (the sacerdotal order) is one alone, yet it has various degrees of dignity and power. The first degree is that of those who are simply called priests, and of whose functions we have hitherto been speaking.
>
> "The second is that of Bishops, who are placed over the various dioceses to govern not only the other ministers of the Church, but the faithful also, and to promote their salvation with supreme vigilance and care. ... Bishops are also called pontiffs. This name is derived from the pagans, who thus designated their chief priests."[115]

By the 1940's, a change in thinking had occurred and the episcopate (bishopric) was seen as an Order in its own right.[116] This is the stance taken by the post-Vatican II Church, which declares there are only three Orders – Bishops, Priests, and Deacons[117] – and abolished the minor orders in 1968.[118] Since the minor Orders were not given from God but were created by the Church to fill certain

---

[115] *Catechism of the Council of Trent*, Part II, Ch VII, n. 50. The CCC comes closest in n. 1557.

[116] Pope Pius XII, *Sacramentum Ordinis*, November 30, 1947, lists the Diaconate, Presbyterate, and Episcopate as the Sacred Orders. **See also Ott, Ludwig.** *Fundamentals of Catholic Dogma*. Book Four, Part III, Chapter VI, §2 for a more detailed discussion.

[117] 1983 Code of Canon Law, can 1009 §1: "The orders are the episcopate, the presbyterate, and the diaconate." **See also** CCC 1554.

[118] Pope Paul VI, *Pontificalis Romani*, June 18, 1968. The abolition of the minor Orders is what accounts for any apparent differences between the CCC and the Catechism of Trent regarding this subject. http://www.catholicliturgy.com/texts/pontrecognitio.txt (Dec. 9, 2014)

needs,[119] this suppression need not bother us in any significant way.

d. When the Character Is Imprinted.
Without getting bogged down in details, it's enough to say that in the pre-Vatican II Church, the question of "when" the sacramental character was imprinted seemed to be an open one. The *Summa Theologiae*, for example, is of the opinion that every Order, including the minors, imprints a character:

> "Wherefore since a character is a sign whereby one thing is distinguished from another, it follows that a character is imprinted in each Order."[120]

The *Catechism of the Council of Trent* says nothing explicit on the subject one way or the other, but seems to agree with the *Summa* in a section we've already quoted: "but [the character] is greater or less in the inferior ministers in proportion as their ministry approaches the Sacrament of the Altar."[121]

In the post-Vatican II Church, the character is said to be imprinted upon ordination to the Diaconate, and its nature is very loosely defined if we were to go by the CCC alone,[122] though Canon Law shows perfect agreement with pre-Vatican II teaching. We'll return to this point shortly.

e. Holy Orders as an Initiation. Its Levels.
As an initiation, the ranks of Holy Orders signify an even more progressive interaction with God's grace/energies. In

---

[119] *Fundamentals of Catholic Dogma.* Book Four, Part III, Ch VI, §2.
[120] Supplement, Q. 35, Art. 2.
[121] *Catechism of the Council of Trent*, Part II, Ch VII, n. 57.
[122] CCC 1570.

Order, the recipient is imprinted with a character and given what's technically called the "power of order," the power to confect sacraments officially in the name of the Church, and especially the power to bring Jesus Christ down to earth under the appearances of bread and wine.

In the highest level of Order – the Episcopate – the recipient is able to initiate others into all levels of Church life and practice. While I would not say that Order is a "higher" initiation than Confirmation, I would say that Order is a different kind of initiation, in that it is one of two ways the Church perpetuates herself here on earth (the other is Matrimony and the begetting of children).

It would seem there is a definite spirituality behind the sacrament of Holy Orders, and this is why I think the minor orders are important, even if they weren't of divine institution. The progression of grades, from the four minor orders and up to the three majors, breaks up the powers and responsibilities of Holy Orders into degrees, and thus gives the candidate a chance to experience it a little at a time, and to know what they're getting into, and to know whether they can handle it. Not everybody's cut out for the priesthood, and the sooner one realizes what they can handle (one way or the other), the better.

f. Power of Order versus Power of Jurisdiction.

Before passing on from our discussion on Holy Orders, it's important to relate one important feature about the character, namely the nature and limitations of the power derived from this initiation. On the one hand, there is what the recipient receives in his soul, the "power of Order."[123] On the other hand, there's whether the recipient has

---

[123] Ott, Ludwig. *Fundamentals of Catholic Dogma*. Book Four, Part III, Chapter VI, §4, n. 2.

permission from the Church to use those powers, and this is called "power of Jurisdiction." This latter is defined as:
> "The moral right to govern the faithful in the Catholic Church. Also called the power of ruling (potestas regiminis), which, by divine institution, belongs to the Church founded by Christ."[124]

In simple English, the power of Jurisdiction can only be given by the Church's hierarchy, while the power of Order is dependent upon the character imprinted in Holy Orders. This is the distinction between "licit" and "valid" that we find in Catholic theology.

f-1. The Power of Order and Validity.

We learn from St. Augustine that clerics who leave the Church retain their ordinations, and the sacraments can be administered even by those in schism:
> "For the sacrament of baptism is what the person possesses who is baptized; and the sacrament of conferring baptism is what he possesses who is ordained. And as the baptized person, if he depart from the unity of the Church, does not thereby lose the sacrament of baptism, so also he who is ordained, if he depart from the unity of the Church, does not lose the sacrament of conferring baptism. For neither sacrament may be wronged. ... and we act rightly who do not dare to repudiate God's sacraments, even when administered in schism."[125]

---

[124] Fr. John Hardon, S.J., *Modern Catholic Dictionary*. 1999. Inter Mirifica. Available online at: (Retrieved December 10, 2014). http://www.therealpresence.org/dictionary/adict.htm.
[125] Augustine. *On Baptism*, Book I, ch 1, n. 2. (December 10, 2014). http://www.newadvent.org/fathers/14081.htm.

St. Thomas expounds upon this, telling us that on account of the sacramental character, any one who has been ordained is capable of validly administering the sacraments, including heretics, schismatics, and those who were excommunicated:

> "But such as are ordained while separated from the Church, have neither the power rightly, nor do they use it rightly. But that in both cases they have the power, ... And since the consecration of the Eucharist is an act which follows the power of order, such persons as are separated from the Church by heresy, schism, or excommunication, can indeed consecrate the Eucharist, which on being consecrated by them contains Christ's true body and blood ..."[126]

As we have seen, the Council of Florence (*Decree for the Armenians*, DZ 695) confirmed the doctrine of the sacramental character, and in the same paragraph it also tells us:

> "All these sacraments are dispensed in three ways, namely, by things as the matter, by words as the form, and by the person of the minister conferring the sacrament with the intention of doing as the Church does; if any of these is lacking the sacrament is not fulfilled."

And the Council of Trent, says this:

> "If any one saith, ... that he who has once been a priest, can again become a layman; let him be anathema."[127]

---

[126] *Summa Theologiae*. Part III, Q. 82. a. 7. In article 8 he adds, in regards to degraded (defrocked) priests: "And thus it is evident that the degraded priest can perform this sacrament."
[127] Council of Trent, Session XXIII, Canon 4.

In more recent times, Pope Leo XIII tells us, when discussing Anglican Orders:

> "A person who has correctly and seriously used the requisite matter and form to effect and confer a sacrament is presumed for that very reason to have intended to do (*intendisse*) what the Church does. On this principle rests the doctrine that a Sacrament is truly conferred by the ministry of one who is a heretic or unbaptized, provided the Catholic rite be employed."[128]

What this ultimately means is that according to Catholic doctrine, the power to confect the Sacraments can be found both inside and outside the Catholic Church. So long as the "form, matter, and intent" are correct, the Sacrament is *valid*, meaning a true Sacrament actually happened. Period.

f-2. Power of Jurisdiction and Liceity.

Power of Jurisdiction is something that will take less time to discuss than power of Order, mainly because it has less to do with theology and everything to do with *permission*. We've seen it defined as "A moral right to govern," and what that really means is: "Do you have permission from the Pope/local bishop to do what you're doing?"

If a person has this permission, then he has power of Jurisdiction and his actions are *licit* and acts with *liceity*. If he does not, then his actions (without permission) are called *illicit*. That's really all there is to say about power of Jurisdiction.

---

[128] *Apostolicae Curae*, September 18, 1986, n. 33. Pope Leo concluded that Anglican ordinations were invalid owing to defect of intention and form. He affirmed the Catholic principle that sacraments performed outside the Catholic Church are valid if done in the Catholic manner.

To put it another way, the difference between validity and liceity can be compared to driving a car. One can *validly* drive a car – that is, take it from point A to point B – with or without a license. However, one cannot *licitly* drive a car without a license. While liceity is important for the good order of any society, it's important not to confuse man-made laws with divine institutions.

This distinction between validity and liceity is found within Canon Law and treatises on Sacramental Moral Theology, which describe conditions under which a Sacrament is "licit" or "illicit." Even canon Law recognizes its own limits in this matter, where we read:
"Sacred ordination never becomes invalid"[129]

And we read elsewhere:
"There is no such penalty as the deprivation of the Power of Order."[130]

This is also why Rome habitually refrains from public pronouncements on consecrations performed by schismatic bishops, but will denounce those consecrations as illicit. This was the rationale in 1976 when the Vatican denounced the Palmar de Troya consecrations by Abp Ngo Dinh Thuc,[131] and in 2006 – contrary to the interpretations of Wikipedia and the Catholic blogosphere – only pronounced

---

[129] *1917 Code of Canon Law*, c. 211. *1983 Code of Canon Law*, c. 290.
[130] *1983 Code of Canon Law*, c. 1338.
[131] Sacred Congregation for the Doctrine of Faith. *Decree concerning certain unlawful priestly and episcopal ordinations.* September 17, 1976. n. 3: "whatever about the validity of their orders, the Church does not recognize their ordination nor shall it do so" (December 10, 2014).
http://www.vatican.va/roman_curia/congregations/cfaith/documents/rc_con_cfaith_doc_19760917_illegitimas-ordinationes_en.html.

on the "canonical status" of the four Episcopal consecrations performed by Abp. Emmanuel Milingo.[132]

Of course, this brings us to a problem with the concept of liceity in terms of the big picture: *Everybody is somebody's schismatic. Everybody is somebody's heretic.*

Think about it. The Catholic Church declares that her hierarchy alone was lawfully established by Christ, and that all outside here are schismatics, heretics, infidels, or apostates.[133] This means that to the Catholic mentality, the only liceity is that which eats, sleeps, and breathes under the shadow of the Vatican. Amongst the Eastern Orthdox – who follow the "Cyprianic doctrine" and thus make no distinction between validity and liceity – nobody outside her umbrella is lawful or even *able* to confect the Sacraments (in fact, the Russian Orthodox Church teaches that non-Orthodox aren't even baptized!). We can say the same thing for the Anglicans (who have their own church law), the Old Catholics in Germany and Holland, and pretty much every church on the face of the planet!

This is a point where I openly dissent from the hierarchy, as I tend to look at it this way: if your faith is primarily invested in "team spirit," "institutional loyalty," and "a

---

[132] Vatican Press Office, September 26, 2006. Both the Wikipedia article and the lay Catholic blogosphere have taken this to mean the consecrations were pronounced invalid, but the Vatican is incapable of such a pronouncement unless there were a known defect in the form, matter, or intent. To do otherwise transgresses both Catholic theological principles and Canon Law, which we've amply discussed and documented thus far.

[133] *1983 Code of Canon Law*, c. 1364, §2. Heretics, apostates, and schismatics are automatically (*latae sententiae*) excommunicated – that is, put outside the Church – and infidels (non-Christians) were never members of the Church in the first place.

spirit of partisanship," then liceity should be the overriding factor for you. If, however, you're able to see past the borders of communities of men, past them and towards the source from which it all came, then the first concern should be one of validity, with liceity being of little concern. My own position is closer to the latter, as unthinking partisan loyalty means nothing to me.

g. Conclusions Drawn.
Ultimately, when one considers the initiations of Baptism, Confirmation, and Holy Orders, one has to stand in awe at the grandeur of a spiritual system so complicated and at once so simple. Complicated, in that there are all these subtle distinctions between "licit" and "valid" and the different ranks and orders. But at the same time simple, because Baptism, faith, and a virtuous life are all that's needed to get into heaven.

We have seen how these three Sacraments serve as initiations into the energy that powers Catholicism, God's grace as distributed through His Son, Jesus Christ, and we have talked about how that works. We also see that God's grace is not limited to any one hierarchy, but that the "spirit goes where it wilt," regardless of the boundaries of heresy or schism. So whether in the Catholic Church, or the Orthodox Churches, or even the small churches that dot the landscape of the "Independent Sacramental Movement,"[134] I hold that each of them possesses these initiations, and if

---

[134] The Independent Sacramental Movement (ISM), also called the "Independent Catholic Movement," refers to small churches descending from groups that broke from Rome, Anglicanism, or Orthodoxy in various waves, for different reasons, and at different points in history. The best modern treatment is found in Plummer, John, *The Many Paths of the Independent Sacramental Movement*. 2006. Apocryphile Press. ISBN-13: 978-0977146123.

they would each get over their prejudices and ego problems, those initiations could lead to a powerful spiritual life for Christian souls indeed!

THE HOLY EUCHARIST AND ITS PLACE IN THE SPIRITUAL LIFE

We said earlier that the post-Vatican II Church views the Eucharist as a Sacrament of initiation, right after Baptism and Confirmation. This is part of a fuller scheme, where the modern "conciliar" Church divides the Sacraments into three categories: the *Sacraments of Initiation* (Baptism, Confirmation, Eucharist), *Sacraments of Healing* (Penance, Extreme Unction), and the *Sacraments of Service* (Holy Orders and Matrimony).[135]

Prior to Vatican II, the Sacraments were divided into two categories: the *Sacraments of the Dead* (Baptism and Penance) and the *Sacraments of the Living* (Confirmation, Eucharist, Extreme Unction, Holy Orders, and Matrimony), based on whether they were intended for a recipient in a "state of grace."[136]

While both of these schemes and categorizations are man-made, they can both be helpful. They can be helpful because they assist us in comprehending the Sacraments' place in our lives. And of all the Sacraments, none

---

[135] CCC 1210-1211. Also 1212, 1421, 1534.

[136] This scheme does not seem to have official sanction, but is found in various catechisms and textbooks on religion. Deharbe's *A Full Catechism of the Catholic Religion*. 1876. Catholic School Book Company. p. 247. (Dec 10, 2014) https://books.google.com/books?id=J749AAAAYAAJ&pg. **See also** Coppens, Charles, S.J., *A Systematic Study of the Catholic Religion*. 1903. B. Herder Book Company. n. 232. (December 10, 2014). https://archive.org/details/systematicstudy00coppuoft.

illustrates the intersectionality of our lives with the life of the Catholic community so much as the Eucharist.

To understand that statement fully, it helps to understand that the Catholic Church takes the doctrine behind the Eucharist – that the bread and wine are changed really, truly, and substantially into the Body, Blood, Soul, and Divinity of Christ, and that only the appearances ("accidents") of the bread and wine remain – she takes this belief VERY SERIOUSLY. Hence, the life of the Church leads towards and draws from the Eucharist, because as much as Christ is truly present in the Eucharist, THE EUCHARIST IS CHRIST.

This is why the entirety of Catholic life is oriented towards the Eucharist (and by extension the Mass), because the Eucharist is what grounds the Church in her founder. In **Baptism**, we become members of Christ's Church and are able to receive the other Sacraments. In **Confirmation**, we become soldiers of Christ, strengthened and armed in faith. In **Penance**, our souls are cleansed and again made ready to partake of Christ in the Sacrament of the Altar. In **Extreme Unction** we are prepared to meet Christ in the world to come. In **Holy Orders** we are given the Power to make Christ present to others. And finally, in **Matrimony**, we are called to give birth to others who will encounter Christ as we do. The entirety of Catholic life is oriented towards the Eucharist, because the entirety of the Catholic life is oriented towards Christ.

1. The Real Presence
What I said above was a strong statement, and could easily be appalling to non-Catholic readers as well as Catholics who were poorly catechized (an all-too-common phenomenon these days), so allow me to explain. When I

mention that "the Eucharist is Christ," it's a logical conclusion from the doctrine of the *Real Presence*, which states that Jesus is truly present in the Eucharist.

The seed of the Real Presence doctrine is found in multiple places in Scripture, beginning with the narrative of the Last Supper, where Jesus said "This **IS** my body."[137] In no place did he say "This is a symbol of my body."[138]

We likewise have the testimony of St. Paul, who writes to the Christians in Corinth about the dangers of misusing the Eucharist:

> "For all who eat and drink without discerning the body, eat and drink judgment against themselves. For this reason many of you are weak and ill, and some have died."[139]

Paul is talking about "unworthy communion," which refers to receiving the Eucharist while in a state of sin, but this passage raises a more interesting point: when was the last time anybody died from ordinary bread or ordinary wine?

By the end of the first century, the *Didache* tells us:

---

[137] Matthew 26:17-30. Mark 14:12-26. Luke 22:7-39.

[138] This is the belief of Reformed Protestantism. While Lutheranism affirms that the Sacraments confer grace (*Augsburg Confession*, Articles IX and X), Reformed theology reduces the Sacraments to mere symbols with no efficacy. This is rooted in Ulrich Zwingli (the father of the Reformed churches) who said, amongst other things: "The sacraments we esteem and honor as signs and symbols of holy things, but not as though they themselves were the things of which they are the signs. For who is so ignorant as to try to maintain that the sign is the thing which it signifies" *An Exposition of the Faith*. 1530. http://divdl.library.yale.edu/dl/FullText.aspx?qc=AdHoc&q=3164&qp=6. (Retrieved December 11, 2014).

[139] 1 Corinthians 11:29-30.

"Let no one eat and drink of your Eucharist but those baptized in the name of the Lord; to this, too the saying of the Lord is applicable: 'Do not give to dogs what is sacred.'"[140]

Around 110 A.D., St. Ignatius of Antioch writes the following while on his way to martyrdom in the arena:

"They abstain from the Eucharist and from prayer, because they confess not the Eucharist to be the flesh of our Savior Jesus Christ, which suffered for our sins, and which the Father, of His goodness, raised up again. Those, therefore, who speak against this gift of God, incur death in the midst of their disputes."[141]

In the middle of the second century, St. Justin Martyr also affirms the Real Presence:

"For not as common bread and common drink do we receive these; but in like manner as Jesus Christ our Savior, having been made flesh by the Word of God, had both flesh and blood for our salvation, so likewise have we been taught that the food which is blessed by the prayer of His word, and from which our blood and flesh by transmutation are nourished, is the flesh and blood of that Jesus who was made flesh."[142]

Iranaeus of Lyons, around the end of the second century, tells us:

"When, therefore, the mingled cup and the manufactured bread receives the Word of God, and

---

[140] *Didache* 9:5.
[141] *Epistle to the Smyneans.* n. 7. (Retrieved December 11, 2014). http://www.newadvent.org/fathers/0109.htm.
[142] *First Apology.* ch. 66.

the Eucharist of the blood and the body of Christ is made, from which things the substance of our flesh is increased and supported, how can [the heretics] affirm that the flesh is incapable of receiving the gift of God, which is life eternal, which [flesh] is nourished from the body and blood of the Lord, and is a member of Him?"[143]

While we again run the risk of overkill, we see there's no question that early Christians did **not** believe the Eucharist was a mere symbol, but the testimony is plain that they believed the elements truly became the Body and Blood of Christ. Of course, none of this talks about *how* the bread and wine become the Body and Blood of Christ, only that they do.

As to the "how," there is no specific hypothesis that's supported directly by Scripture. The Catholic Church, moved by Aristotelian metaphysical concepts of "substance" (a thing as it is in itself) and "accidents" (what a thing looks/smells/feels/sounds/tastes like), defined this process as *Transubstantiation* at the Fourth Lateran Council in 1215 A.D.

> "His body and blood are truly contained in the sacrament of the altar under the forms of bread and wine, the bread and wine having been *changed in substance*, by God's power, into his body and blood, so that in order to achieve this mystery of unity we receive from God what he received from us."[144]

---

[143] *Against Heresies*. Book V, ch. 2, n. 3. (December 11, 2014). http://www.newadvent.org/fathers/0103502.htm.

[144] Fourth Lateran Council, Confession of Faith. (December 11, 2014). http://www.ewtn.com/library/COUNCILS/LATERAN4.HTM.

By the sixteenth century, the Protestant Revolt challenged the doctrine of Transubstantiation from all quarters. Luther claimed that Transubstantiation held the Eucharist a prisoner of "Aristotelian metaphysics," but he alone amongst the Reformers defended the Real Presence. While the primary confession of his church (the *Confessio Augustana*)[145] doesn't specify a process by which it comes to pass, Luther's own view was what he called "Sacramental Union" (often incorrectly called *Consubstantiation*): Jesus was truly present, but the bread and wine remained.[146]

Ulrich Zwingli taught that the Sacraments were mere symbols, tokens of what we do for God and lacking in any kind of grace whatsoever.[147] John Calvin tried to find a position halfway between Luther and Zwingli, stating that Jesus was present in the Eucharist only as a spiritual presence in the room, because His body was *localiter circumscriptus*, or "locally constrained" in heaven:

> "I now come to the hyperbolical mixtures which superstition has introduced. Here Satan has employed all his wiles, withdrawing the minds of men from heaven, and imbuing them with the perverse error that Christ is annexed to the element of bread. And, first, we are not to dream of such a presence of Christ in the sacrament as the artificers of the Romish court have imagined, as if the body of Christ, locally present, were to be taken into the

---

[145] AC, art. X: "Of the Supper of the Lord they teach that the Body and Blood of Christ are truly present, and are distributed to those who eat the Supper of the Lord; and they reject those that teach otherwise." http://bookofconcord.org/augsburgconfession.php. (Dec. 11, 2014).

[146] *Luther's Works*, Vol. 37, pp. 299-300.

[147] Quoted in a previous footnote. Zwingli's approach is technically called "Real Absence" or "Memorialism," and my personal term for it is "Nonsubstantiation."

hand, and chewed by the teeth, and swallowed by the throat. ... As we cannot at all doubt that [Christ's body] is bounded according to the invariable rule in the human body, and is contained in heaven, where it was once received, and will remain till it return to judgment, so we deem it altogether unlawful to bring it back under these corruptible elements, or to imagine it everywhere present. And, indeed, there is no need of this, in order to our partaking of it, since the Lord by his Spirit bestows upon us the blessing of being one with him in soul, body, and spirit. The bond of that connection, therefore, is the Spirit of Christ, who unites us to him, and is a kind of channel by which everything that Christ has and is, is derived to us."[148]

To put an end to all this foolishness, the Council of Trent clearly defined that Transubstantiation is the official teaching of the Catholic Church:

"And because that Christ, our Redeemer, declared that which He offered under the species of bread to be truly His own body, therefore has it ever been a firm belief in the Church of God, and this holy Synod doth now declare it anew, that, by the consecration of the bread and of the wine, a conversion is made of the whole substance of the bread into the substance of the body of Christ our Lord, and of the whole substance of the wine into the substance of His blood; which conversion is, by

---

[148] Calvin, John. *Institutes of the Christian Religion*. Book IV. Chapter 17. n. 12. The reader will notice a general thread throughout the *Institutes*: Calvin typically rails against Catholicism and then advocates the opposite of what Catholics believe, apparently for no reason other than that Catholics believe it. (Retrieved December 11, 2014). http://www.ccel.org/ccel/calvin/institutes.vi.xviii.html.

the holy Catholic Church, suitably and properly called Transubstantiation."[149]

The foregoing quote retains the status of official Catholic doctrine, and the CCC reiterates it in full.[150]

2. The Real Presence for a Catholic
For a devout Catholic, the Real Presence is more than the arguments and decrees we've cited. It's something more than an intellectual debate or an ideological construct, even more than just an official dogma of the Church. For a devout Catholic, transubstantiation is a palpable reality, every bit as real as the birds in the air, the trees in the forest, and the water in the streams. Our God is often called a Living God, and it is through our living that we best encounter and experience Him: whether that living takes place through the drawing of breath, through love for our fellow living creatures, or through the eating of God's own flesh in the Sacrament of the Altar.

In the previous sections, much has already been said about the Sacraments of Baptism, Confirmation, and Order, and we have seen how the Christian receives progressive initiations. Each initiation is intended to configure him to Christ and be His worthy vessel – "servants of Christ and

---

[149] Council of Trent, Session XIII, ch. 4. Protestant views are clearly anathematized in the canons of that session.
[150] CCC 1376. Some may say this stance is softened in CCC 1374: "… is not intended to exclude the other types of presence as if they could not be 'real' too …" This is a quotation from Paul VI, *Mysterium Fidei*, n. 39, and the document refers to other ways Jesus is present in the community of believers (nn. 35-39), not to other theologies of Jesus being present in the Eucharist. (Retrieved December 11, 2014).
http://www.vatican.va/holy_father/paul_vi/encyclicals/documents/hf_p-vi_enc_03091965_mysterium_en.html.

dispensers of God's mysteries"[151] – yet it is singularly by way of the Eucharist that we are *filled* with Christ Himself.

In the Latin Mass, during the part known as the Offertory, there is a prayer said while the celebrant pours water and wine into the chalice, the *Deus, qui humanae substantiae*, which translates: "O God, who hast wonderfully crafted the dignity of the human substance and hast more wonderfully reformed it, grant unto us, through the mystery of this water and wine, to become partakers of His divinity, who vouchsafed to become a partaker of our humanity."[152]

The text of this prayer is important in understanding the nature of the Eucharist in relation to our spiritual life, as it illustrates the exchange which takes place between God and man in context of this Sacrament. While by the Sacraments of initiation we are made into vessels containing degrees of Christ's divinity and power, it is here, through our participation in the Sacrifice of the Altar, that we are made to become *partakers* in that divinity and power. As we partake of that divinity, so does it fill us and shape us during our pilgrimage on this earth, and so too do we become more and more like unto Christ in His divinity, while at the same time working to perfect our individual humanity.

It is with these things in mind that a Catholic understands the Eucharist, and a Catholic magician understands himself

---

[151] 1 Corinthians 4:1.
[152] The full text of the prayer is as follows: «*Deus, qui humánae substántiae dignitátem mirabíliter condidísti, et mirabílius reformásti: da nobis per hujus aquae et vini mystérium, ejus divinitátis esse consórtes, qui humanitátis nostrae fíeri dignátus est párticeps, Jesus Christus Fílius tuus Dóminus noster: qui tecum vivit et regnat in unitáte Spíritus Sancti Deus: per ómnia sáecula saeculórum. Amen.*»

as being filled with God's grace to bring about change on this physical plane.

SPIRITUAL CLEANSING IN THE SACRAMENT OF PENANCE

When we move from the Sacraments of the Living to the Sacrament of Penance, we find there are classic grimoires of ceremonial magic making reference to it; they require the operator to receive Confession before undertaking a planned magical operation.[153,154] Likewise, the Church directs faithful Catholics to make confession prior to receiving Communion,[155] and the priest to confess his sins before saying Mass[156] or performing an exorcism.[157]

---

[153] One example is the *Sworn Book of Honorius*, folio 13v: "First he that shall work must be very penitent and truly confessed of all his sins." http://www.esotericarchives.com/juratus/juratus.htm. 06/27/2015.

[154] Another example is the *Grimoire of Pope Honorius*, based on the *Sworn Book*. It begins: "The person who desires to invoke the perverse "Spirits of Darkness must observe a three days' fast; he must also confess and approach the Holy Altar." www.hermetics.org/pdf/grimoire/grimoireofhonorius.pdf. 06/27/2015.

[155] Council of Trent, Session XIII, chapter 7: "Now ecclesiastical usage declares that ... no one, conscious to himself of mortal sin, ... ought to approach to the sacred Eucharist without previous sacramental confession." See also CCC 1385.

[156] Burchard's *Ritus Servandus in Celebratione Missae*, which appeared in every altar Missal from 1502 to 1967, begins by saying the priest should make sacramental confession prior to celebrating Mass. As of the 1962 edition, the reference to Confession was removed while the remainder of the text is mostly intact. The three editions of the Novus Ordo's *General Instruction of the Roman Missal* (1969, 1975, and 2002; English translations 1974, 1985, and 2011) seem to have dropped this rubric and text entirely.

[157] *Rituale Romanum*, Title XI, Chapter 2, n.1: "The priest ... shall have been confessed, or at least made a detestation of sin ..." (My translation)

Why is this? How could such a Sacrament as Penance, which has by now fallen into almost complete disuse within the modern Church, be so important to one's spirituality as to be required before partaking in the Church's spiritual nourishments? Many of us seem to have imbibed the Protestant accusation that the confessional is nothing other than a ploy to engender guilt and low self-esteem in the minds of the faithful, a means to collect information on the Church's subjects and their loved ones, a way to keep the people under the clergy's thumb, and yet another of many ways to keep the laity from thinking for themselves.[158] Nothing could be farther from the truth.

To understand, let us begin at about 28 A.D. or so, the year when Our Lord came back from the dead and gave His Apostles the power to forgive sins. This is spelled out in John 20:22-23:

> "When [Jesus] had said this, he breathed on them and said to them, 'Receive the Holy Spirit. If you forgive the sins of any, they are forgiven them; if you retain the sins of any, they are retained.'"

As we can see, the Apostles were given the choice of whether to forgive or retain people's sins, but nowhere does it say they had the power to read people's minds. This leads to the question: how could they know which sins to forgive or retain, unless they are first told which sins they're being asked to forgive? This makes spoken

---

[158] This can make for a fascinating line of inquiry in and of itself, yet alas it's beyond the scope of this discussion. For those interested in further exploration, a good overview with sources can be found at *The Catholic World Report*, "American Anti-Catholicism and the Confessional," http://www.catholicworldreport.com/Item/2358/american_anticatholicism_and_the_confessional.aspx (Retrieved June 29, 2015)

confession a logical necessity, because without it the Confessor would be clueless as to which sins to forgive or retain. And speaking from experience, there are cases where it's better to retain (a confession given under obvious false pretenses, for example).

While it can be fun to trace the Church's practice in administering this Sacrament from the earliest days of public penitence to the rise of one-on-one confession,[159] it would suffice for our purposes to discuss the effects of this Sacrament and why its reception is beneficial to the spiritual life, let alone the life of a practicing magician. In so doing, it will first be necessary to define what constitutes sin, what its nature is, and how it affects us both mentally and spiritually.

In the section on Baptism, much time was devoted to the discussion of Original Sin and its effects upon Adam's descendants. Yet there is another classification of sin, called **actual sin**, which refers to those sins we commit on our own and especially after Baptism.

Do not misunderstand this, as actual sins can be committed before Baptism, but through that sacrament they are also

---

[159] Many of the Early Fathers talk about Confession, beginning with the *Didache* 14:1, *"On the Lord's Day gather together, break bread, and give thanks, after confessing your transgressions so that your sacrifice may be pure."* Also of interest is Tertullian's exhortation in his *De Paenitentia* 10:1, *"Yet most men either shun [confession], as being a public exposure of themselves, ... I presume (as being) more mindful of modesty than of salvation; just like men who, having contracted some malady in the more private parts of the body, avoid the privity of physicians, and so perish with their own bashfulness."* http://www.newadvent.org/fathers/0320.htm. Retrieved June 29, 2015.

washed away.[160] But what exactly is sin? Is sin something we do that makes God angry at us just because we went against His authoritarian "because I said so?" No, it is rather an abuse (or at best a less-than-fully informed use) of our free will, in which we choose a temporary, lesser good over the more lasting, greater good. The spiritual danger arising from choosing this lesser good, therefore, is now to be found in how it shows irresponsibility and lack of love towards God (idolatry, blasphemy, etc.), or unloving /irresponsible behavior towards our neighbor (rape, murder, theft, and any number of other things).[161]

Think of it this way: God is not only the author of heaven, earth, animals, and man, but He is also the author of human nature and all nature in general. This means He knows and understands our nature better than any of us ever will, and so His commandments have always been enjoined so that we (having been deprived of the *donum scientiae*) may better be able to know and do what is in our best interest in terms of our relation to God, our neighbor, and ourselves. Ultimately, therefore, what is in God's best interest is also in our long-term best interest, while the temporary, immediate pleasures offered by a short-term temptation can many times end up with destructive consequences running counter to that interest.

---

[160] Augustine, *De Peccatorum Meritis et Remissione*, I, ch. 20: "…by the regeneration of the Spirit there is effected the remission not of original sin only, but also of the sins of man's own voluntary and actual commission." http://www.newadvent.org/fathers/15011.htm. 6/29/2015.
See also Roman Catechism II, 2, 42 and CCC 1263.

[161] The best definition of Actual Sin I've found comes from the 1979 *Book of Common Prayer*, p. 848, used by Episcopal Church USA, a definition with which a Catholic could easily agree: "Sin is the seeking of our own will instead of the will of God, thus distorting our relationship with God, with other people, and with all creation."

This brings us to the natural consequence of sin, known as damnation. As sin is the choice of a lesser good that may ultimately run against the best interest of the sinner, so damnation is the inevitable consequence of making that choice. The way I usually describe it in conversation is with the illustration of a hot stove. If a child puts his hand on a hot stove, his hand is burned. This is not because the stove is "angry" or "out to get him," but only because the burning is a natural consequence of placing a hand on a hot stove. In this sense, damnation has nothing to do with "being evil," or with "making God angry," but is simply a matter of cause and effect, because every deed a man does will eventually come back and take its toll. This is the nature of sin and damnation.

With this in mind, we can now discuss which effects of sin are removed by the sacrament of Penance. Just as we've noticed that certain sacraments leave a mark on the soul, so too does sin leave a mark. Fortunately, this mark is not permanent, and can be seen as dirt which collects on our soul with every sinful act, until such a point that we become so opaquely encrusted that the soul can no longer perceive God's light shining upon us, nor can we (or others) the divine spark that shines from within. As magic is primarily a manifestation of the divine light shining through us, it becomes progressively more difficult for us to perceive the light, and thence to manifest it when we are in such a filth-covered state.[162]

If we apply the Principle of Correspondence to sin, we would find that the spiritual effect of sin begets a psychological effect. Psychologically, when a person sins,

---

[162] This paragraph is my own interpretation of the psychological and spiritual effects of sin on one's soul. Though not drawn from official sources, I believe it doesn't contradict the official sources, either.

the process establishes itself just like a drug addiction. First he commits a sin and may feel some revulsion to it, but then he may desire to do it more and more, until such point that it seems perfectly natural and he becomes completely insensitive to the harm or damage which it may cause to others. Even when he does not wish to do it (killing, for example), he can still become desensitized to the act and get to the point of not even caring anymore.

This is why in the sacrament of Penance, the filth encrusted on our souls is stripped away, and our spirits become gently polished to a "like-new" shine with the rouge-cloth of God's loving glory: *"For there is no sin, however great or horrible, which cannot be effaced by the Sacrament of Penance, and that not merely once, but over and over again."*[163] Likewise, the Church teaches that *"Re-established or strengthened in the communion of saints, the sinner is made stronger by the exchange of spiritual goods among all the living members of the Body of Christ, whether still on pilgrimage or already in the heavenly homeland."*[164]

Through the Sacrament of Penance, we are reminded of God's love for us even in moments of weakness, and we are also reminded, by way of that "squeaky-clean" feeling, how much the dirt accumulated by our sins had kept us from seeing God's light and perhaps kept others from seeing ours. Far from being a tool of manipulation at the hands of a corrupt clergy, this sacrament helps us to put things in perspective and keeps us clean and pure.

---

[163] Roman Catechism, II, 5, 23
[164] CCC 1469. A footnote to this entry references *Lumen Gentium*, nn. 48-50, though that passage refers more to the life of the Church in general than to Penance in particular.

INITIATION AND REINFORCEMENT: FREQUENT RECEPTION OF THE SACRAMENTS

We now reach the point where we much close this chapter, likely to the relief of our less theologically-interested readers. I completely understand that many readers might dismay at the theological and not overtly magical catechesis at the heart of this chapter, and I really wish it hadn't been necessary to go into so much detail. Sadly, it was necessary.

It was necessary because most Catholics never learned the basics of the faith, not even those who allegedly had good catechism classes. Instead, they were compelled to remember various formulations by rote, with more emphasis placed on obligation and blind obedience than on actually learning the faith or developing a vibrant spirituality. This is unfortunate, for if the laity had actually been *taught* the contents of the faith and had a vibrant spirituality been *encouraged*, then fewer would leave the Church for Protestantism, Neopaganism, or Atheism, and the problems that face the modern Church may never have found soil in which to grow in the first place.[165]

Since we now have the theological foundations out of the way, this seems like a good time to illustrate their applications, how the sacraments work in combination to support one's spiritual life, and how they give the practitioner what he or she needs at a given point in time.

In many an initiatory tradition, spiritual helps are provided to the initiate, and they generally take the place of two

---

[165] In fact, the Catholic school system may well be the largest suppliers of new Pagans in the country! This is easily tested by asking your Pagan friends how many of them went to Catholic school.

types: 1) an initiation, and 2) a reinforcement. As previously mentioned at the beginning of this chapter:

> *"In the first place, we would do well to concentrate our attention upon the seven Sacraments, which in and of themselves are pure rituals of Transcendental Magic, that is, rituals of magic which are focused on the devotee's initiation into a spiritual current, and then on his continued purification and ever closer connection with Deity. In this manner, we transcend the limitations of this world, its necessities, and its hardships, and as we draw even more nigh to Deity, so too do we, as a side effect, gain power over those things and circumstances which once restrained us."*

Using this paragraph as a starting point, we could say that an "initiation" is the former, bringing the **initiand** (i.e. "the person about to be initiated") into contact with the spiritual current that runs through a particular tradition, and a "reinforcement" is the latter, which reinforces the initiate's contact with that current by keeping the initiate mentally and spiritually clean and increasing his contact and growth within the current of that tradition.

Now some of us may ask, "What does this guy mean by the word 'current?'" Simply put, a current is a spiritual energy at the focus of a given spiritual tradition; this "energy" can be a blind energy, or it can be the power of some deity who is at the head of that tradition. To the Jedi Order, for example, that current is the Force, while to the Catholic Church that current is Christ, who in the Catholic tradition "surrounds us, penetrates us, and binds us all together."[166]

---

[166] The Lorica of Saint Patrick says this beautifully:
Christ with me, Christ before me, Christ behind me,

Thus, it is through Baptism, Confirmation, and Order that we are put into different levels of contact with the power of Christ (which can be called the "Christ-current," meaning that we are put in special, intimate contact with Christ's power and strength), in ways that have already been previously discussed; this is why we refer to them as "initiations," while the sacraments of Penance and the Eucharist are referred to as "reinforcements."

For those who may be wondering about the other two sacraments, we can say that Matrimony is a type of initiation (in which two people are initiated into a life where they both work together for sanctification), and Extreme Unction is a very unique type of reinforcement, in that it totally cleanses the soul; we must also remember that, under ideal conditions, it is accompanied by Holy Viaticum ("Last Communion"), thus the soul is thoroughly cleansed and empowered in preparation for its last breath.

This interplay of initiation and reinforcement is something which must be considered in the life of every Catholic, especially those Catholics who desire to practice the magic arts. For with initiation we are given the right and the privilege to speak as a representative of the society in which we are initiated, and particularly in the name of that society's current or deity. The reinforcements are what keep us strong in that current, and are the means by which we develop power to practice the magical arts and manifest our desires here on the earth below.

Christ in me, Christ beneath me, Christ above me,
Christ on my right, Christ on my left,
Christ when I lie down, Christ when I sit down,
Christ in the heart of every man who thinks of me,
Christ in the mouth of every man who speaks of me,
Christ in the eye that sees me,
Christ in the ear that hears me.

- *Chapter Two: Catholicism as an Initiatory Magical System* -

With that in mind, it is hoped that the reader is given food for thought as we proceed to the next chapter.

"Fructus arboris seduxit nos, Filius Dei redemit nos. Salvator mundi, salva nos: qui per crucem et Sanguinem tuum redemisti nos, auxiliare nobis, te deprecamur, Deus noster." – Liturgy for Good Friday

CHAPTER THREE: THE SACRAMENTALS

FOREWORD FOR CHAPTER THREE

In the previous chapter, we discussed the sacraments in the context of initiation/reinforcement, as well as their underlying theology. In this chapter, we begin to look at the sacramentals – other rituals whose purpose is to apply the Christ-current to every day life, and thus serve as "practical reinforcements" – and we shall do so in terms of their import and application as practical magical operations.

So, what's a sacramental, some may ask. Sacramentals are defined in the Baltimore Catechism as: "holy things or actions of which the Church makes use to obtain for us from God, through her intercession, spiritual and temporal favors." (Q. 469)[167]

As for what the sacramentals do for us, the Catechism is far clearer in listing five benefits which we may derive from their usage: actual grace, forgiveness of venial sin, remission of temporal punishment, health of body and material blessings, and protection from evil spirits. And finally, the Catechism tells us that sacramentals break down into two types: blessings and exorcisms.[168] As a third category, the term "sacramental" can also refer to an item which has been blessed and has a religious or sacred use: holy water, rosaries, scapulars, medals, and so on and so forth.

Now comes what is perhaps the most important question, and this is what effects us the most: *who* is able to perform

---

[167] *Baltimore Catechism No. 2 Revised Edition*, Confraternity of Christian Doctrine, 1941
[168] *Ibid.*, q. 471-472

the sacramentals? Popular thought has it that only a priest or bishop could give a blessing or perform an exorcism, which is even reflected in the wording of the Catechism.

Notice that I say "popular thought," however, because the actual teaching is quite different. Though not commonly spelled-out in published books (except the excellent 1940's catechetical work *My Catholic Faith*[169] and part 2 of the *Malleus Maleficarum*[170]), it is taught that the laity are able to administer blessings, but when they do so they do it in their own name, and not as official ministers of the Church. This was finally translated into the realm of public catechesis with the 1994 *Catechism of the Catholic Church*, which states: "Sacramentals derive from the baptismal priesthood: every baptized person is called to be a 'blessing,' and to bless."[171]

The above having been said, I feel it necessary to state that I am not one for "over-empowering" the laity or encouraging them to pretend at being priests, however I do strongly believe that the laity deserve to know exactly what their rights are. And the clergy (retired, resigned, or still active), have a sacred obligation to tell them. Suffice to say that sacramentals are the bread and butter of a Catholic magician, as this comprises the realm in which most go about their work.

---

[169] *My Catholic Faith*. The Most Reverend Louis LaRavoire Morrow. 1949. My Mission House. Kenosha, Wisconsin. In the section on Sacramentals, Morrow tells us:
"***The laity can bless, but not in the name of the Church.*** *Thus we have the custom of parents blessing their children when they leave the house, at the Angelus, or when they go on a journey. In these private blessings, the more pious the person giving the blessing, the greater the effect."* (bold and italics in the original)
[170] See footnote 7 in Chapter One.
[171] *Catechism of the Catholic Church*, n. 1669: «A sacerdotio oriuntur baptismali: omnis baptizatus vocatur ut sit benedictio et benedicat.»

Now that we know what the sacramentals are, what they do, and who may perform them, let us delve into the realm of their magical composition and applications!

BLESSINGS

As already established, blessings take the chief place amongst the sacramentals. These are the rituals most commonly employed by priests ("Father, will you bless my cat? My car? My belly? And while you're at it, how about all the beer in my fridge? Pretty please?"), as well as being the most predominant domain of a Catholic magician's practice. The reason is that not only do blessings cover those rites for any object, but they also cover any rite or prayer through which we invoke the divine power to aid us in our life. Thus, most spells and incantations also fall into the realm of blessings, so long as their object is compatible with the teachings of the Church.

According to the Roman Ritual, the blessings of the Church generally follow a particular format.[172] They begin with two versicles, each followed by a response, the celebrant then says "Let us pray," and then a prayer – usually short, sweet, and to-the-point – is said over the object to be blessed, normally with the Sign of the Cross being made over the object, person, or place being blessed. At the end of the blessing, the object is sprinkled thrice (and in silence) with Holy Water:

> The priest shall always stand with head uncovered. In the beginning of the blessing he shall say the following, unless otherwise noted:

---

[172] This is the format used in the pre-Vatican II Church. The post-Vatican II Church uses a different format, as found in *The Book of Blessings*. The reader is encouraged to look into both formats and determine which works better for him.

Chapter Three: The Sacramentals

V. *Our help is in the name of the Lord.*
R. *Who made heaven and earth.*
V. *The Lord be with you.*
R. *And with thy spirit.*

Then he shall say the prayer, one or many, as noted in its proper place.
Afterwards he sprinkles the blessed oject with holy water and – where noted – incenses it, while saying nothing.[173]

There are other rubrics concerning vestments (wearing surplice and red or white stole), but we're not so much concerned with the trappings and props here, as we are with the essence of the rites themselves. To which end, let us look at the versicles and general format of a blessing.

As a simple example, let's use the Blessing of Beer that can be found in the Appendix to the Roman Ritual. It reads as follows:

BENEDICTIO CEREVESIAE[174]

Latin	English
V. Adjutórium nostrum in nómine Dómine.	V. Our help is in the name of the Lord.
R. Qui fecit caelum et terram.	R. Who made heaven and earth.
V. Dóminus vobíscum.	V. The Lord be with you.
R. Et cum spíritu tuo.	R. And with thy spirit.
Orémus.	Let us pray.
Béne✝dic, Dómine,	Bless✝, O Lord, this

---
[173] *Rituale Romanum*. 1947 editio typica. Tit. VIII, cap. 1. *De Benedictionibus Regulae Generalis*. rubric 7. (My translation)
[174] *Rituale Romanum*. 1947 editio typica. Appendix, n. 58.

creatúram istam cerevésiae, quam ex ádipe fruménti prodúcere dignátus es: ut sit remédium salutáre humáno géneri: et praesta per invocatiónem nóminis tui sancti, ut, quicúmque ex ea bíberint, sanitátem córporis, et ánimae tutélam percípiant. Per Christum Dóminum nostrum. R. Amen. *Et aspergatur aqua benedicta.*	creature of beer, which thou hast vouchsafed to produce from the kernel of grain, that for the human race it may be an healing remedy: and grant, through the invocation of Thy holy name, that whosoever shall drink from it may find health in body and protection of soul. Through Christ our Lord. R. Amen. *And it is sprinkled with Holy Water.*

Since this may be the reader's first encounter with the written format of Catholic ritual, it seems prudent to describe the format's main conventions:

>**1.** Red or *italic* type denotes an instruction or a rubric, which means that it is not read aloud, but merely an action performed by the celebrant. Black type denotes text which is read aloud, whether it be a prayer, an address to another person, and so forth.
>**2.** The letter "V," in red, denotes that the following text is a versicle read by the celebrant. The letter "R," also in red, denotes a response, which is spoken by the celebrant's assistant(s) or the congregation; if there are no assistants, the celebrant voices the responses himself.
>**3.** The red cross in the text of a prayer (✠) is an instruction to make the sign of the cross. In a blessing, it is usually made over the object to be

blessed right as the word next to the symbol is being read.

4. The letter "N.," which is especially found in connection with a person, represents a person's name. It means "insert name here."

To begin our analysis of the blessing, let's start by looking at the versicles which begin it:
"Our help is in the name of the Lord."
Here, the celebrant is making clear the source of the power, the "help" upon which he is drawing. All power comes from God, and all power which is within ourselves comes from God as well.

"Who made heaven and earth."
This comes as an answer to the question: how powerful is He? How much is He able to help us? So when the assistants answer with this versicle, they are in effect telling us: "Well, if God's powerful enough to create heaven and earth, He should have no problem helping us!"

"The Lord be with you."
In the first versicle, the celebrant was identifying his power source, which is the Lord. Now, he is implying a blessing upon his assistants and upon all present, thus inviting them to have a share in that help and in that power.[175]

"And with thy spirit."
Here, the assistant makes and completes a circuit of power, flowing from God, to the celebrant, to the assistants, and then back to the celebrant. The power is focused into a specific circuit, and will find its grounding when it is

---

[175] Even if the celebrant is alone, he should still say this versicle, because it tacitly acknowledges a link between himself and the rest of the body of believers.

discharged into the specific object which is being blessed (in this case, the beer). Which brings us to the next part.

With the words "Let us pray," the celebrant is announcing that even though he has already identified the source of his power and created a circuit of that power, the time has now come for him to call upon that power and channel it into the object being blessed. The text of the prayers is normally short and to-the-point, and the Sign of the Cross seals the energy into the object itself. The blessing is asked and the reason for the blessing is specified, to which the people answer "Amen," signifying that it has been done.

Finally, the object is sprinkled with Holy Water, to signify that it has been "baptized" and dedicated to God's service as well as to the service of man, having been delivered from the "old life" of a profane object, and into a "new life" as a creature of God.

If the reader were to look over the format of blessings given in the Ritual, he would notice that some blessings are more complex than others, and some have more versicles than others (*Domine, exaudi orationem meam* being the most common). Since an English translation of the 1964 Ritual is easily available on the internet, the reader is encouraged to look for it and analyze it.[176] It's not the best translation, to be sure, but it is still good enough for the reader to figure out the system used in constructing the rituals, and to devise his own should the need ever arise.

---

[176] The Ritual can be found on EWTN's website, as two text files. https://www.ewtn.com/library/PRAYER/ROMAN1.TXT and http://www.ewtn.com/library/prayer/roman2.txt (Retrieved 11/27/14)

EXORCISMS

Having discussed blessings, which take the first place amongst the sacramentals, we now move on to exorcisms, which occupy the second place. In most people's minds, exorcism is irrevocably linked to Hollywood (*The Exorcist*) or to sensationalist pamphlets (*Begone, Satan!*) which tell stories of dramatic, grueling demonic possessions and of ultra-heroic clerics who fight the demon tirelessly until their patient is liberated. In reality, the sacramentals of exorcism apply to a lot more than just these kinds of cases!

On the more regular, day-to-day basis, the Church makes frequent use of her power of exorcism, both independently as exorcism proper, as well as in her rites for consecrating any person or object to God's use or mission. Generally, the use of exorcism is more "pre-emptive" in nature, designed to clean out a person or object "just in case" there might be any evil forces or energies hanging around. That's the reason why water and salt are exorcised before being combined and blessed as Holy Water, or why St. Benedict medals are exorcised before being blessed to ward off evil, and even why babies are exorcised before Baptism. There is nothing necessarily evil about the water, salt, medal, or babies; we're just making sure the recipient is clean before going forward. It's just like washing your vegetables before you eat them.

Of the rites of exorcism proper, there are two kinds listed in the Roman Ritual. The first is called the *Ritus Exorcizandi Obssessos a Daemonio* (Rit. Rom., Tit. XI, cap. 2, also commonly called "solemn exorcism"), and the second is the one composed by Pope Leo XIII, the *Exorcismus Contra Satanam et Angelos Apostaticos* (ibid., Tit. XI, cap

3, also called "short-form exorcism").[177] The first is the rite used for exorcising a person possessed by a demon, while the second can be used for a more general form of spiritual warfare, and is especially suited to use with cleansing a locality where one finds either an evil spirit, or just "bad vibes."

Since the texts for these rites of exorcism are easily enough found on the internet, I see no reason to reproduce them here.[178] What is important (especially in the solemn exorcism) is that one begins by receiving the sacraments of Penance and the Eucharist, and then invokes the help of Almighty God and the Saints in Heaven. After that, the evil spirit is addressed in forceful language and commanded to depart, and finally a prayer is said to God either for more power or in thanks for having defeated the adversary. The solemn form is a lot more involved and drawn out than the short form, yet the elements are all still there.[179]

And as an aside, for those who wish to question the right of the laity to administer sacramentals, the short form/Leo XIII exorcism was intended to be used by the laypeople.

In addition to these two "official" forms of exorcism, there is also what could be called a third kind, which is used in conjunction with a blessing. As the first two types could be called *combative* exorcisms, I would call the third kind *pre-*

---

[177] These are the rites for the pre-Vatican II Church. The post-Vatican II Church's rite is in the book *De Exorcismis et Supplicationibus Quibusdam*, published in 1999.

[178] http://www.laudatedominum.net/files/exorcismale.pdf. Retrieved 11/28/2014

[179] As a personal note, each exorcist's mileage will vary. However, I've found the short form to be more useful in human cases as well as for objects and locations.

emptive exorcisms, designed to clean a person or object before evil can even get close enough to touch it. Into this category fall baptismal exorcisms, exorcisms over salt, water, objects, and so on and so forth, many of which we find peppered through the pages of the Ritual.

Since the combative exorcisms are stand-alone rites, the reader is free to peruse them in order to get a feel for how they are constructed. The more commonly-used exorcisms over objects, much like the blessings, are written along a similar and easy-to-follow format:

1. The usual versicles:
V. Adjutórium nostrum in nómine Dómini.
R. Qui fecit caelum et terram.

2. Exorcism:
This is addressed to the object receiving the exorcism, usually beginning with the formula "I exorcise thee, creature of N.," and culminates into commanding that all evil leave the object. The Sign of the Cross is used, especially whenever any person of the Trinity is mentioned, and the reason for the exorcism is mentioned by way of the purpose the object is to have after it has been exorcised and blessed. The common ending for an exorcism is the form "…our Lord Jesus Christ, who shall come to judge the living and the dead, and the world by fire. R. Amen."

3. More versicles:
V. Dómine, exáudi oratiónem meam.
   (Lord, hear my prayer.)
R. Et clamor meus ad te véniat.
   (And let my cry come to You.)
V. Dóminus vobíscum.
R. Et cum spíritu tuo.
Orémus.

4. Actual prayer of blessing:

This is the place where the object is formally blessed, and charged with the energy of the Christ-current that dedicates it and consecrates it to its new purpose in life. It follows the exact same format as the blessings described above, the Sign of the Cross is commonly used in conjunction with the words "bless" and "sanctify," and the prayers end with the usual endings (which we'll discuss in the next chapter).

5. Sprinkling with Holy Water.

Examples of this pattern range from the relatively simple to the relatively complex, some even including multiple exorcisms, prayers, and others even incorporating the Leo XIII exorcism mentioned above. Perhaps the most straightforward example of this pattern may be found in the blessing of oil (Rit. Rom., Tit. VIII, cap. 19), which text is fully given below:

BENEDICTIO OLEI

Latin	English
V. Adjutórium nostrum in nómine Dómini.	V. Our help is in the name of the Lord.
R. Qui fecit caelum et terram.	R. Who made heaven and earth.
Exorcismus	*Exorcism*
Exorcízo te, creatúra ólei, per Deum ✝ Patrem omnipoténtem, qui fecit caelum et terram, mare, et ómnia, quae in eis sunt. Omnis virtus adversárii, omnis exércitus diáboli, et omnis incúrsus, omne phantásma sátanae eradicáre, et effugáre ab hac	I exorcise thee, creature of oil, through God ✝ the Father almighty, who hath made the heaven, the earth, the sea, and all things contained therein. May all power of the adversary, all the devil's hosts and incursions, every phantasm of Satan be eradicated, and

creatúra ólei, ut fiat ómnibus, qui eo usúri sunt, salus mentis et córporis, in nómine Dei ✠ Patris omnipoténtis, et Jesu ✠ Christi Fílii ejus Dómini nostri, et Spíritus ✠ Sancti Parácliti, et in caritáte ejúsdem Dómini nostri Jesu Christi, qui ventúrus est judicáre vivos et mórtuos, et sáeculum per ignem.
R. Amen.

V. Dómine, exáudi oratiónem meam.
R. Et clamor meus ad te véniat.
V. Dóminus vobíscum.
R. Et cum spíritu tuo.
Orémus.
Dómine Deus omnípotens, cui astat exércitus Angelórum cum tremóre, quorum servítium spirituále cognóscitur, dignáre respícere, bene✠dícere, et sancti✠ficáre hanc creatúram ólei, quam ex olivárum succo eduxísti, et ex eo infírmos inúngi mandásti, quátenus sanitáte percépta, tibi Deo vivo et vero grátias ágerent: praesta, quáesumus; ut hi, qui hoc oleo, quod in tuo nómine

take flight from this creature of oil, that it may be unto all who make use of it a healing remedy of mind and body; in the name of God ✠ the Father almighty, and of Jesus ✠ Christ His Son our Lord, and of the Holy ✠ Ghost, the Paraclete, and in the love of our same Lord Jesus Christ, who shall come again to judge the living and the dead, and the world by fire. R. Amen.
V. Lord, hear my prayer.
R. And let my cry come unto Thee.
V. The Lord be with you.
R. And with thy spirit.
Let us pray
Lord God almighty, unto whom the hosts of Angels stand in awe, and whose spiritual service is recognized, vouchsafe, we beseech Thee, to look upon, to bless✠, and to sanctify✠ this creature of oil, which Thou hast brought forth from the sap of olives, and which Thou hast commanded for anointing the infirm: so that, insofar as they have been made well, they shall give thanks to

bene✠dícimus, usi fúerint, ob omni languóre, omníque infirmitáte, atque cunctis insídiis inimíci liberéntur, et cunctae adversitátes separéntur a plasmáte tuo, quod pretióso sánguine Fílii tui redemísti, ut numquam laedátur a morsu antíqui serpéntis. Per eúmdem Dóminum nostrum Jesum Christum, Fílium tuum: Qui tecum vivit et regnat in unitáte Spíritus Sancti Deus, per ómnia sáecula saeculórum.
R. Amen.

Thee, O Living and True God. Grant, we pray Thee, that they who will use this oil which we bless✠ in Thy name, may be delivered from all suffering, all infirmity, and all the wiles of the enemy: let it be a means of averting any kind of adversity from man, made in Thine image and redeemed by the precious Blood of Thy Son, so that they may never again suffer the sting of the ancient serpent. Through the same Lord, Jesus Christ, Thy Son, who liveth and reigneth in the unity of the Holy Ghost, God, forever and ever.
R. Amen.

Et aspergatur aqua benedicta.

And it is sprinkled with Holy Water.

As we can see, the pattern is very straightforward and to-the-point, something which many liturgical historians consider to be a hold-back from the practical and austere spirit of the Roman people. In fact, the majority of rites in the Roman Ritual tend to be rather austere and goal-oriented, combining reverence with good ritual theory and psychology.

I should probably say a few words here about the post-Vatican II rites, which do not always fit this format. Sometimes they can be minimalist (the rite for blessing Holy Water, for example), and other times they are overly long and drawn-out, containing multiple scriptural readings and prayers that don't always indicate their purpose or channeling of energy. One quickly notices a marked aversion to any sort of imperative exorcism, and the tendency is to avoid blessing the object itself, but to direct a blessing towards the people who will use the object. I say these things not to disparage the Novus Ordo rite, but simply to illustrate the difference between the two ritual systems. Those interested in surveying the difference are encouraged to peruse the Roman Ritual side-by-side with *The Rites I and II* and *The Book of Blessings*, which together form the Novus Ordo equivalent of the Ritual, and to determine which system speaks most to them personally.

SACRAMENTALS PERFORMED BY THE LAITY: *EX OPERE OPERATO* VS. *EX OPERE OPERANTIS*

Earlier, we had discussed in small detail whether the sacramentals may be performed by the laity, although they're generally thought of as the exclusive right of priests and bishops. This begs the question, what's the difference?

According to classic theology, the difference rests in the character of Holy Orders, as well as the difference between validity and liceity. Through the character of Orders, the cleric is given a guarantee that any sacrament he administers will be valid, because it is Christ who confects the sacrament *through* the priest, and not the priest himself confecting it. This is called *ex opere operato*, or "by the work operated," as the flow of the Christ-current through him is so strong that neither the priest's orthodoxy nor his sinfulness can pollute it, provided the priest works with the proper form, matter, and intent of the sacrament in question.[180] For this reason, the orders and sacraments of certain heretics (Arians, Monophysites, and a number of Gnostic Groups, for example) are considered to be valid.[181]

When it comes to the sacramentals, they don't have this *ex opere operato* thing working for them, regardless of whether they are performed by a cleric or by a layperson. Rather, they draw their efficacy from a principle called *ex opere operantis*, or "from the work of the one working." This means that the efficacy of the work is determined by the virtue and merit of the operator, or the person performing the work. In other words, one's faith, virtue, and spirituality are all factors in determining whether this blessing will stick, and then how much it will stick. As individuals, a priest is no different from a layperson when it comes to these criteria.

The only real difference is that a priest is authorized to bless or exorcise in the name of the Church, while a layperson does so in his or her own name. In both cases, both act as members of the Church, and it is the Church's faith that prays with the one blessing or exorcizing. No matter what collar may be around the individual's neck, the sacramentals are performed as part of the Church's prayer

---

[180] Council of Trent, Sess. VII, Canon xii: "If any one saith, that a minister, being in mortal sin,-if so be that he observe all the essentials which belong to the effecting, or conferring of, the sacrament,-neither effects, nor confers the sacrament; let him be anathema."

[181] *Summa Theologica*, Supp., 38: *"When a bishop who has fallen into heresy is reconciled he is not reconsecrated. Therefore he did not lose the power which he had of conferring Orders. Further, the power to ordain is greater than the power of Orders. But the power of Orders is not forfeited on account of heresy and the like. Neither therefore is the power to ordain. Further, as the one who baptizes exercises a merely outward ministry, so does one who ordains, while God works inwardly. But one who is cut off from the Church by no means loses the power to baptize. Neither therefore does he lose the power to ordain."*

in, with, and through Christ to manifest His glory here in the world.

Come Holy Ghost, Creator Blest

CHAPTER FOUR: PRAYERS, DEVOTIONS, AND GESTURES

THE MENTAL ATTITUDES OF PRAYER

In this chapter, we find ourselves discussing a subject near and dear to the Catholic's devotional life, one upon which many books and articles have been written: prayer. It is also in prayer that we find ourselves at the heart of the magician's practical life.

On page 27, we referred to magic as "applied theology." And on page 29 we mentioned that the lower planes are able to influence the higher by means of petition. Thus it is by prayer that we, here on earth, send our petitions upwards to God who is above, and move Him to shine His light upon us, moving that light in such a way as to manifest those things we desire.

Older prayer books often describe two kinds of prayer: mental and vocal. There is a third kind of prayer, called corporeal. These terms are pretty self-explanatory, in that mental prayer (also called meditation) is performed by way of our thoughts, vocal with our voice, and corporeal by way of various gestures and postures. This means that everything we think, say, and do sends a message to God (who sees and hears all of it), and therefore qualifies as a type of prayer.

When we understand that everything is a type of prayer, we find ourselves in a better position to understand the concept of actual sin. In contrast to Original Sin, we must remember that Actual Sin is when we, of our own free will, choose a lesser good over a greater good. Now, if everything we think, say, and do is sending God a message, then by our thoughts, words, and actions we are telling Him exactly how much we love Him and how much we really want to do with Him, even when we're not realizing it!

This also helps us understand Jesus' words in the Gospel of Matthew, that if a man is angry at his brother, he is already guilty of murder, and that if a man lusts after a woman, he has already committed adultery. (Mt. 5:22 and 28, respectively). Understand that we have no control over what thoughts or feelings will enter our heads, so the sin (or virtue) lies in how we deal with them. If these thoughts come to us and we dismiss them, taking no pleasure from the thought, then we do not sin. However, if we think these things and dwell upon them, enjoying them, and desiring them, then we have consciously prayed for these things to happen, and actually caused them to happen on another plane (remember the Law of Mentalism). This is where we commit sin.

For prayer to be most effective, one must understand that it depends heavily upon the Laws of Correspondence and of Mentalism. The reason is that our prayers' intentions and forms originate in our minds, are felt in our hearts, and find themselves physically manifested by being voiced through our lips. The Law of Mentalism should be obvious here.

The next Law, the Law of Correspondence, is also of supreme importance. According to this Law, all the planes are in alignment. If you voice the words for a prayer when neither your mind nor heart truly want it, then you pray out of alignment with yourself, and this non-alignment may cause nothing at best, absolute chaos at worst.

Thus when we pray, we are best to remember the words of St. Teresa of Avila:

> *"I do not say mental prayer rather than vocal, for, if it is prayer at all, it must be accompanied by meditation. If a person does not think Whom he is addressing, and what he is asking for, and who it is that is asking and of Whom he is asking it, I do not consider that he is praying at all even though he be constantly moving his lips. True, it is sometimes possible to pray without paying heed to these things, but that is only because they have been thought about previously; if a man is in the habit of speaking to God's Majesty as he would speak to his slave, and never wonders if he is expressing himself properly, but merely utters the words that come to his lips because he has learned them by heart through constant repetition, I do not call that prayer at all -- and God grant no Christian may ever speak to Him so!"*[182]

One could go even further than this, and not just say "think what you're saying," but also say "think and feel what you're saying." If one has read any books on magic, especially on creative visualization (which in itself is mental prayer), he will already have received this advice: the mind, heart, and lips must all be focused on the same thing, so that the various planes of one's consciousness shall be aligned and the manifestation of one's desire shall come through.

PRACTICAL ASPECTS OF PRAYER COMPOSITION

This section should prove to be a review of material already known to a well-informed Catholic, as the mechanics of prayer are something we've been taught ever

---

[182] St. Teresa of Avila, *Interior Castle*, ch. 1

- Chapter Four: Prayers, Devotions, and Gestures -

since childhood. As children, we had to learn the basic prayers (Our Father, Hail Mary, Apostle's Creed, Glory Be) before we could receive our First Communion. We grew up surrounded by the prayers and mystery of the Mass. We're encouraged to light candles for our prayer intentions, and to seek out the intercession of the Saints as if talking to a close friend. Not to mention Benediction, the Rosary, the Novenas to this or that Saint, and so many other devotions that fill our prayer books. If anyone were to question whether the Catholic Church possesses a complete and valid magical system, here would be the place to look for that answer.

In a general sense, one could look at prayer as an outpouring of the soul to God, with or without words. In a more specific sense, it is the alignment of the physical, emotional, mental, and spiritual aspects of oneself that sends up this outpouring to the heavens, whereby God moves the Uncreated Light and showers His graces/energies upon us. However, when dealing with vocal prayer, it must be said that a certain structure is necessary. Yes, the petitioner is best to use his or her own words, just as an architect is best to design his or her own house; but if that house is not based upon sound architectural principles, it often will not stand.

In constructing a solid prayer (which can even be done *ex tempore*), the practitioner is advised to peruse the old prayer books, study the Rituals, the Liturgy, and the Divine Office of the Church, as well as those written by the Saints, and see what makes these prayers so great or efficacious, what features they all have in common. A cursory investigation will find that these prayers generally employ a great deal of imagery, while at the same time being specific and to-the-point about what they ask for. In the Official prayers of the Church, we have an even more noticeable structure and uniformity, along with rules for how each prayer is ended.

Fortunately, we don't always need that much structure in our individual prayers. It can be a good thing to have certain established patterns for use in group rites, so that everyone in the group will have something he or she can count on, and can help them attain the proper headspace for meditation and piety; but in a person's private and individual prayers, let it be said that God loves each of us for who we are, and personal experience has shown that He listens best to our heart when authentically expressed. Trappings and ceremonial conventions can either help or hinder, depending on how close (or far removed) they are from the person's individuality, yet it is hoped that these observations will prove themselves of assistance to anybody looking for ways to add a little structure to their devotional compositions.

Moving right along, we noted that many of the great prayers tend to make use of imagery. Generally, this imagery is a reference to some narrative in Scripture or in Church History, to the life of a Saint, or to someone else who has been helped by God's power or a Saint's intercession. The blessing of a boat furnishes us with an excellent example:

> "Lord, be well disposed to our prayers, and by your holy hand bless ✠ this ship (boat) and its passengers, as you were pleased to let your blessing hover over Noah's ark in the Deluge. Reach out your hand to them, Lord, as you did to blessed Peter as he walked upon the sea. Send your holy angel from on high to watch over it and all on board, to ward off any threat of disaster, and to guide its course through calm

waters to the desired port. Then after a time, when they have successfully transacted their business, may you in your loving providence bring them back with glad hearts to their own country and home. We ask this of you who live and reign forever and ever. *R.* Amen."[183]

We see here that the prayer wastes no time in getting to its purpose, yet we also have two references to Biblical history, the ark of Noah and Peter walking on the water. The imagery clearly serves no purpose to God, for He has no need to be reminded of the things He has done in the past; He knows all and remembers all. What this imagery does serve is a purpose for us, because it reminds us that God has helped people in similar circumstances, and it also establishes in our minds a historical relationship between God and others who have followed Him. In essence, therefore, the use of poetic, Biblical, and historical imagery helps us plant ourselves in eternity and find our place in it, and give us hope in the sense that as God has manifested the prayers of others, He will certainly do so for us.

It also helps us to note the aesthetic value behind using such images. Not only do they remind us of history, they also help draw our mind into focus and help us visualize what we're looking to do with this prayer. As such, this device helps immensely with getting ourselves to align vocally, emotionally, mentally, and spiritually. This is exactly what many of us need, especially in times of great distress or distraction. Thus, when one composes his own prayers, he is encouraged not only to ask directly for what

---

[183] *Benedictio Navis*, Rit. Rom., Tit. VIII, cap. 9

he needs, but also to take a moment and reflect upon God's, the Blessed Mother's, or the Saint's history of whom or where help has been given.

Another convention, at least in the Western Church, is the manner in which prayers are ended. The unofficial prayers of the Church have no special ending, but the official prayers, those found in the Missal and the Breviary, are concluded according to specific formulae, with the intention of making sure we indicate that it is through Christ that we ask for what we need.

These are described in detail, in the General Rubrics for the Roman Missal:

> 115. The conclusion of the prayers – in the Mass even as in the Office – is this:
> a) if an oration is directed to the Father, it is concluded: Through our Lord Jesus Christ, Thy Son, who liveth and reigneth with Thee in the unity of the Holy Ghost, God, forever and ever. Amen;
> b) if an oration is directed to the Father, but in its beginning there is made a mention of the Son, it is concluded: Through the same our Lord, etc., as above;
> c) if an oration is directed to the Father, but in its ending there is made a mention of the Son, it is concluded: Who liveth and reigneth with Thee in the unity of the Holy Ghost, God, forever and ever. Amen;
> d) if an oration is directed to the Son, it is concluded: Who livest and reignest with God the Father in the unity of the Holy Ghost, God, forever and ever. Amen.

- Chapter Four: Prayers, Devotions, and Gestures -

e) if in the oration there has been made a mention of the Holy Ghost, , in the conclusion is said: ... in the unity of the same Holy Ghost, etc.

116. Whensoever noted in the liturgical books, other peculiar conclusions are also to be observed.[184]

For the reader's knowledge, the most common "peculiar conclusion" to be encountered happens when a prayer is addressed to the Son, where the ending "Who livest and reignest forever and ever. Amen." is found. There are also the endings for exorcisms, which could be considered "peculiar conclusions," and which have already been discussed in Chapter Three.

So why bother with these endings for prayers? What purpose do they serve? To answer those questions, we have to think in terms of the spiritual current that we discussed in Chapter Two. As the imagery in a prayer helps remind us of others who have been initiated into that current and how they've been helped by it, it's here in these conclusions we see that current identified as the power-source through which our prayers operate; we "plug ourselves in" to Christ, the power source that lights us up and sets the world on fire!

So *in fine*, it may or may not help us, as individuals, to construct our prayers along the lines of ecclesiastical formulae, though from these formulae, and especially from

---

[184] *Rubricae Generales Breviarii ac Missalis Romani*, Tit. XVII «De Conclusionie Orationum», rubrics 115-116 (my translation). The post-Vatican II Missal also observes the same endings, as found in *Institutio Generalis Missalis Romani*, n. 54.

at least endeavoring to structure our prayers as the Church does, it can help us to become more conscious that we speak as representatives of the Church and as initiates through which her powerful current flows.

DEVOTIONS AND NOVENAS

St. Alphonsus of Ligouri has often been quoted as saying, "Those who got into heaven got there because they prayed. Those who did not get into heaven did not get there because they did not pray."

In prayer, we open up our souls to God and pour out to Him our inmost hopes and desires, sharing with Him our needs, our wants, our dreams, and our love for Him. In devotion, however, we go a little bit further.

In essence, a devotion is an exercise that commonly involves repetitive prayer and/or meditation. A devotion could take the form of a mental exercise (reading sacred literature), a vocal prayer (self-explanatory), or even a complete ritual (such as the Stations of the Cross).

The word "devotion" itself comes from the Latin "*devotio*" and means "sacrifice," and with devotion, we not only devote ourselves to God (often in exchange for some want or need being fulfilled), but we also give something of ourselves to Him. This gift is most commonly a sacrifice of time, such as spending so much time each day praying the devotion, as well as a gift of the mental and verbal faculties used in being focused upon the exercises given in the devotion. Perhaps the most perfect example can be found in the Rosary.

The Rosary, which most Catholics have known since childhood, is a complete devotion which incorporates mental, vocal, and in some small measure corporeal prayer,

Chapter Four: Prayers, Devotions, and Gestures

making it a mini-ritual. Its verbal component resides almost entirely on the basic prayers we learn as children, but by using these repetitively, we focus our minds upon one or other of fifteen "mysteries," or various scenes in the life of Jesus and Mary. Corporeally, we begin and end with the Sign of the Cross, kiss the crucifix before beginning, and slide our fingers across the beads to help us keep track of our prayers.

Each of these fifteen (note that I said fifteen, *not* twenty![185]) mysteries is associated with something called a "spiritual fruit," basically a virtue that we aspire to gain or cultivate through our meditating on its respective mystery. Thus in this devotion we sacrifice our time, the use of our minds, our lips, and our hands, in exchange for a development in virtue and for the fulfillment of multiple promises which our Lady is said to have made for those who recite the Rosary.

That being said, it should be obvious that the Rosary also has a lot of what could be considered magical uses, in that often a Rosary is recited while the operator has the specific intention to manifest something into his or her life. Examples of this could be passing an exam, finding enough food or money to feed one's children, protection from one's enemies, and so on and so forth. It is perfectly lawful

---

[185] This reference is made to the fact that the traditional Rosary has fifteen Mysteries, also called "decades" because of the ten Hail Mary's said while meditating on each one. The post-Vatican II Church has seen the addition of five more "Luminous" Mysteries, added by Pope John Paul II in his encyclical *Rosarium Virginis Mariae*, dated October 16, 2002. Though the individual Catholic is free to use these Mysteries if he so desires and to his benefit, they have been firmly rejected by Traditional Catholics. Please see Christopher Ferrara's article "Bugnini's Ghost" (*Christian Order*, May 2003) for a more thorough treatment of the subject.

to pray for these things with a Rosary (or most any other devotion, for that matter), and here we see processes of the magic arts unmasked in Catholic devotion.

Another form of devotion is the Novena, which can be any form of prayer or other devotion, whether a rosary, attending Mass, or even a set of "homebrew" prayers said over a period of nine days. Within Catholicism, the number nine is associated with a number of actions in her ritual: the *Kyrie eleison* is said nine times, there are nine Propers in the Mass, the priest turns to face the people nine times (including the sermon and the people's Communion), and there are nine prayers in the Offertory. The Latin *novem*, "nine," is also the source of the word "novena," and this custom takes its origin from the actions of the Apostles in the Upper Room.

The story of the "Upper Room" is that after Jesus ascended into heaven, the Apostles were afraid of the civil authorities. Because they were afraid, they hid in the upper room at Mary's apartment, where they waited and prayed for nine days. On the tenth day, the Jewish feast of Shavuos,[186] the Holy Ghost came upon them and they went out to preach to each person in his own language. That day about three thousand people converted to the Jesus Movement and were baptized (Acts 2:1-41). Catholic children are told this was the first Pentecost, the "birthday of the Church."

---

[186] Shavuos (Hebrew: שָׁבוּעוֹת), or the Feast of Weeks, is the Jewish feast that takes place fifty days after Passover, celebrating the reception of the Torah at Mount Sinai. By Jesus' time, many Jews spoke Greek as their first language and called the feast "Pentecost" (Greek: Πεντηκοστή), which is where the Christian term comes from.

There is really not much that can be said about novenae that hasn't already been said about devotions, except that they place an emphasis on the number nine. The same ritual, prayer, or devotion is done consecutively for nine days, and the operator's attention is concentrated on his purpose throughout that entire time, which causes a concentration of energy to build up and thus manifest even more strongly.

COMMON RITUAL GESTURES AND ACTIONS

Thus far, we have discussed aspects regarding the composition of prayers and explained the use of devotions and novenae. In this section, we move from the *orational* to the *ceremonial*, or, in other words, from the art of prayer to the art of ceremony and ritual.

In ecclesiastical parlance, a ceremony is roughly equivalent to a small mini-ritual, which composes a larger rite. For example, the Mass is a big ritual composed of a number of small rituals, and the most notable is perhaps the Elevation of the Host and Chalice. Other examples would be the *Confiteor*, the *Munda Cor Meum*, the *Lavabo*, the Elevation, and the *Per Ipsum*, but the Elevation is by far the most recognizable.

As for the size or length of a ceremony, it has no fixed length or complexity, and can be as simple as the Sign of the Cross or as complex as the *Asperges me*.[187] However, each ceremony is composed of one or more basic gestures and/or actions, which is what we shall endeavor to discuss here.

---

[187] The *Asperges* is a common name for the sprinkling of the people with holy water before Mass. It is found in the Roman Ritual under the title *Benedictio Populi cum Aqua Benedicta*, Rit. Rom., Appendix, *De Benedictionibus*, cap. 1

1) The first such gesture, and the one most familiar to every Catholic, would be the Sign of the Cross. This sign is made with the right hand, and is most commonly used in conjunction with the *Trinitarian Invocation*: "In the name of the Father, and of the Son, and of the Holy Ghost. Amen."

This sign is also made over various objects or people that the operator intends to bless, and as such it is a sign of invoking, sending, or sealing energy. When the operator crosses himself, he is receiving energy (which is why we cross ourselves at Mass when the priest blesses us; he sends energy, and we receive it). When he crosses another person or object, he is sending energy. For this reason, it is common to cross oneself at the versicle "Our help is in the name of the Lord," with which the operator not only acknowledges the source of power, but invokes it into himself. When he signs the person or object that he blesses, he then takes that power which was invoked and projects it into that person or object.[188]

2) The second most familiar gesture is that of joining one's hands. When the operator has nothing to do with his hands, he joins them together, palms facing each other, fingers extended, with the right thumb crossed over the left.[189] This is a position that denotes private prayer (public or official prayer is indicated by the *Orans* posture, and its use is restricted solely to clergy), and also denotes receptivity

---

[188] It should also be noted here that there are two forms of the Sign of the Cross, the *Great Sign* in which the operator uses his entire hand, and the *Small Sign* in which the operator uses only his thumb.

[189] Cf. Rev. Laurence O'Connell, *Book of Ceremonies*, p. 31, "When your hands are unoccupied, hold them joined before your breast; the fingers should be extended and touching each other, and should point upward at an angle of about twenty degrees; the right thumb is over the left."

- Chapter Four: Prayers, Devotions, and Gestures -

to God's influence. It is also a sign of inner calmness, and if the reader would just try it for a moment, he or she may find at least a momentary effect in that direction.

3) Two rather different, yet not necessarily opposed, positions are those of standing and kneeling. Kneeling is a position for denotes private prayer, penitence, or adoration in its highest kind, and it's for this reason that we kneel while receiving Communion, because the Body of Christ is being placed upon our tongue and into our bodies; for this reason we should all the more certainly adore Him.

Of similar import to kneeling is genuflection, an act of adoration shown only to God. This is often done while the operator is in the middle of a prayer said while standing, but then comes to a passage of such import that adoration must be shown. The Creed and the Last Gospel are primary examples of this.[190]

Standing, on the other hand, is used in public ritual, when the celebrant is praying for the people assembled, when the celebrant represents the people, or when the celebrant is exercising his authority as an initiate of the Church. This is why the operator stands when he blesses or stands when he exorcises, yet kneels when he entreats God or gives thanks.

4) Another action which comes into play is the bowing of the head. Technically there are three kinds of bows, called slight, moderate, and profound, which are held to

---

[190] When the Nicene Creed is said during the Latin Mass, the practice is to genuflect from the words "descéndit de coelis" to "et homo factus est." During the Last Gospel, the practice is to genuflect at the words "et Verbum caro factum est." In both cases, the adoration is to the act of God becoming human. In the post-Vatican II Mass, the practice is to bow one's head during this part of the Creed, while the Last Gospel has been suppressed.

correspond to three different levels of reverence (*dulia, hyperdulia, latria,* respectively[191]).

What's important for the layperson is that when reading sacred texts, he bows the head at the name of Jesus or Mary, during the recitation of the *Gloria Patri,* and briefly at the conclusion of a prayer. If the prayer's conclusion starts with "Through Our Lord," he bows at those words. If it begins with "Who liveth and reigneth," then this is where he would bow.

The above has been a description of the actions for which a layperson or a cleric in Minor Orders would have the most use. I have not discussed other gestures or postures relating primarily to the priesthood, such as the *Orans,* because is it primarily a difference between public and private prayer, placing it outside the scope of our discussion.

"The continual prayer of a just man availeth much." (James 5:16)

---

[191] In short, *latria* means "worship," and is given to God alone. *Hyperdulia* means "extra-special reverence," and is the level of reverence we show to the Mother of God. *Dulia* simply means "reverence," and refers to the manner in which we show respect to the Saints.

CHAPTER FIVE: GETTING STARTED

In the first four chapters of this work, we have discussed theology and magical theory in terms of Catholic doctrine and ritual. We have discussed the sacraments and sacramentals, prayer, and certain gestures found in the Catholic ritual system. At this stage, we take that theory and translate it into practice.

DEVELOPING THE SPIRITUAL LIFE
This is the first step that one takes on the road to practicing as a Catholic magician. The reason for this is that magic is not only just "applied theology," but it is also "applied spirituality." That is, its effectiveness is dependent upon the relationship between worshipper and Worshipped. As God is the source of all power, we can only function as magicians because He allows us to use that power. This means it's absolutely necessary that the aspiring magician build up a genuine prayer life and develop a personal relationship with Him.

The word "genuine" is important, because the practitioner cannot pray just for the purpose of accumulating power. No. Magic is a side effect of a vibrant spiritual life, but not an end purpose in itself. Devotions performed for any reason other than sheer love of God become an act of hypocrisy, and be assured that God will see the devotee's true intentions.

So how does one go about developing such a prayer life? The first step lies in finding time to pray every day. It can be a simple prayer in your own words, or it can be a prayer found in your prayer book, it can be a daily Rosary, or another devotion that you feel draws you closer to God. In all events, the first step is regular daily prayer and meditation.

Take time each day to quiet yourself, to meditate on God's majesty and love, and to devote yourself to Him. If you wish, you may also visualize yourself being covered and imbued with the light of the Trinity (see pp. 225-227). There are many ways to go about this, and each person will likely find the best way for himself through means of intuition.

Perhaps most importantly, one should strive insofar as humanly possible to be the best person that he or she can be. Receive the sacraments regularly, behave reverently in dealing with God, and deal fairly and charitably with your neighbor. If you examine the people around you, you'll find that those who have the most "personal power" also tend to have strong personal integrity and moral character. You'll also notice that their morality does not stifle or repress their individuality, but enhances it.

This means that along with prayer and meditation, the way to start is by working on your moral character. The instructions of St. Ignatius of Loyola can be helpful, as he suggests writing down every time you commit a particular sin or habit you wish to break. The idea is that in being forced to pay attention to it, you become more aware of that action and can find a way to reduce the activity. Also, you can find out what makes you act in such a way and work on it at the source.

Meditation, building moral character, and prayer. Make a point of developing a strong prayer life. My highest recommendation is that you pray the Rosary every day, because it has the side benefit of helping you to learn how to focus your mental faculties for extended periods.[192] Thus you work on developing your relationship with God, with our Lord, and with the Blessed Mother, and you also learn how to focus your mind and will. These fruits cannot be overestimated.

Finally, you should make it a point to receive the sacrament of Penance and attend Mass regularly and attentively, meditating on each part of the whole ritual and reflecting upon its significance to you. Many older prayer books contain prayers and meditations which cover each part of the Mass, and the reader is encouraged to seek these out for the help and the insight they offer.

After keeping at this for at least a month, you should be able to perceive definite signs of improvement in your mental and spiritual faculties. Once you've observed this program for at least that month, continue on to the next section.

IN THE RITUAL CHAMBER

While the reader is working on his spiritual life (a process which should never stop), he should also work on setting aside some space – be it a corner, extra room, basement, attic, etc. – which he can devote strictly to spiritual and magical exercises. He performs devotions, meditates, and practices magic in this space. He does nothing in this space that is not related to his spirituality, and in this manner sets up the area with a specific "vibe."

---

[192] To pray the Rosary effectively, it is good to visualize a scene of the mystery being meditated upon, or to visualize oneself within the scene. This is why the Rosary can be a powerful aid to developing visualization and concentration.

In this space there should be a table (we will call it a *mensa*, Latin for "tabletop"), preferably longer than it is wide. It should be covered with a white cloth and have a crucifix either standing upon it or on the wall above it. At the corners there should be two white candles, one at each corner. Many practitioners call them "altar candles," which is appropriate. They are white because white vestments are worn on feasts of Our Lord, indicating under whose auspices one's magic operates. The operator should also keep all magical-related objects and paraphernalia in this area.

HOLY WATER
After setting aside the working area, the first thing the magician should learn is the blessing of Holy Water. He should always have some on hand, since holy water is used for the blessing and consecration of almost all objects and accessories, and innumerable other uses that range from healing sickness, driving off demons, and so on and so forth. My advice is to bless it in large quantities.

The ingredients for Holy Water are water and salt, and the form of blessing provides the practitioner with a good way to start learning ritual. With this in mind, the ritual is given below, in both Traditional and Novus Ordo form:[193]

---

[193] The Traditional Blessing is taken from the *Rituale Romanum*, Tit. VIII, cap. 2, «Ordo ad Faciendam Aquam Benedictam», translated substantially by Phillip Weller and slightly revised by myself; the Novus Ordo Blessing is taken from the Sacramentary, "Rite of Blessing and Sprinkling Holy Water," translated by the International Commission for English in the Liturgy.

Chapter Five: Getting Started

Traditional Rite

Latin	English
1. *In dominicis, et quandocumque opus sit, praeparato sale et aqua munda benedicenda in operatorio, Celebrans, superpelliceo et (si clericus est) stola alba vel violacea indutus, primo dicit:* V. Adjutórium nostrum in nómine Dómini. R. Qui fecit caelum et terram.	1. *On Sundays, or whenever water must be blessed, the salt being prepared and the clean water to be blessed in the working-space, the celebrant, invested in surplice and white or purple stole (if a cleric), first says:* V. Our help is in the name of the Lord. R. Who made heaven and earth.
2. *Deinde absolute incipit exorcismum salis:* EXORCIZO te, creatúra salis, per Deum ✠ vivum, per Deum ✠ verum, per Deum ✠ sanctum, per Deum, qui te per Elíseum Prophétam in aquam mitti jussit ut sanarétur sterílitas aquae: ut efficiáris sal exorcizátum in salútem credéntium; et sis ómnibus suméntibus te sánitas ánimae et córporis; et effúgiat atque discédat a loco in quo aspérsum fúeris omnis phantásia, et nequítia, vel versútia diabólicae fraudis, omnísque spíritus immúndus, adjurátus per eum qui ventúrus est	2. *Then he absolutely begins the exorcism of salt* I exorcise thee, creature of salt, by the living ✠ God, by the true ✠ God, by the holy ✠ God, by God who ordered you to be thrown into the water-spring by Eliseus to heal it of its barrenness. May you be a purified salt, a means of health for those who believe, a medicine for body and soul for all who make use of you. May all evil fancies of the foul fiend, his malice and cunning, be driven afar from the place where you are sprinkled. And let every unclean spirit be repulsed by Him who is

judicáre vivos et mórtuos et sáeculum per ignem.
R. Amen.

Orémus. *Oratio*
IMMENSAM cleméntiam tuam, omnípotens aetérne Deus, humíliter implorámus, ut hanc creatúram salis, quam in usum géneris humáni tribuísti, bene✠dícere et sancti✠ficáre tua pietáte dignéris: ut sit ómnibus suméntibus salus mentis et córporis; et quidquid ex eo tactum vel respérsum fúerit cáreat omni immundítia omníque impugnatióne spiritális nequítiae. Per Dóminum. R. Amen.

Dicitur absolute:
EXORCIZO te, creatúra aquae, in nómine Dei✠Patris omnipoténtis, et in nómine Jesu✠Christi, Fílii ejus Dómini nostri, et in virtúte Spíritus✠Sancti: ut fias aqua exorcizáta ad effugándam omnem potestátem inimíci, et ipsum inimícum eradicáre et explantáre váleas cum ángelis suis apostáticis, per virtútem ejúsdem Dómini

coming to judge both the living and the dead and the world by fire.
R. Amen.

Let us pray.
Almighty everlasting God, we humbly appeal to your mercy and goodness to graciously bless ✠ and sanctfy ✠ this creature of salt, which you have given for mankind's use. May all who use it find in it a remedy for body and mind. And may everything that it touches or sprinkles be freed from uncleanness and any influence of the evil spirit; through Christ our Lord.
R. Amen.

It is said absolutely
I exorcize you, creature of water, in the name of God ✠ the Father almighty, in the name of Jesus ✠Christ, His Son, our Lord, and in the power of the Holy ✠Spirit. May you be a purified water, empowered to drive afar all power of the enemy, in fact, to root out and banish the enemy himself, along with his fallen angels. We ask this

- Chapter Five: Getting Started -

nostri Jesu Christi: qui ventúrus est judicáre vivos et mórtuos et sáeculum per ignem. R. Amen.

Orémus. *Oratio*
DEUS, qui ad salútem humáni géneris máxima quaeque sacraménta in aquárum substántia condidísti: adésto propítius invocatiónibus nostris, et eleménto huic, multímodis purificatiónibus praeparátio, virtútem tuae bene☩dictiónis infúnde; ut creatúra tua, mystériis tuis sérviens, ad abigéndos dáemones morbósque pelléndos divínae grátiae sumat efféctum; ut quidquid in dómibus vel in locis fidélium haec unda respérserit cáreat omni immundítia, liberétur a noxa. Non illic resídeat spíritus péstilens, non aura corrúmpens: discédant omnes insídiae laténtis inimíci; et si quid est quod aut incolumitáti habitántium invídet aut quiéti, aspersióne hujus aquae effúgiat: ut salúbritas, per invocatiónem tui sancti nóminis expetíta,

through the power of our Lord Jesus Christ, who is coming to judge both the living and the dead and the world by fire. R. Amen.

Let us pray.
O God, who for man's welfare established the most wonderful mysteries in the substance of water, hearken to our prayer, and pour forth your blessing ☩ on this element now being prepared with various purifying rites. May this creature of yours, when used in your mysteries and endowed with your grace, serve to cast out demons and to banish disease. May everything that this water sprinkles in the homes and gatherings of the faithful be delivered from all that is unclean and hurtful; let no breath of contagion hover there, no taint of corruption; let all the wiles of the lurking enemy come to nothing. By the sprinkling of this water may everything opposed to the safety and peace of the occupants of these homes be banished, so that in calling on your holy name they may

ab ómnibus sit impugnatiónibus defensa. Per Dóminum. ℟. Amen.

3. Hic ter mittat sal in aquam ad modum crucis, dicens semel:
Commíxtio salis et aquae páriter fiat, in nómine Pa✠tris, et Fi✠lii, et Spíritus✠Sancti. ℟. Amen.

℣. Dóminus vobíscum.
℟. Et cum spíritu tuo.
Orémus.*Oratio*
DEUS, invíctae virtútis auctor, et insuperábilis impérii Rex, ac semper magníficus triumphátor: qui advérsae dominatiónis vires réprimis: qui inimíci rugiéntis saevítiam súperas: qui hostíles nequítias poténter expúgnas: te, Dómine, treméntes et súpplices deprecámur, ac pétimus ut hanc creatúram salis et aquae dignánter aspícias, benígnus illústres, pietátis tuae rore sanctífices; ut ubicúmque fúerit aspérsa, per invocatiónem sancti nóminis tui omnis infestátio immúndi spíritus abigátur,

know the well-being they desire, and be protected from every peril; through Christ our Lord. ℟. Amen.

3. Thrice he puts the salt into the water in the sign of the cross, saying only once:
May this salt and water be mixed together; in the name of the Father ✠, and of the Son, ✠ and of the Holy ✠ Spirit. ℟. Amen.

℣. The Lord be with you.
℟. And with thy spirit.
Let us pray.
God, source of irresistible might and king of an invincible realm, the ever-glorious conqueror; who restrain the force of the adversary, silencing the uproar of his rage, and valiantly subduing his wickedness; in awe and humility we beg you, Lord, to regard with favor this creature thing of salt and water, to let the light of your kindness shine upon it, and to hallow it with the dew of your mercy; so that wherever it is sprinkled and your holy name is invoked, every assault of the unclean

terrórque venenósi serpéntis procul pellátur, et praeséntia Sancti Spíritus nobis, misericórdiam tuam proscéntibus, ubíque adésse dignétur. Per Dóminum.
R. Amen.

spirit may be baffled, and all dread of the serpent's venom be cast out. To us who entreat your mercy grant that the Holy Spirit may be with us wherever we may be; through Christ our Lord.
R. Amen.

Novus Ordo Rite[194]
After greeting the people (if any be present) the celebrant remains standing at his chair.
A vessel containing the water to be blessed is placed before him.
Facing the people, he invites them to pray, using these or similar words:

Dóminum Deum nostrum, fratres caríssimi, supplíciter deprecémur, ut hanc creatúram aquae benedícere dignétur, super nos aspergéndam in nostri memóriam baptísmi. Ipse autem nos adiuváre dignétur, ut fidéles Spirítui, quem accépimus, maneámus.

Dear brethren (brothers and sisters), let us humbly beseech the Lord our God to bless this water he has created, which will be sprinkled on us as a memorial of our Baptism. May he help us by his grace to remain faithful to the Spirit we have received.

After a brief silence, he joins his hands and continues:
Option A:
Omnípotens sempitérne | Almighty ever-living God,

---

[194] *Ordo ad Faciendam et Aspergendam Aquam Benedictam.* Appendix II of the *Missale Romanum*, editio tertia, Libreria Editrice Vaticana. 2002. Translation from *The Roman Missal, Third Edition*, International Commission for English in the Liturgy. 2011.

Deus, qui voluísti ut per aquam, fontem vitae ac purificatiónis princípium, étiam ánimae mundaréntur aeternáeque vitae munus excíperent, dignáre, quáesumus, hanc aquam ✠ benedícere, qua vólumus hac die tua, Dómine, communíri. Fontem vivum in nobis tuae grátiae renovári et ab omni malo spíritus et córporis per ipsam nos deféndi concédas, ut mundis tibi córdibus propinquáre tuámque digne salútem valeámus accípere. Per Christum Dóminum nostrum.
R. Amen.

who willed that through water, the fountain of life and the source of purification, even souls should be cleansed and receive the gift of eternal life; be pleased, we pray, to ✠ bless this water, by which we seek protection on this your day, O Lord. Renew the living spring of your grace within us and grant that by this water we may be defended from all ills of spirit and body, and so approach you with hearts made clean and worthily receive your salvation. Through Christ our Lord.
R. Amen.

Option B. *Or:*
Dómine Deus omnípotens, qui es totíus vitae córporis et ánimae fons et órigo, hanc aquam, te quáesumus, ✠ benedícas, qua fidénter útimur ad nostrórum implorándam véniam peccatórum et advérsus omnes morbos inimicíque insídias tuae defensiónem grátiae consequéndam. Praesta, Dómine, ut, misericórdia tua interveniénte, aquae vivae

Almighty Lord and God, who are the source and origin of all life, whether of body or soul, we ask you to ✠ bless this water, which we use in confidence to implore forgiveness for our sins and to obtain the protection of your grace against all illness and every snare of the enemy. Grant, O Lord, in your mercy, that living waters may always spring up for our salvation,

semper nobis sáliant in salútem, ut mundo tibi corde appropinquáre póssimus, et omnis córporis animáeque perícula devitémus. Per Christum Dóminum nostrum. R. Amen.

and so may we approach you with a pure heart and avoid all danger to body and soul. Through Christ our Lord. R. Amen.

Option C. *Or (during the Easter season):*

Dómine Deus omnípotens, précibus pópuli tui adésto propítius; et nobis, mirábile nostrae creatiónis opus, sed et redemptiónis nostrae mirabílius, memorántibus, hanc aquam ✚ benedícere tu dignáre. Ipsam enim tu fecísti, ut et arva fecunditáte donáret, et levámen corpóribus nostris munditiámque praebéret. Aquam étiam tuae minístram misericórdiae condidísti; nam per ipsam solvísti tui pópuli servitútem, illiúsque sitim in desérto sedásti; per ipsam novum foedus nuntiavérunt prophétae, quod eras cum homínibus initúrus; per ipsam denique, quam Christus in Jordáne sacrávit, corrúptam natúrae nostrae substántiam in regeneratiónis lavácro renovásti. Sit ígitur haec

Lord our God, in your mercy be present to your people's prayers, and, for us who recall the wondrous work of our creation and the still greater work of our redemption, graciously ✚ bless this water. For you created water to make the fields fruitful and to refresh and cleanse our bodies. You also made water the instrument of your mercy: for through water you freed your people from slavery and quenched their thirst in the desert; through water the Prophets proclaimed the new covenant you were to enter upon with the human race; and last of all, through water, which Christ made holy in the Jordan, you have renewed our corrupted nature in the bath of regeneration. Therefore, may this water be for us

aqua nobis suscípti baptismátis memória, et cum frátribus nostris, qui sunt in Pascháte baptizáti, gáudia nos tríbuas sociáre. Per Christum Dóminum nostrum.
R. Amen.

a memorial of the Baptism we have received, and grant that we may share in the gladness of our brothers and sisters who at Easter have received their Baptism. Through Christ our Lord.
R. Amen.

Where it is customary, salt may be mixed with the holy water. The celebrant blesses the salt, saying:

Súpplices te rogámus, omnípotens Deus, ut hanc creatúram salis benedícere ✚ tua pietáte dignéris, qui per Elíseum prophétam in aquam mitti eam jussísti, ut sanarétur sterílitas aquae. Praesta, Dómine, quáesumus, ut, ubicúmque haec salis et aquae commíxtio fúerit aspérsa, omni impugnatióne inimíci depúlsa, praeséntia Sancti tui Spíritus nos júgiter custódiat. Per Christum Dóminum nostrum.
R. Amen.

We humbly ask you, almighty God: be pleased in your faithful love to bless ✚ this salt you have created, for it was you who commanded the prophet Elisha to cast salt into water, that impure water might be purified. Grant, O Lord, we pray, that, wherever this mixture of salt and water is sprinkled, every attack of the enemy may be repulsed and your Holy Spirit may be present to keep us safe at all times. Through Christ our Lord. *R.* Amen.

Then he pours the salt into the water in silence.

The operator is free to utilize whichever form he chooses. What matters most is the effectiveness of the blessing being bestowed.

- Chapter Five: Getting Started -

It should be noted that only a small pinch of salt needs to be blessed for mixing into the water. If the operator chooses to bless a larger quantity of salt, he or she is free to do so, and the leftover salt can be used for many purposes, even cooking. The way I do it by using the same amount I would normally use, sprinkling it onto my food with the Sign of the Cross as I'm cooking it, and saying: *"May almighty God bless this food (soup, pasta, sauce, etc.), and deliver us from all our infirmities, injuries, and pains, in the name of the Father, and of the ✝Son, and of the Holy Ghost. Amen."*[195]

After blessing the holy water, the operator now has the principal tool for blessing and cleansing himself, his tools, candles, implements, and the entirety of the working space. Generally, this is done by dipping his hand into the water and crossing himself, or by using a sprinkler to sprinkle whom or what he intends to bless. This can be done after reciting a blessing, or as an act of blessing in and of itself.

At least once a week, the operator should sprinkle Holy Water around the working space to keep it clean, so that no muddled vibrations, negativity, or confused thoughts or feelings will be allowed to take root. In essence, you are "washing down" the ritual space and the mensa, keeping it clean and keeping out any evil or negative thoughts/thought-forms/entities that may creep in. You may even notice that it "feels" different after you've done it, too.

---

[195] This blessing is composed by myself, and the original Latin text is: «Benedícat istum cibum (*vel* istam suppam, *vel* istam pastam, *vel* istam salsam, *etc.*), et líberet nos ab ómnibus infirmitátibus, injúriis, et poenis nostris, in nómine Patris, et Fí✝lii, et Spíritus Sancti. Amen.»

The rite for sprinkling with Holy Water is called the *Asperges Me*, given below in its entirety.[196]

> *The celebrant, vested in the color of the day, approaches the mensa, takes up the aspersorium (or his fingers, if he has no aspersorium), and sprinkles the mensa thrice, then himself, then his assistants (if there be any). Then he begins singing the Antiphon* Sprinkle me, *while he proceeds to sprinkle the people and the working-space.*
>
> *Antiphon:* Thou shalt sprinkle me, O Lord, with hyssop, and I shall be cleansed: Thou shalt wash me, and I shall be made whiter than snow. *Ps. 50, 3* Take pity on me, O God, according to Thy great mercy. Glory be to the Father, and to the Son, and to the Holy Ghost. As it was in the beginning, is now, and ever shall be, world without end. Amen.
>
> *And he repeats the Antiphon* Sprinkle me, O Lord.
>
> *In Easter Time, however, to wit Passion Sunday up until Pentecost inclusive, the following Antiphon is recited or chanted:*
>
> I saw water flowing from the temple, from the right side, alleluja: and all unto whom the water flowed were saved, and they shall say: alleluja, alleluja. *Ps. 117(118):1* Confess to the Lord,

---

[196] Rit. Rom., Appendix, *De Benedictionibus*, 1, «Benedictio Populi cum Aqua Benedicta». The translation given is my own, though the rubrics have been adapted for use by a solitary layperson practicing in a house with no one assisting. A very similar form is employed in the «*Benedictio Domorum extra Tempus Paschale*» – the blessing of houses outside the Easter season – found in Rit. Rom., Tit. VIII, cap. 5

for He is good: for His mercy endureth forever.
Glory be to the Father, etc.
And the Antiphon I saw water flowing *is repeated. On Trinity Sunday the Antiphon* Sprinkle me, O Lord *is resumed, as above.*

The Antiphon being finished in the aforesaid method, the celebrant who sprinkles the water, having returned to the mensa, stands facing it, with his hands joined, and says:
V. Show us, O Lord, Thy mercy. *(Paschal Time:* Alleluia.*)*
R. And grant us Thy salvation. *(Paschal Time:* Alleluia.*)*
V. Lord, hear my prayer.
R. And let my cry come unto Thee.
V. The Lord be with you.
R. And with thy spirit.
Let us pray.
Graciously hear us, O holy Lord, almighty Father, eternal God: and vouchsafe to send Thine holy Angel from heaven; that he may guard, cherish, protect, visit, and defend all who dwell within this house. Through Christ our Lord. R. Amen.

In the post-Vatican II rite, the celebrant sprinkles in silence while a choir sings an antiphon or hymn, and afterwards he returns to the altar, faces the people, joins his hands and says: "*May almighty God cleanse us of our sins, and through the eucharist we celebrate make us worthy to sit at his table in his heavenly kingdom. R. Amen.*"[197]

---

[197] The operator may and should omit the reference to the Eucharist. He may even replace this formula with the closing prayer given in the traditional rite.

BLESSING ONE'S IMPLEMENTS

Now that the operator has set up a ritual working-space, prepared some holy water and cleansed the working area, it is time to bless the implements. Logically, the first thing to be blessed would be the mensa, because that's the point of focus for most of what the magician will be doing. One might note that I call the table a "mensa" and not an "altar," as it is commonly called by many authors. My reason is two-fold.

First, the word "mensa" refers to the table-top of an altar. Second, in my mind the word "altar" – and I derive this from in traditional Catholic parlance – refers specifically to a slab of marble containing relics from two saints, upon which Mass is celebrated; some people may call this an "altar-stone." Since we're not referring to such a stone, I find the word "mensa" preferable.

However, even though it may not be a "proper" altar, the mensa is still a place where most of the magician's attention will be fixed, and so it will prove to be a "point-of-contact" between God and man. This gives the term "mensa" another meaning, because it is not just a table. The mensa is a special table, a "Table of Light."

Since the Church has no particular rite for blessing such a table, the formula given below is of my own composition, the "Blessing of a Table of Art."[198]

---

[198] Not only does this illustrate an example of the "Who livest and reignest" peculiar conclusion mentioned in Chapter Four, but it also furnishes an example of how one can construct one's own blessings with the use of the Church's formulae.

BLESSING OF A TABLE OF ART

V. Adjutórium nostrum in nómine Dómini.
R. Qui fecit caelum et terram.
V. Dóminus vobíscum.
R. Et cum spíritu tuo.
Orémus.
DOMINE Jesu Christe, per cujus vitam, mortem, et resurrectiónem aperuísti nobis lucem caelestem, et super cujus altária sacrifícium Córporis, Sánguinis, ánimae et divinitátis tuae illúminat vitam spirituálem nostram: bene☩dícere digneris et sancti☩ficáre istam mensam, ut fiat mensa lucis divínae, super quam manifesténtur ómnia propósita in méntibus eórum uténtium ad orándum te in glorificatiónem nóminis tui, et ad majórem manifestándam preséntiae Spíritus ☩ Sancti in orbem terrárum. Qui vivis et regnas in sáecula saeculórum.
R. Amen.
Et aspergatur aqua benedicta.

V. Our help is in the name of the Lord.
R. Who made heaven and earth.
V. The Lord be with you.
R. And with thy spirit.
Let us pray.
O Lord Jesus Christ, through whose life, death, and resurrection Thou hast opened unto us the heavenly light, and upon whose altars the sacrifice of Thy Body, Blood, soul and divinity illuminates out spiritual life: vouchsafe to ☩bless and ☩sanctify this table, that it may be a table of divine light, upon which may be made manifest every purpose which is in the minds of those who shall use it for praying to Thee in glorification of Thy name, and to the greater manifestation of the presence of the Holy ☩Ghost throughout the entire world. Who livest and reignest forever and ever. *R.* Amen.
And it is sprinkled with holy water.

The holy water is sprinkled thrice, in the form of a cross, while the celebrant says nothing. This is the usual procedure of sprinkling anytime the rubric calls for it, unless the rite specifically says otherwise.

Now that the mensa has been blessed, it is covered with a white cloth which doesn't need any particular blessing. If you feel the need to bless it, a few sprinkles of Holy Water should suffice.

The next thing to bless would be the Crucifix, if it is not blessed already. The form for this is as follows:[199]

V. Adjutórium nostrum in nómine Dómini.	V. Our help is in the name of the Lord.
R. Qui fecit caelum et terram.	R. Who made heaven and earth.
V. Dóminus vobíscum.	V. The Lord be with you.
R. Et cum spíritu tuo.	R. And with thy spirit.
Orémus. *Oratio*	Let us pray.
Rogámus te, Dómine sancte, Pater omnípotens, aetérne Deus: ut dignéris bene✝dícere hoc signum Crucis, ut sit remédium salutáre géneri humáno; sit solíditas fídei, proféctus bonórum óperum, redémptio animárum; sit solámen, et protéctio, ac tutéla contra saeva jácula inimicórum. Per Christum Dóminum nostrum. R. Amen.	We beseech Thee, holy Lord, Father almighty, eternal God: that Thou mayest vouchsafe to ✝bless this sign of the Cross, that it may be a saving help to mankind; let it be a bulwark of faith, and encouragement to good works, the redemption of souls; let it be a consolation and a protection, and a shield against the cruel darts of the enemy; through Christ our Lord. R. Amen.

---

[199] Rit. Rom., Tit. VIII, cap. 24., «*Solemnis Benedictio Crucis*»

Chapter Five: Getting Started

Oremus. *Oratio*
BENE✠DIC, Dómine Jesu Christe, hanc Crucem, per quam eripuísti mundum a potestáte dáemonum, et superásti passióne tua suggestórem peccáti, qui gaudébat in praevaricatióne primi hóminis per ligni vetíti sumptiónem. *Hic aspergatur aqua benedicta.* Sanctificétur hoc signum Crucis in nómine Pa✠tris, et Fí✠lii, et Spíritus ✠Sancti; ut orántes, inclinantésque se propter Dóminum ante istam Crucem, invéniant córporis et ánimae sanitátem. Per eúndem Christum Dómunim nostrum.
R. Amen.
2. postea Celebrans ante Crucem genuflexus ipsam devote adorat, et osculatur, et idem faciunt quicumque voluerint.

Let us pray.
✠Bless, O Lord Jesus Christ, this Cross, by which Thou hast delivered the world from the power of demons, and by Thy passion conquered the tempter of sin; who rejoiced in the first man's fall in eating of the forbidden tree. *Here he sprinkles the Cross with Holy Water.* May this sign of the Cross be ✠hallowed in the name of the ✠Father, and of the ✠Son, and of the Holy ✠ Ghost; that those who kneel and pray in honor of our Lord before this Cross may find health in body and soul. Through the same Christ our Lord. R. Amen.
Afterwards the celebrant genuflects and devoutly adores the Cross, and whosoever wishes may do the same.

The Crucifix is now blessed, and may be placed upon the mensa or hung on the wall. The next step would be to bless the "altar candles," which follows the standard blessing as given in the Ritual:[200]

V. Adjutórium nostrum in nómine Dómini.	V. Our help is in the name of the Lord.
R. Qui fecit caelum et terram.	R. Who made heaven and earth.
V. Dóminus vobíscum.	V. The Lord be with you.
R. Et cum spíritu tuo.	R. And with thy spirit.
Orémus *Oratio*	Let us pray.
DOMINE Jesu Christe, Fili Dei vivi, béne✠dic cándelas istas supplicatiónibus nostris: infúnde eis, Dómine, per virtútem sanctae Cru✠cis, benedictiónem caeléstem, qui eas ad repelléndas ténebras humáno géneri tribuísti, talémque benedictiónem signáculo sanctae Cru✠cis accípiant, ut, quibuscúmque locis accénsae, sive pósitae fúerint, discédat príncipes tenebrárum, et contremíscant, et fúgiant pávidi cum ómnibus minístris suis ab habitatiónibus illis, nec praesúmat amplíus inquietáre, aut molestáre serviéntes tibi omnipoténti Deo: Qui vivis et regnas in	Lord Jesus Christ, Son of the living God, ✠bless these candles at our humble request. Endow them, Lord, by the power of the holy ✠Cross, by an heavenly blessing, Thou who gavest them to humankind to dispel the darkness; let the blessing that they receive by the sign of the holy ✠Cross be so effectual that, wherever they are lighted or places, the princes of darkness may tremble and depart from these places, and flee in fear, along with all their legions, and never more dare to disturb or molest those who serve Thee, almighty God; who livest and reignest forever and ever.
	R. Amen.

---

[200] Rit. Rom., Tit. VIII, cap. 3, «*Benedictio Candelarum*»

sáecula saeculórum.
R. Amen.

| Et aqua benedicta aspergantur. | And they are sprinkled with holy water. |

As a side note, the order in which these items are being blessed isn't necessary, nor is it mandatory. Rather, I am simply listing them in the order in which they would likely be placed on the mensa. Holy water, admittedly, must be blessed first, because it's needed for blessing the other objects, but all the others needn't happen in any particular order.

These are the basic things needed for the purpose of practicing as a Catholic mage. It may seem quite simple when compared with many other magical systems, yet the faith Jesus gave us is equally simple, and look at the wonderful things it has accomplished for so many people!

THE USE OF CANDLES

We now arrive at the part that everybody's been waiting for: the theory is done, the spiritual preparation is underway, and the implements have been blessed; now how do we start casting spells?

Well, that's the problem. We don't cast spells, at least not on my watch. The word sounds so childish and so puellile[201] that it doesn't deserve to be used in connection with the processes of Catholic magic, no matter how simple. We might practice theurgy,[202] we might perform operations, and we definitely confect sacramentals. But we *don't* cast spells!

---

[201] Puellile: a word that I made up, meaning "little girl-ish."
[202] Theurgy: from the Greek θεουργία. Magic rites based on the invocation of deity.

As I said earlier, one's magical operations are sacramentals insofar as they result in conferring actual graces and thus an increase in the operator's faith in Christ. If you pray for money to feed your kids, for example, and the money comes, then an actual grace has been granted; this usually leads to one's faith being edified. This is what I mean when saying magic is a sacramental. Therefore the term "sacramental" is preferable to "spell," because it more accurately describes what we're doing here.

Most of the operations which you'll do, at least when starting out, will involve candles and prayer. Most of your own work, especially later on, will be composed according to what you find works best for you, and likely determined by your individual situation. As such, the directions in this book are meant as a guideline to help you organize your practice, but never as a hard-and-fast rule. Please bear this in mind as you go along.

The Catholic magician is faced with many choices for the candles used in ritual; the three most common options are: tapers, votives, and seven-day candles. Tapers can be found in almost any retail store, while votive and seven-days are the same types of candles you find at the side altars in a church, made either of colored wax, or a white "insert" inside a colored glass sleeve. In all things of this sort, the best choice is whichever works best for you. Generally speaking, votive candles are better suited for single-burns or one-day rites, while seven-day candles are better suited for longer rituals such as novenae or other continuous devotions. Tapers fit somewhere in between.

Once you light a candle, you should not blow it out unless there's a grave necessity. The light of the candle signifies the light of Christ in the world, while the act of burning a candle is representative of an offering made to Christ, the

- Chapter Five: Getting Started -

Blessed Mother, or the Saint whom you are invoking. As an offering is most acceptable when it is pure and undisturbed, you don't want to disturb the offering by extinguishing and re-lighting the candles. True, some rites will involve extinguishing and re-lighting, but the general rule of thumb is to let the candles burn themselves all the way down.

For the candles themselves, you may have noticed that I mentioned they come in different colors. One will find that different authors give different reasons for their colors and different attributions, though the general meanings are the same. According to Vito Quattrocchi in his *Sicilian Benedicaria*,[203] these colors have their roots in those used by the Catholic Church in her vestments and the colors she associates with the Saints.

The colors the Church has used in her ceremonial have a long and varied history, and the custom of using different colors for different seasons seems to have come about in the ninth century. Pope Innocent III is the first to mention a scheme of four colors used in the Roman Rite, and he mentions red, white, black, and green; violet was considered a variant of black, rose was used on the feast of martyrs, and yellow for confessors.[204] Later on, violet became distinguished from black and treated as its own

---

[203] Vito Quattrocchi, *Sicilian Benedicaria: Magical Catholicism*, 2003, self-published.
[204] Pope Innocent III. *De Sacro Altaris Mysterio*. Book I, ch. 64: "Now the principal colors are four, by which the Roman Church distinguishes her sacred vestments according to the properties of the days: white, red, black, and green." At the end of the chapter Innocent speaks of other colors, saying: "To these four [colors], others are referred: to red, the scarlet color; to black, violet; to green, saffron. Although to some: rose refers to martyrs, saffron to confessors, and the Lily to virgins." (my translation)

color, creating the five-color scheme codified by Pope St. Pius V in the Roman Missal of 1570.[205]

We should note that prior to 1570, the choice of color was more a matter of custom than of obligation, and even after 1570 different color schemes were permitted if they had an established use of 200 years or longer.[206] Prior to the codification of the 1570 Missal, each local church could well have had its own system of colors. Some may have worn only black and white vestments, while others had more colors than the rainbow.[207]

These colors are known to many older Catholics, yet younger Catholics are generally not taught about them, which is why we're discussing the subject here. So kids, if you ever get the chance, take a peek into your parents' and grandparents' old hand missals or prayer books. Trust me; you'll be downright floored by how much your catechism teachers kept away from you!

---

[205] *Missale Romanum.* 1570. General Rubrics, Title XVIII: "The paraments of the altar, the Celebrant and ministers should be in the color common to the Office and Mass of the day, according to the use of the Roman Church: which five colors she is accustomed to use: white, red, green, violet, and black." (my translation)

[206] Pope St. Pius V. *Quo Primum Tempore.* 1570. "This new rite alone is to be used unless approval of the practice of saying Mass differently was given ... at least 200 years ago, or unless there has prevailed a custom of a similar kind ... for a period of not less than 200 years ..." (translation from http://www.papalencyclicals.net/Pius05/p5quopri.htm. retrieved 11/29/2014.)

[207] One example of "more colors than the rainbow" would be the Sarum Use, a variant of the Roman Rite followed in England prior to the Protestant Reformation. This is the source for the custom of wearing the gray/white "Lenten Array" found in some Anglican churches. There is also debate that the Sarum Use is the source of wearing blue vestments during Advent, though "Advent Blue" seems just as likely to have come from the Scandinavian Lutheran churches.

- Chapter Five: Getting Started -

As to the colors, the five main colors are as follows:
1. **White** is the color or purity, innocence, and joy. It is worn on high Feast-days, feasts of Our Lord and Our Lady, and the times immediately after Christmas and Easter, during the second half of the rite of Baptism, and during the sacraments of Matrimony and Confirmation.

As a magician, this joy also translates to spirituality, and this association with Our Lord and Our Lady translates to protection and intercession. Traditionally, because white light contains all the colors of the rainbow, white candles may also be used as a substitute for any other candle color except black.

2. **Red** is the color of blood, the Holy Ghost, and of love, particularly the love of God. It is the color for all Masses of the Holy Ghost, for Ordinations (which invoke the Holy Ghost), Feasts on which the suffering and the Cross of Christ are called to mind (except for Good Friday), and the feast-days of the Apostles and Martyrs, who shed their blood for the love of God.

Magically red, as the color of blood, is also a color of power and energy; it can symbolize the divine energy of the Holy Ghost, and it can also symbolize raw, physical energy and strength. It can also be used for human love, which ideally is a reflection of the divine love.

3. **Green** is the color of hope, of growth, and of fertility. As a liturgical color, it is worn used on the Sundays after Epiphany and the Sundays after Pentecost (what the Novus Ordo calls "Ordinary Time"), as well as on all ferias (weekdays) that do not have a Saint's feast assigned to them.

Magically, this color is most often employed in fertility and money rituals. The association with fertility comes from green's place as the predominant color in nature, and its association with money stems from the fact that one needs to fertilize the soil upon which the money crop can grow, before any growth can take place. Hence fertility and growth are but two sides of the same coin.

4. **Violet** is the color of humility and of penance, suffering and fasting. It is worn during Advent and Lent, as well as during the Ember Days and the Rogations, as well as during while administering the first part of the rite of Private Baptism and the sacraments of Penance and Extreme Unction. It is also a color of Kingliness, as the soldiers put a purple robe on Jesus (John 19:2, Mark 15:17), and is used in the rite of exorcism.

Magically, this makes violet a color associated with kingly power, especially Christ's kingly power, and also with purification. We can glean that, when the priest changes from violet to white vestments in the old rite of Baptism, violet is used for the process of purification, while white refers to the actual purity itself.

5. **Black**, as the opposite of white and a heavier analogue of violet, is the color of mourning and deep sorrow. It is traditionally used on Good Friday, when the Church mourns Jesus' death, on November 2 ("All Soul's Day") when the Church prays for the souls in Purgatory, and in all funerary Masses and rites of burial.

Magically, this is not a color I recommend using; I know it's used within other magical traditions, but within the Church's ritual its associations with death are all too overwhelming. In fact, this is so overwhelming that the term "Black Mass" authentically refers to a funeral Mass, on account of the black vestments; its association with evil came about when a funeral Mass is offered for a person still living, with the intent of bringing about that person's death.

These are the basic liturgical colors first recognized by Innocent III and later codified by St. Pius V. There are other colors, too, which are or were allowed in the Church's liturgy, and which have likewise left their mark on popular magical practices:
    1. **Rose** – a purplish-pink mixture – is a combination of red, white, and violet, and a sign of love and penance, or subdued joy. In Innocent III's time, it was worn on the feast-days of Martyrs, who suffered (violet) and shed their blood (red) for the love of Christ (white). It is now used on only two feast-days of the year: Gaudete, the third Sunday of Advent; and

Laetare, the fourth Sunday of Lent. The reason is to reflect the Church's joy at these penitential seasons being halfway over.

Interestingly enough, the magical use of this color is to accelerate things into manifestation, denoting it as a combination of red (energy) and violet (power). I find this to be curious, and speculate that this may stem from the older association with the Martyrs, based on the old logic that Martyrdom granted instant entry into heaven, or, as one could say, "accelerated their manifestation" into the heavenly Kingdom.

2. **Gold** is allowed to be worn on any day that is normally white, red, or green, and in practice it is usually worn on Christmas Day and Easter Sunday, where it denotes a high degree of joy bordering on ecstasy. It also denotes the Sun shining down upon us, as it is during the Christmas and Easter celebrations that we see the Son shining forth in radiant glory. The color gold refers to worth, to virtue, and to the glory of God.

Magically, this color is used to bring a great deal of energy into the operation, like a ray of the sun piercing into – and through – the cloud covering of a gloomy world, and then burning away the clouds to reveal a bright, blue sky. The color gold can also be used to overcome opposition and manifest the glory of God through your operations.

3. **Blue**, as a liturgical color, is forbidden in the Roman Rite, except with very special exceptions; for example, in Spain and certain Spanish-speaking countries it is used for the feast of the Immaculate Conception. In the Eastern Churches (where local custom prevails) and in the Carmelite and Mozarabic[208] Rites, blue may be worn on feasts of the Blessed Mother. Though blue was replaced by white in Rome, it still remains the Blessed Mother's color within the realm of popular devotion and religiosity. In the Episcopalian and some Lutheran churches, blue is also used for Advent as a symbol of hope and of waiting with Mary for Jesus' arrival; this hope can also be applied to her intercessions on our behalf.

Both devotionally and magically, blue is applied in a special way to ask the Blessed Mother's intercession, and represents the peace, protection, and prosperity that is obtainable through her pleading our case before the Father.

4. **Yellow**, another forbidden color, was once used for the feasts of Confessors, who professed the faith with joy and gladness even up till death. While the Martyrs died a death of red blood for their faith, the Confessor was able to die a death upon which the yellow rays of happiness shone.

---

[208] Mozarabic Rite: The Liturgy traditionally celebrated used in southern Spain, until being suppressed by the Novus Ordo Missae in 1969.

Magically, this means that yellow can be used to represent happiness, in imitation of the happiness of the Confessors.

The student of folk magic and candle magic will notice that these nine colors – white, red, green, violet, black, rose, gold, blue, and yellow – are the most common colors used in magical practice, and we now see how these colors derive their meaning from the historic color schemes of the Catholic Church.

There are other colors not found in the Liturgy, however, which can be formed from combinations of two or more liturgical colors. Brown, for example, is commonly used in candle magic to manifest things to the material plane; one would be hard-pressed to explain this in terms of the Church's color scheme, but it's effectively a mixture of red and green, the power of the Holy Ghost and the color of growth and fertility. Using this example as a guide, it is possible to find colors which will suit any purpose the magician has in mind.

In an operation using candles, you should have at least one candle representing you, in a color either related to your purpose or representing the patron saint associated with your purpose (pp. 179-208). For example, if you're looking to find a new job, you would use a green candle for growth or a yellow one for St. Joseph, the patron saint of workers. Since we're on the subject, if a Saint is to be invoked, you may also want a picture of that Saint on your mensa. A Holy Card, especially a relic card, is perfect, but if you can obtain a first-class relic, then so much the better!

Now you would make the Sign of the Cross and light your two "mensa candles," and underneath the candle representing you, you may place a piece of paper or

- Chapter Five: Getting Started -

parchment whereon you have written your name and your purpose. For example: "A new job comes to N."

If you wish, you may choose to anoint the candles with an oil that corresponds to your purpose. New Age, Pagan, and Occult shops carry a great variety of these oils, with names like "Money Drawing," "Come to Me," and so forth. The Church offers us an alternate option, as she provides the faithful with oils specially blessed and consecrated in honor of the Saints. These oils must be officially blessed in the name of the Church, and therefore a priest or bishop must bless them; if you've ever held or used these oils, you'd understand what I mean. You'll find St. Michael oil, St. Francis oil, St. Peregrine oil, and so many others designed specifically to invoke the powers of the Church Triumphant on your behalf.

In looking for a job, you could place a green seven-day candle on your mensa and anoint it with St. Joseph oil. To anoint it, you can either rub the oil across the top of the candle with your right thumb, or you can poke a long screwdriver down the length of the candle and pour the oil in the hole. As you apply the oil, you say "Through the intercession of St. Joseph, and Christ's most loving mercy, may almighty God grant me the grace a new job. Amen." This formula can be adapted for any Saint and for any purpose, and the wording can be changed into something more comfortable for you.

Next you would step back, compose your thoughts, and contemplate the good that finding a new job will bring you, and how thankful you will be to God for helping you find one. When you've contemplated this enough, step forward, hands joined, and pray in your own words that God will grant you the grace of a new job through St. Joseph's intercession. Make sure to pray "through the Name of

Jesus our Lord," as it is through God the Son that a Christian's prayers will ultimately be answered.

After this, you would proceed to light the candle. While you light the candle, say "As I light this candle, so does a new source of employment come to N. Amen."

As the candle burns, you would take a few moments to visualize yourself with a new job, visualize the paycheck, having your rent, mortgage, bills, or whatever paid, and the things you can do once you get that job. Whatever your purpose, be honest with yourself and allow yourself to feel happy while you're visualizing. The happier you genuinely allow yourself to feel, and the more honest you are with yourself and with God, the more effective your prayers will be.

Once you've visualized for a reasonable amount of time, say another prayer in your own words praying that God will help you. After this, make the sign of the Cross and extinguish your mensa candles. However, you want to leave the primary candle burning. Put all thoughts of the rite outside your mind for the time being, and do not disturb the candles or blow them out.

Now once every day, until your candle burns itself out, you want to light the mensa candles and repeat this process. On the day the mensa candle burns out, you make a special prayer to God giving Him thanks for having fulfilled your prayer. For this, speak in the past tense, even if your desire has not been fulfilled; the reason for this is to show you have faith in Him, and also because psychologically it will help you to overcome doubt or fear.

Chapter Five: Getting Started

So far, this is the most basic form of candle magic usable for a Catholic, and you will find these sacramentals to be quite efficacious under normal circumstances. There are other methods for dealing with multi-aspect problems, such as having a candle for each aspect of the problem to be solved, or offering a Rosary while the candle burns, and so on and so forth. These and more advanced procedures will be covered in a future book dedicated solely to candle magic, but unfortunately they are beyond the scope of a book that's simply aiming to present the basic facts and theological principles of Catholic magical practices.

Angels Show Sir Galahad the Holy Grail

CHAPTER SIX: ANGELS AND SAINTS

> "I love the Saints of olden time,
> The places where they dwelt;
> I love to pray where Saints have prayed,
> And kneel where they have knelt."
> – *From the hymn "I Am a Faithful Catholic"*

Historically, Protestants have made many accusations against Catholics. Of these, one of the best-known is the Catholic attachment to the Saints. Starting with Calvin, the **cult of the Saints** was considered idolatry,[209] and with Middleton, the Protestant bias became something of a matching game wherein authors would play "match that saint to that Pagan deity."[210] During the nineteenth century, there was even an attempt to draw direct comparisons between Catholicism and Hinduism![211]

So what is it about the Catholic (and Orthodox) devotion to the Saints that yanks the Protestant chain? Is it their doctrine of *Soli Deo Gloria*,[212] or is it their insistence on

---

[209] Calvin, *Institutes of the Christian Religion*, III, 12, 1: "In the same way, too, for some ages past, departed saints have been exalted to partnership with God, ... At the same time, being deluded by these entanglements, we go astray after divers gods." (June 30, 2015) http://www.ccel.org/ccel/calvin/institutes.iii.xiii.html

[210] Middleton, Conyers. *A Letter from Rome, Showing an Exact Conformity between Popery and Paganism.* 1729. https://archive.org/details/drmiddletonslett00midd. June 30, 2015.

[211] Poynder, John. *Popery in Alliance with Heathenism.* 1835. https://books.google.com/books?id=cIIBAAAAQAAJ&dq=poynder+popery+and+hinduism&source=gbs_navlinks_s. June 30, 2015.

[212] *Soli Deo Gloria*, or "Glory to God Alone." One of the **Five Solas** of the Protestant Revolt, it means that God is to be approached and glorified directly with no intermediaries: not the Saints, not the Angels, and certainly not Mary.

seeing themselves as slaves devoid of free will in regard to things spiritual?[213 and 214]

Unlike the Protestant, the Catholic neither lives in a universe devoid of spiritual diversity, nor does he serve as a slave to a cruel God who, before the beginning of time, decreed that some would be welcome into heaven and others would be condemned to hell just because He said so.

Unlike the Protestant, the Catholic is master of his or her own destiny, free to choose God's offer of salvation and free to reject it. Unlike the Protestant, the Catholic lives in a universe filled with spiritual helpers who will help him or her in times of need and distress,[215] and these helpers are described in the doctrine of the **Tripartite Church.**

THE TRIPARTITE CHURCH
In the Apostles' Creed, we say "I believe in the Communion of Saints." But what is meant by this term, "Communion of Saints?"

---

[213] John Calvin's doctrine of predestination is well-known. See his *Institutes of the Christian Religion*, III, 21, 5. "All are not created on equal terms, but some are preordained to eternal life, others to eternal damnation; and, accordingly, as each has been created for one or other of these ends, we say that he has been predestinated to life or to death." http://www.ccel.org/ccel/calvin/institutes.v.xxii.html. June 30, 2015.
See also Luther's *On the Bondage of the Will*. Retrieved June 30, 2015. http://www.covenanter.org/Luther/Bondage/bow_toc.htm.

[214] The Catholic position affirming free will is expressed in the Council of Trent, Session VI, c. 4: "If any one saith, that, since Adam's sin, the free will of man is lost and extinguished; ... let him be anathema."

[215] This is true of Reformed Protestantism. Lutheranism concedes that the Saints pray for us all the time and thus opposes invocation as an unnecessary exercise. *Apology to the Augsburg Confession*, XXI. (Retrieved 6/30/2015) http://bookofconcord.org/defense_20_saints.php

This term, in the Apostle's Creed after the words "the holy Catholic Church," serves to remind us that the Church is more than just the faithful here on earth, and that the Church continues further out than what we see here during our lifetimes. Instead, the Church consists of three parts: the **Church Triumphant** in heaven, the **Church Militant** on earth, and the **Church Suffering** in purgatory.[216]

Interrelationship of Church Members

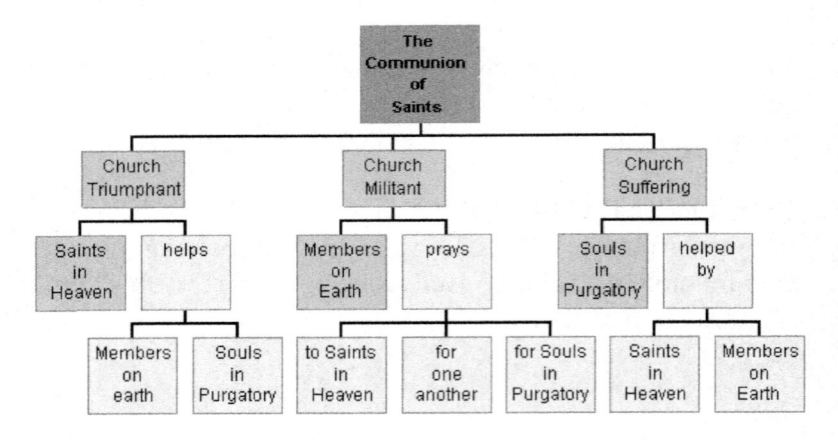

```
                    The Communion of Saints
        ┌───────────────────┼───────────────────┐
   Church Triumphant    Church Militant    Church Suffering
    ┌─────┴─────┐       ┌─────┴─────┐       ┌─────┴─────┐
  Saints      helps   Members      prays  Souls        helped
    in                   on                  in           by
  Heaven                Earth             Purgatory
              ┌──────┴──────┐   ┌──────┬──────┐   ┌──────┴──────┐
          Members        Souls  to Saints  for    for Souls   Saints    Members
            on            in      in       one       in         in        on
           earth       Purgatory Heaven  another Purgatory    Heaven     Earth
```

1. The Church Triumphant (*Curia Triumphans*): is comprised of all the Angels, Saints, Blesseds, and everybody else in heaven, who have conquered the wiles and temptations of the adversary in life and now have earned their reward in the next world. These blessed souls watch over and intercede on behalf of the other two parts of the Church. Since this part of the Church sees and knows

---

[216] Ott, *Fundamentals*, IV, II, 21: "In the following exposition the concept Church is taken in the wider sense to designate all those redeemed and sanctified by the grace of Christ whether on earth, in Purgatory or in Heaven. The Church in this wider sense is usually called the Communion of Saints."

the God on a personal basis, they know more about him, his rules, and the way he thinks than the rest of us presently do. Therefore, they could be said to use this special knowledge and act as our lawyers in God's court, helping us to get the favors we ask for and/or need.[217]

2. The Church Militant (*Curia Militans*): This is you and me, all baptized persons in communion with the Catholic Church, we who are supposed to be fighting the good fight against the wicked adversary. Of course we don't always fight the good fight, but that's another story.

Our relationship is that we receive help and intercession from the Church Triumphant, and in turn we help the Church Suffering by means of prayers, indulgences (we can pass our indulgences on to them), and our own petitions on their behalf before the Divine Throne.[218]

3. The Church Suffering (*Curia Patiens*): These are the people who didn't make it to heaven, but aren't quite bad enough to go to hell, either. Thus God, in his infinite mercy, decided to still give them a way of getting into heaven, a state of the soul which we call purgatory.[219] Since nothing impure can enter heaven, purgatory is

---

[217] Roman Catechism, I, 10, 8. "The Church triumphant is that most glorious and happy assemblage of blessed spirits, and of those who have triumphed over the world, the flesh, and the iniquity of Satan, and are now exempt and safe from the troubles of this life and enjoy everlasting bliss."

[218] Roman Catechism I, 10, 9: "The Church militant is the society of all the faithful still dwelling on earth. It is called militant, because it wages eternal war with those implacable enemies, the world, the flesh and the devil."

[219] Roman Catechism I, 6, 5: "Among them is also the fire of purgatory, in which the souls of just men are cleansed by a temporary punishment, in order to be admitted into their eternal country, into which nothing defiled entereth." See also CCC 1030-1032.

something like a spiritual washing machine where the stains of venial sin (or temporal guilt remaining from mortal sin) are washed away so these souls can eventually be received into heaven. Those in purgatory folks are commonly referred to "The Poor Souls."

In the big scheme of things, the Poor Souls are said not to be able to pray for themselves, which leaves them dependent on our prayers and intercessions on their behalf. However, they are still able to pray and intercede for us in the Church Militant.[220] Nobody knows the holiness of another person, yet I would wager that most people end up in purgatory, which includes our ancestors. Along these lines, I would say that so long as we do so in good faith, there's nothing wrong with asking for our ancestors to assist us with their prayers.[221]

LATRIA AND DULIA

Since Protestants (and Neopagans converted from Protestantism) often charge that veneration of the Saints is no different from praying to Pagan gods, we would do well briefly to review the Church's teaching on the subject.

The way the Church speaks to the Angels and the Saints is not the same way the Church speaks to God. When she speaks to God, it is out of a spirit of worship, which is technically called **latria**, from the Greek word λατρεία meaning "worship." In the Church's liturgy, the acts of

---

[220] There is debate on whether the Poor Souls can pray for us, and the Church has never issued an official declaration. A good starting point would be the 1911 *Catholc Encyclopedia* article on Purgatory, under the heading "Invocation of Souls." (Retrieved July 1, 2015) http://www.newadvent.org/cathen/12575a.htm

[221] The Roman Catechism only describes the Church Triumphant and Militant. The CCC discusses all three in a very general manner (nn. 954-962), but without giving names to the parts of the Church.

bowing, incensation, genuflection, kneeling, and so forth are considered gestures of latria and reserved for God alone.

When the Church invokes the Angels or the Saints, she speaks in a manner of **dulia**, from the Greek word δουλεία, meaning "reverence." She speaks to the Angels and Saints as one would speak to a revered and cherished friend, oftentimes as a friend able and willing to help us out of a tight spot.

Lastly, there is a special category within Catholic devotion, called **hyperdulia**, from ὑπέρδουλεία, meaning "extra special reverence." There is only one person who receives hyperdulia, and that person is the Blessed Virgin Mary.

With these concepts in mind, it's possible to move onward, where we'll first discuss the concepts involved in working with the Angels, and then the concepts for working with the Saints.

WORKING WITH THE ANGELS

In the Roman Missal, we find a list of votive Masses for the various days of the week which can be said on a "ferial" day (i.e. a weekday when there's no Saint's feast). Of these, we find a special Mass given for Tuesdays, which is called the Mass of the Angels. What sets this Mass apart is that it's the only votive Mass where the *Gloria in Excelsis* is always said.[222]

Actually, it is of great efficacy to have a priest offer Mass for your intentions, and in this Mass the Angels are called upon to help you, especially in the Collect (also called the

---

[222] *Rubricae Generales Missalis Romani*, Titulus VIII «De Diversis Missae Partibus», rubrics 431e and 432c.

"Opening Prayer").[223] There is also a "Little Office of the Angels," which we share on page 171 of this book, and Catholic children around the world are taught the prayer to the Guardian Angel:
> Angel of God, my guardian dear,
> To whom His love commits me here.
> Ever this day (night) be at my side,
> To light and guard, to rule and guide. Amen.[224]

Older Catholic prayer books are filled with prayers to the Angels, and we need not look far to find a Chaplet dedicated to St. Michael and the Nine Angelic Orders.[225] We further find that in the Biblical Book of Tobit, the Archangel Raphael identifies himself to the young Tobias as "one of the seven Angels who enter and serve before the glory of the Lord." (Tobit 12:15)

This list of examples can go on for a long time, and Catholic piety traditionally places a great deal of faith in Angelic watchfulness and intercession. But how much does the average Catholic really know about the Angels?

---

[223] The Collect reads: "O God, by a marvelous order you arrange the ministries of angels and of men. Graciously grant that our lives will be assisted and helped by those who always minister to you in heaven. Through our Lord, etc." (my translation)

[224] The original Latin is: "Angele Dei, qui custos es mei, me tibi commíssum pietáte supérna; hódie (hac nocte) illúmina, custódi, rege et gubérna. Amen."
The history of the prayer is discussed at the *Thesaurus Precum Latinarum* website, given below. (Retrieved November 29, 2014).
http://www.preces-latinae.org/thesaurus/Basics/AngeleDei.html

[225] This chaplet dates to 1751, when St. Michael is said to have appeared to a Portuguese nun named Antónia d'Astónaco. The devotion was approved by Pope Pius IX in 1851. The text of the devotion may be found at:
http://www.ewtn.com/devotionals/prayers/chaplet-of-st-michael.htm.
(Retrieved November 29, 2014.)

Does he know the names of any more than three of them? Can he name the Nine Orders from which the Angels come, and the areas over which they have charge? Does he even have a good working relationship with his *own* Guardian Angel?[226] Nine times out of ten, I'd bet his answer to all these questions is likely "No."

THE NINE ORDERS
This being said, let us start out with a quick foundational course in Catholic Angelology, which is most strongly influenced by a book called the *Celestial Hierarchies*, written in Greek in the fifth century and attributed to an unknown author commonly called "Pseudo-Dionysius."[227] This is the book that laid the foundation for the Catholic conception of the nine Orders of Angels: Seraphim, Cherubim, Thrones (or, *Erelim* or *Ophanim*), Dominions (or, *Lordships* or *Hashmalim*), Virtues (or, *Strongholds*), Powers (or, *Authorities*), Principalities (or, *Rulers*), Archangels, and Angels.

These nine Orders, in turn, are grouped together into three "Hierarchies," or groups of three Orders each. Each Triad is grouped based on its distance from the throne of God, with the first being nearest to God and the third being nearest to earth:
First Hierarchy: Seraphim, Cherubim, Thrones
Second Hierarchy: Dominions, Virtues, Powers

---

[226] Pope John XXIII once gave sound advice to Catholic parents on this subject, though sadly it still goes unheeded: *"Teach the children that they are never alone, that an angel is at their side. Show them how to have a trusting conversation with the angel, who is a good advisor and intercedes for you and helps you in your needs."*

[227] The original title is Περὶ τῆς Οὐρανίας Ἱεραρχίας ("Upon the Heavenly Hierarchies"), and an English translation can be found here: http://www.tertullian.org/fathers/areopagite_13_heavenly_hierarchy.htm. (Retrieved November 29, 2014.)

Third Hierarchy: Principalities, Archangels, Angels

The names of the Orders are themselves taken from Scripture,[228] and each Order is said to have its own specialized function as well as another function in relation to the other Orders within its Hierarchy.

According St. Thomas Aquinas, this grouping into three Hierarchies was done according to their share of access to the Universal knowledge:[229]

> "For it was shown above, in treating of the angelic knowledge, that the superior angels have a more universal knowledge of the truth than the inferior angels. This universal knowledge has three grades among the angels. For the types of things, concerning which the angels are enlightened, can be considered in a threefold manner.
>
> First as preceding from God as the first universal principle, which mode of knowledge belongs to the first hierarchy, connected immediately with God, and, 'as it were, placed in the vestibule of God,' as Dionysius says.
>
> Secondly, forasmuch as these types depend on the universal created causes which in some way

---

[228] **Seraphim**: Isa 6:1-8. **Cherubim**: Gen 3:24 and Ez 28:14-16. **Thrones**: Col 1:16 (Ophanim in Dan 7:9). **Dominions**: Eph 1:21 and Col 1:16. **Virtues**: Eph 1:21. **Powers**: Eph 3:10 and 6:12. **Principalities**: Eph 1:21 and 3:10. **Archangels**: 1 Thes 4:16 and Jude 1:9. **Angels**: all throughout the Bible.
[229] *Summa Theologica*, I, Q. 108

- Chapter Six: Angels and Saints -

are already multiplied; which mode belongs to the second hierarchy.

Thirdly, forasmuch as these types are applied to particular things as depending on their causes; which mode belongs to the lowest hierarchy. ... In this way are the hierarchies distinguished on the part of the multitude of subjects."

Before we continue, it might be well to point out that while Pseudo-Dionysius was influential, it was by no means the only categorization of angelic Orders in existence, nor did the Celestial Hierarchy codify all angelology for generations to come. Many schemes came before and after, and the modern Catholic conception of the Angelic Orders is more of a synthesis from many of these sources.[230]

As to what could be called the "functions and responsibilities" of each Order, there seems to be some difference of opinion amongst various sources. However, here is a brief list of the basics:

1. **Seraphim** are the highest Order of the Angels. The name is Hebrew for "Burning Ones" (שְׂרָפִים), and they are

---

[230] As an example, the fourth-century *Apostolic Constitutions* (once mistakenly attributed to Pope St. Clement I) gives eleven angelic Orders: Seraphim, Cherubim, Aeons, Hosts, Powers, Authorities, Principalities, Thrones, Archangels, Angels, Dominions. Also in the fourth century, **St. Jerome** gives us seven: Seraphim, Cherubim, Powers, Dominations, Thrones, Archangels, Angels. In the twelfth century, **St. Hildegard von Bingen** gives nine Orders in three Hierarchies: 1. Seraphim, Cherubim; 2. Thrones, Dominations, Principalities, Powers and Virtues; 3. Arch-angels and Angels. **Modern angelology** often draws on all of these sources, as well as St. Thomas Aquinas and the writings of **Dante Alighieri**.

described in Isaiah 6:2 as having six wings and standing around the throne of God. The Seraphim are purifiers, having purified Isaiah's lips with a burning coal, and Aquinas tells us their essence is a superabundance of divine love. He also tells us that in addition to being able to cleanse, the Seraphim have the quality of brightness and are also able to give perfect enlightenment. This suggests that the Seraphim possess the highest knowledge of any of the angelic Orders, and can be called on for any of these three purposes.

2. **Cherubim**, the second Order, have a name that means "Strong ones" (כְּרוּבִים) in Hebrew. It is a Cherub who was said to guard the gates to the Garden of Eden (Genesis 3:24), and they are described as having four wings and four faces: those of a man, an eagle, a lion, and a bull.[231] Pope St. Gregory the Great associates them with a plenitude of knowledge, sublime actions, and the vision of the Creator which is theirs by virtue of their dignity.[232] By virtue of their strength and four faces that see in all directions, they can also be called upon as guardians and protectors.

3. **Thrones** are the third of the Angelic Orders, the last members of the first Hierarchy, and are the carriers of the throne of God, hence the name. According to St. Gregory the Great, they are also called thrones because they God sits on them when He makes judgments, and God's justice is administered through them.[233] In Christian angelology, they are depicted as large, sparkling, topaz-colored wheels

---

[231] Ezekiel 1:6-10. These creatures are not referred to as Cherubim until chapter 10:20.
[232] Pope St. Gregory the Great. *Homily 34 on the Gospels*, section 10. The original Latin text is available on Google Books.
[233] Ibid.

covered with many eyes,[234] and also called the Ofanim (Hebrew אוֹפַנִּים, "wheels") or the Erelim (Hebrew אֶרְאֶלִּם, "valiant ones"), while in Jewish angelology, the Wheels and Thrones/Valiant Ones are considered two separate Orders.[235] The thrones may be called upon for God's justice, and also to gain greater wisdom and understanding, as these two qualities are at the root of God's sense of justice.

4. **Dominions** or **Dominations** are the highest Order of the second Hierarchy, the fourth of the Angelic Orders. They have also been called the Hashmalim (Hebrew חַשְׁמַלִּים, loosely "Electric Ones" or "Amber Ones," taken from Ezekiel 1:4), and Pseudo-Dionysius says the name of Dominions "denotes a certain unslavish elevation ... superior to every kind of cringing slavery, indomitable to every subserviency."[236] Pope Gregory the Great speaks of them as a sort of enforcer of Divine obedience,[237] and we can call upon them to enforce obedience to legitimate authority (but only if you know for a fact that authority is legitimate and not being abused!), or to cultivate the virtue of obedience in ourselves. This can also mean cultivating obedience to the laws of nature and helping ourselves perform better in our careers, relationships, and lives.

---

[234] Ezekiel 1:15-18

[235] Jewish angelology divides the heavenly hosts into ten Orders, which are not immediately reconcilable with the Catholic system: 1. **Hayyos Ha-Kadesh** ("Holy Living Creatures"), 2. **Ofanim** ("Wheels"), 3. **Erelim** ("Valiant Ones"), 4. **Hashmalim** ("Electric Ones"), 5. **Seraphim** ("Burning Ones"), 6. **Malakhim** ("Angels"), 7. **Elohim** ("Godly Beings"), 8. **Benei Elohim** ("Sons of Godly Beings"), 9. **Cherubim** ("Mighty Ones"), and 10. **Ishim** ("Man-like Beings"). The Jewish angelic hierarchy is normative in modern books on ceremonial magic.

[236] *Celestial Hierarchies.* Chapter VIII, sec. 1.

[237] *Homily 34 on the Gospels*, section 10.

5. **Virtues**, the fifth Angelic Order, take their name from Ephesians 1:21 (Greek dynameis, δυνάμεις, "virtues" or "powers"[238]). According to Pseudo-Dionysius, "the appellation of the Holy Virtues denotes a certain courageous and unflinching virility, for all those Godlike energies within them."[239] And Gregory says "For those called Virtues are doubtless those spirits through whom signs and miracles frequently happen."[240] They are called upon to give strength: strength to overcome obstacles, strength to conquer vices and bad habits, strength to persevere on our path, and all other kinds of strength in our lives.

6. **Powers**, the sixth in the list of Orders, take their name from Ephesians 3:10 (Greek exousiai, ἐξουσίαι, "authorities"), and refer to power in the sense of authority. Pseudo-Dionysius says that the Powers work toward the administration of divine authority in the sense of keeping everything in good order, and Gregory tells us that the Powers have dominion over evil spirits (his words: "for to their might the adverse powers have been subjected"), and that they may keep the forces of evil from tempting the hearts of men.[241] They may be called upon for help with the proper exercise of authority, for protection against temptation, against evil spirits, or against one's enemies.

7. The **Principalities**, who sit at the top of the third Hierarchy, take their names from the Latin *principatus*, itself a translation of the Greek ἀρχαὶ, "Rulers" (*archai*, itself from ἀρχή, arché, "beginning") mentioned in

---

[238] The word "power" here is in reference to strength and ability to accomplish one's objectives, not "power" as in authority.
[239] *Celestial Hierarchies*. Chapter VIII, sec. 1.
[240] *Homily 34*, section 10. (my translation)
[241] Ibid.

Ephesians 3:10. St. Gregory says of them: "And they are called Principalities, who themselves stand above the good spirits of the Angels themselves, while they distribute to their other subjects whatever needs to be done, having authority over them for the exercise of divine ministries."[242] In language easier to understand, Fr. Raphael V. O'Connell, S.J., tells us this: "In all that appertains to the salvation of mankind, whether it be question of persons of rank or of low degree, of individuals or communities, they have authority over the angels and archangels and are the intermediaries through whom the divine will is intimated to them."[243]

We quickly see that the Principalities are more than just rulers; they are delegators and therefore organizers. This point is emphasized by St. Thomas Aquinas, when he says: "Now in the execution of any action there are beginners and leaders; as in singing, the precentors; and in war, generals and officers; this belongs to the 'Principalities.'"[244] This tells us that not only can the Principalities be called upon as beginners and organizers, they can be called upon as inspirers, as any good organizer must also be able to inspire the people he or she leads. We call upon them for wisdom in governing ourselves and those under our care, for inspiration and success in whatever works we undertake (art, music, business, etc.), and for the right use of the abilities God has trusted to our minds and bodies.

---

[242] Ibid. (my translation)
[243] O'Connell, Raphael V. *The Holy Angels*. Chapter 18c, "Principalities." http://theholyangels.wordpress.com/principalities/. (Retrieved December 1, 2014).
[244] *Summa Theologiae*. Part I. Question 108. Article 6.

8. Eighth in line are the **Archangels**, whose name comes from the Greek *archangelos* (ἀρχάγγελος, "high-ranking messenger") possibly a translation of the Hebrew rav-malakh (רַב-מַלְאָךְ, "great messenger"). The New Testament only uses this word twice, in 1 Thessalonians 4:16 (when the archangel will blow the trumpet) and Jude 1:9 (when the archangel Michael argued with Satan).

Three archangels are named in the Bible: **Michael** (מִיכָאֵל, "Who is like God?"), **Gabriel** (גַּבְרִיאֵל, "strength of God"), and **Raphael** (רְפָאֵל, "healer of God"). In the book of Tobit, Raphael says indentifies himself as "one of the seven who stand before the Lord" (12:15); we are given another reference to seven angels who stand before the Lord in Revelations 8:2. These are the Archangels, with Gabriel similarly identifying himself as an "angels who stands before the Lord" in Luke 1:19, and Michael specifically referred to as an Archangel in Jude 1:9.

These are the three Archangels recognized by Catholicism, so what of the other four? Before we get to that, a brief history lesson might be in order. At the Council of Rome in 745, Pope St. Zachary wanted to clarify the Church's teaching about the Angels. In order to eliminate confusion and discourage Angel-worship, he struck the names of the other four Archangels from the list, leaving only the three who are explicitly named in Scripture. This is why one needs to do some legwork to find the other Angels' names, and while these do turn up from time to time in private devotions, they are not found in the official prayers of the Church.[245]

---

[245] This ban was reaffirmed by John Paul II in 2002, according to an article in *The Telegraph*:
http://www.telegraph.co.uk/news/worldnews/europe/italy/1390845/Vatican-bans-rogue-angels.html (Retrieved December 2, 2014).

Chapter Six: Angels and Saints

The names of the other four Archangels have been given in various (sometimes conflicting) lists over the centuries, and come mostly from pesudopigraphical[246] books like Second Esdras and the Books of Enoch. In these books, we find a fourth Archangel by the name of **Uriel** (אוּרִיאֵל, "light of God"); of the remaining four, his is the most commonly mentioned in private devotions.[247]

While the names of Raphael, Michael, Gabriel, and Uriel are constant, the lists of names are inconsistent regarding the other three. The Eastern Orthodox Church lists the other three as **Yehudiel** or **Jegudiel** (יְהוּדִיאֵל, "praise of God"), **Sealthiel** (שְׁאַלְתִּיאֵל, "prayer of God"), **Barachiel** (בְּרָקִיאֵל, "lightning of God"). We also commonly encounter the names **Anael** (הַנִּיאֵל, "joy of God"), **Suriel** (Aramaic זהריאל, "command of God"), **Zadkiel** (צַדְקִיאֵל, "righteousness of God"), and even names of possible Greek derivation such as **Metatron** (מֶטָטְרוֹן, possibly from μετὰ θρόνος, "next to the throne") and Sandalphon (סָנְדַלְפוֹן, possibly from συνάδελφος, "fellow brother" or from σανδάλιον, "sandal").[248] Suffice to say that no list can be considered definitive, and everyone has taken a stab at making their "best guess" at some time or another.

---

[246] Books of the *Pseudepigraphia*, ranking below the *Deuterocanonicals* in terms of religious literature. While the Catholic Church does not recognize them as inspired, they can offer the reader insight into the cultural beliefs and practices of the people who wrote them.

[247] And example of a modern devotion is the "Chaplet of St. Uriel." http://www.rosaryandchaplets.com/chaplets/st_uriel_prayer.html (Retrieved December 2, 2014.)

[248] These Greek etymologies are highly debated and uncertain at best. A grain of salt may go a long way!

While each Order of Angels can be called upon for a certain purpose, the Archangels are called upon individually, and the purpose is usually connected to the Archangel's name. For example, Michael is commonly called upon for protection, Gabriel for strength, Raphael for healing, and Uriel for the light of knowledge. The lists are so large that it's impossible to be comprehensive, and the reader is encouraged to make his or her own researches.[249]

9. The ninth and final Order, the **Angels**, take ther name from the Greek *angelos* (ἄγγελος, "messenger")[250] which in turn is a direct translation of the Hebrew word malakh (מַלְאָךְ, "messenger"). According to Pseudo-Dionysius, the Angels receive the illuminations from all the above orders and are responsible for communicating them to humans, and that the Order of Angels is more concerned with things of this world.[251] According to Fr. O'Connell, our guardian angels are chosen from this Order,[252] and according to me, we can surmise that the Angels are the Order who work most closely with humans. They are the messengers between God and man, and according to Genesis 6, they are the ones who taught us the arts of weapon-smithing, medicine, magic, astrology, writing, and many other arts that we know today. Of course, some of this knowledge was taught against God's will, which led to a second war of the Angels, but the role of the Angels as teachers and guides is well-established, and we can comfortably call upon them for any of these things.

---

[249] Just beware that a lot of authors on the subject aren't exactly informed themselves, or have bought into New Age ideologies, or post information without giving their source, or what have you. If you can evade these pitfalls, you should be good to go.
[250] Compare to the modern Greek *angelia* (αγγελία), "advertising."
[251] *Celestial Hierarchies*. Chapter IX, section 2.
[252] O'Connell, *The Holy Angels*, ch 18c. Link given above.

- Chapter Six: Angels and Saints -

The subject of angelology could be elaborated and extended at great length, and again the reader is encouraged to take up his or her own study.

CALLING ON THE ANGELS

No matter what the operator's intents or purposes, it is first important for him to read about and familiarize himself with each Order's function and in what aspects of life each is able to assist.

Now, in working with the Angels, we will find it easy to consider our purpose and then find the right Order to which this purpose is attributed. For example, if we wish gain strength to conquer life's obstacles, we would look at the Archangel Gabriel, and/or the Angelic Order of the Virtues.

In calling on the Angels, or in calling upon any being in the celestial hierarchies, we must first establish two things: our right to call upon these entities, and permission from Almighty God to call them for our specific purpose.

Let us look at the "Little Office" of the Holy Angels:
Ant: Angels, Archangels, Thrones and Dominations, Principalities and Powers, Virtues of heaven, Cherubim and Seraphim, bless the Lord forever.

V. All ye angels of the Lord, bless the Lord.
R. Sing a hymn and exalt Him above all forever.

Let us pray:
O God, Who in a wonderful manner dost distribute the ministries of angels and of men, mercifully grant that as Thy holy angels ever wait upon Thee to do Thee service in heaven, so

our lives may be defended by them upon earth. Through Christ our Lord. Amen.

Invocation of the Nine Choirs of Angels
O holy Angels, watch over us at all times during this perilous life; O holy Archangels, be our guides on the way to heaven; O heavenly choir of the Principalities, govern us in soul and body; O mighty Powers, preserve us against the wiles of the demons; O celestial Virtues, give us strength and courage in the battle of life; O powerful Dominations, obtain for us dominion over the rebellion of our flesh; O sacred Thrones, grant us peace with God and man; O brilliant Cherubim, illumine our minds with heavenly knowledge; O burning Seraphim, enkindle in our hearts the fire of charity. Amen.

If we examine this devotion, we find the structure consists of an Antiphon, a Versicle, a Collect, and then the Invocation of the Nine Choirs. This is a useful pattern.

Now let's discuss that pattern. First, the purpose of the work is stated through the Antiphon and Versicles, no matter how cryptic such a statement might be: "I intend to contact the Angels for the sake of God's glory and my usefulness." The purpose of the work is stated, setting the mood, theme, and atmosphere for the rest of the work.

Second, a Collect (also called an "opening prayer"). In this case, the prayer used is from the Roman Missal: the *Deus, qui, miro órdine* found in the votive Mass for the Angels on Tuesdays.[253] The Collect accomplishes two things: first, it

---

[253] The original, in full: *Deus, qui, miro órdine, Angelórum ministéria hominúmque dispénsas: concéde propítius; ut, a quibus tibi*

gives the imagery that God arranges the ministries of angels and humans in a marvelous way; second, the Collect then requests of God to fortify our lives through His power.[254] God is thus asked for permission to perform the work, by appealing to the structures He has already put in place for it to be done. In your own prayers, such permission may be asked directly or indirectly, and you may use either your own words, prayers from official sources such as the Missal, Breviary, or Ritual, or other prayers that you find speaking to you in a personal manner. The final arbiter is your own sense of good judgment.

Lastly, in the "Invocation of the Nine Choirs," the Angels themselves are addressed and directed towards specific purposes. In this example, this is the actual discharge of the operation, in which those being petitioned are either asked or sent out to assist you in whatever manner is appropriate to their sphere of influence, and to the reason for your working. Again, either your own compositions or pre-published works may furnish you with the exact wording. With experience, you'll come to realize what works best and what doesn't.[255]

Returning to our pattern of calling Gabriel, we could adapt this pattern of invocation. To begin, we would spend some time meditating on Gabriel and his place in the Angelic Hierarchy, and how he relates to our work. This would help us build an affinity to him, and help form a mental bridge between him and us which would facilitate our work.

---

ministrántibus in caelo semper assístitur, ab his in terra vita nostra muniátur. Per Dóminum.
[254] Though the translation says "defend," the word *muniátur* in the original can also signify fortification. Both meanings are inherent in the prayer.
[255] The only real teacher here is experience!

On the day or night that you wish to perform your work, you would begin by lighting the mensa candles and having either a white or red candle in the mensa's center.[256] Then you would cross yourself with Holy Water (which is best to do before beginning any ritual),[257] and then stand before the mensa.

Standing before the mensa, you would first state your Declaration of Intent, either in your own words or with an antiphon like the one used in the Little Office. Maybe something like "Gabriel, thou Strength-of-God who standest in His presence and shall announce the end of the world, give us strength to bless the Lord and praise Him forever."

After that, you would then kneel and say a short prayer asking the permission of Almighty God to address and direct the Angels towards the fulfillment of your purpose. You could choose any number of approaches to this, though the prayer I use is the *Invocatio Nominis Domini*.

This prayer came about as the result of a dream I had when I was sixteen. In the dream, I was in a magic class and there was an angel teaching it. He wrote something on the blackboard (I can't remember what), and then told me that "when addressing your prayers to God, you must speak in

---

[256] White because that's the color of St. Gabriel's feast-day (March 24 on the pre-Vatican II calendar), or red because you're seeking to invoke the virtue of strength into your life.
[257] It's a good way to help clear the mind and put oneself into the proper headspace.

Christ's name, or else He won't listen."[258] When I awoke, I composed the following prayer:

Prayer: Invocatio Nominis Domini

Deus omnípotens, in nómine Jesu Christi Fílii tui unigéniti ego te imploro, ut dones mihi potestátem imperáre spirítibus ómnibus, bonis vel malis, sine perículum faciéndo mihi vel áliis. Per eúmdem Dóminum nostrum, Jesum Christum, Fílium tuum, qui tecum vivit et regnat in unitáte Spíritus Sancti Deus, per ómnia sáecula saeculórum. Amen.	Almighty God, in the Name of Jesus Christ Thine only-begotten Son I beseech Thee, to grant me the power to command all spirits, good or evil, without causing harm to myself or to anybody else. Through our same Lord Jesus Christ, Thy Son, who liveth and reigneth in the unity of the Holy Ghost, God, forever and ever. Amen.

It's a general-purpose prayer that's served me well to this very day, and you're welcome to use it in your own workings, too, insofar as it brings you positive results.

After the recitation of the *Invocatio*, you would then stand up and say a prayer addressed to the Archangel or Angelic Order associated with your purpose, or both. In the current case of Gabriel, you would ask him to move on behalf of your intentions, and you may also ask him to stir up the

---

[258] This assertion may be disputed by non-Christian readers, whose prayers have worked for centuries, even millennia, without invoking the name of Jesus. I would respond that "speaking in the name of" someone can also mean doing something in the manner that person did, or it can mean speaking with that person's authority. This is a far cry from just sticking "in Jesus' name" to the end of every prayer, as one may work in the same manner Jesus did without even being aware of it, without even believing in him.

entire Order of Virtues to assist him. You are free to make up the wording of this prayer, preferably after reading any legends dealing with Gabriel and/or the Order of Virtues, his/their history of interaction with mankind, and so forth. The more you know about the Angels, the better you will be able to establish an affinity with them, and the more effective your magic will be.[259]

In your prayer (or two prayers, if you wish to address St. Gabriel and the Virtues separately), you should specifically state the kind of strength you seek. Just be ready and keep your eyes open, because it may not come to you through the channels you're expecting. You could receive this strength through a crisis that teaches you to develop it, through meeting a random person who drops some advice, or even an insightful meme that shows up on your Facebook.[260] Therefore we must be willing to keep our eyes open, and be ready when the time comes to receive what it is that we seek.

Once you've addressed the Angels and set them into motion, you would pause for a minute or so (whatever feels natural), and mentally visualize the Angels hovering over you and clothing you in the strength you seek (or going out and doing whatever it is you just asked them). Afterwards you would say a prayer of Thanks to God for having sent the Archangel Gabriel and/or the Order of Virtues on this task for your benefit.

---

[259] This point cannot be over-stressed. It's very much analogous to asking a stranger to do something on your behalf, compared to asking a known and trusted friend. Take time to get to know the Angels and Saints BEFORE you ask them for something!
[260] Yeah, I know that's not likely. But it's still possible.

- Chapter Six: Angels and Saints -

You may want to do this as a Novena, or every day for a week, or just once a week until you find what you seek; the choice is up to you. You may also want to ask a priest to offer a Mass for your intentions (or if you are a priest, offer one for your intentions, either the Mass of the Day or the *Missa Votiva de Angelis* as the rubrics allow); when united with the Blessed Sacrament, our prayers and magic become all the more effective, and we would be fools to ignore such a wonderful gift as this!

This is a good general pattern for use when working with the Archangels and Angels. The more you learn about the Angels, the better you will be able to adapt this pattern or find a better one of your own, and then you will be well on the way to finding your own personal style.

WORKING WITH THE SAINTS
Much of what has been said in regard to working with the Angels also applies to working with the Saints. In fact, all of it applies but with two exceptions.

The first exception is that, while an Angel can act on your behalf of their own God-given power – that is, they can actually go out and fight your battles for you – a Saint is limited to praying on your behalf before the heavenly Court.

The other exception is that it helps to develop a personal relationship with the Saints, especially your patron Saint before asking them to intercede on your behalf. Think of it this way: if we call the Saints our friends, then why should they help us if we only talk to them when we want something? Friends don't do that to each other, and it's rude for us to behave that way toward the Saints.

So how do we do such a thing? How do we develop a personal relationship with our patron or any other Saint? The answer is simple: make time for them. Just sit, meditate, light a candle, and say "Hi" to the saint for no particular reason, other than just to get acquainted. Have a friendly conversation in your mind with him or her, and whatever you do, don't start asking for things unless it's a definite emergency! Just work to get acquainted, and it's from your friendship that good things will start to flow.

Set aside a few minutes each day using a simple exercise like the one below, or you can use something else that works better for you personally.

MAKING CONTACT WITH THE SAINTS
1. On your mensa or home altar, place a holy card or a statue of the Saint of your choice in the center. Either before or to the side of the image, place a candle of the Saint's color on the mensa, and you may also have a flower or object associated with that Saint.

2. Cross yourself in the usual manner, and light the candle, saying: "I come to you in fellowship, Saint N., so that we may come to know each other in friendship and in co-operation. Saint N., may we become fast friends: may I follow your example here on earth, and in heaven may you intercede on my behalf before the throne of Almighty God."

3. Sit comfortably in a chair and relax, using the relaxation/meditation technique of your choice (see pp. 223-225). After that, mentally greet the Saint in your own words, or pray a chaplet to that Saint (if he or she has one), or some other suitable devotion.

- Chapter Six: Angels and Saints -

4. After as long a time as feels appropriate (usually 10-20 minutes), feel free to close the meditation. "Saint N., I have enjoyed our time together. May almighty God bless you, and may we meet again soon."

5. Cross yourself in the usual manner, thus completing the exercise.

Through this exercise, we can become closer with the Saints by talking to them as friends on a social and cordial level, inviting them into our lives to help us, and offering our help to them. This is how we begin taking up a practical application of the doctrine of the Communion of Saints.

A LIST OF COMMONLY-INVOKED SAINTS
Below is a list of some of the more commonly-invoked saints, along with the areas of life which they're said to cover. I would caution that these "areas of life" are a combination of official Catholic teaching and the lore of folk magical practitioners, meaning this list isn't aiming for orthodoxy in the strict sense. I'm not endorsing everything here, so much as cataloging it for the sake of acquainting the reader with this knowledge.

Please note that I have not listed titles of Our Lord or Our Lady, since these are available on any Catholic site on the Internet.

As a quick reference, the Saints are listed by:
Type: this is how the Church classifies her Saints.
(*A* apostle, *Ab* Abbot, *B* bishop, *C* confessor, *D* doctor, *M* martyr, *P* pope, *T* thaumaturge, *V* virgin, *W* Widow)
Feast-Day: The feastday of a Saint is usually the day he or she died, as this is considered to be his or her birthday into heaven.
Liturgical Color: the color worn when offering a votive Mass for that Saint.
Devotional Color: the color of candle usually burned in honor of that Saint.
Symbol: The object commonly pictured along with that Saint in western iconography. Not all Saints have symbols.

1 -St. Agnes, VM
St. Agnes was a Roman virgin who suffered martyrdom at the age of thirteen, rather than lose her virginity.
Feast: January 21
Liturgical Color: Red
Devotional Color: Blue or White
Symbol: Lamb
Invoke to keep a husband faithful, find a soul mate, or reveal dishonesty in a relationship (find out the truth about someone).

2 -St. Alexis, C
The legend of St. Alexis, the "Man of God," tells us that he abandoned wealth and power and lived in poverty and unknown until his identity was revealed after his death.
Feast: July 17
Liturgical Color: White
Devotional Color: Pink
Symbol: Crucifix
Invoke to ask for protection from astral attack, violence and enemies. His emblem is a crucifix.

3 -St. Alphonsus Liguori, BCD

St. Alphonsus is renowned as a great moral theologian and also for his works of devotion. He left a brilliantly successful position as a lawyer to become a priest and devote himself to the care of souls. For this purpose, he founded the Redemptorist Order which would imitate our Savior by preaching in the villages and towns. St. Alphonsus nourished his zeal for souls by humility and prayer. Towards the end of his life, he suffered persecution most patiently and never relaxed his efforts for the salvation of souls. He died in 1787.
Feast: August 2
Liturgical Color: White
Devotional Color: Purple
Invoke to ask for help with sore, aching muscles, joint pain and arthritis. Anything to do with the bones. Also the patron Saint of moral theologians and responsible for our present-day prayers on the Way of the Cross.

4 -St. Aloysius, C

From his infancy St. Aloysius displayed extraordinary purity and devotion to our Blessed Lady. At the age of 17 he entered the Society of Jesus in which he distinguished himself for his detachment from the world, faithfulness to rule, and warm charity towards his brethren. He died a martyr of charity in 1591 from an illness contracted while ministering to the sick during an epidemic in Rome. He is the patron of Catholic youth.
Feast: June 21
Liturgical Color: White
Devotional Color: Blue
Invoke to settle domestic disputes and also banish flu, fevers and contagious diseases.

5 - St. Anne, Mother of Our Lady

We have no historical knowledge of the events of the life of St. Anne, the mother of Our Lady, but the praises of her holiness are sung by many Fathers of the early Church and Christians in all ages have had a tender devotion to her. She is looked upon as the patroness of Christian mothers.

Feast: July 26
Liturgical Color: White
Devotional Color: White

She is the patron Saint of grandmothers, housekeepers, housewives, mothers and women in labor. Petition her for help with the deaf and the blind, and may also be petitioned to help with creating a peaceful and happy home environment.

6 - St. Anthony of Padua, CDT

St. Anthony, a native of Lisbon, entered the Franciscan order with the desire of seeking martytrdom and of practicing perfect poverty. During his life he was famed for his learning and for his wonderful success as a preacher. God worked innumerable miracles through St. Anthony and since his canonization within a year of his death, his fame as a wonderworker has led to worldwide devotion to him, especially in the form of contributing to "St. Anthony's Bread" for the poor. Pope Pius XII conferred on St. Anthony the title of Doctor of the Church.

Feast: June 13
Liturgical Color: White
Devotional Color: Brown
Symbol: Lily

To Invoke: burn a brown candle for special requests, a green candle for financial help or an orange candle to find a husband. St. Anthony's is a wonderworker when it comes to finding lost articles, improving the memory and bringing back a strayed lover.

- Chapter Six: Angels and Saints -

7 -St. Augustine of Hippo, BCD

Aurelius Augustinus was born at Tagaste, in the province of Numidia, to a pagan father and a Catholic mother. After many years spent in licentiousness and philosophical searching, he was finally converted to Catholicism by the prayers of his mother (St. Monica), and was baptized by St. Ambrose of Milan. His great theological and philosophical mind formed and influenced not only the course of Church teaching, but also the whole of Western philosophy and political thinking. His De Civitate Dei is perhaps his greatest and best-known masterpiece, in which he effectively brought the death-blow to the paganism of his day. He is considered the greatest of the Early Fathers, and alongside Aquinas is the foremost Doctor of the Church, though because of his former loose living he is the patron Saint of brewers.

Feast: August 28
Liturgical Color: White
Devotional Color: White

Invoke to defeat followers of Greco-Roman Paganism, to have the gift of eloquence in rhetoric or philosophy, to brew a perfect batch of beer.

8 -St. Barbara, VM

St. Barbara was a native of Asia Minor. After long imprisonment and torture because of her faith, she was beheaded in Nicomedia.

Feast: December 4
Liturgical Color: Red
Devotional Color: Red
Symbol: Tower

Invoke to protect your relationship from rivals, to protect yourself from meddling in-laws, to clear your path of obstacles, to help someone be released from prison and for protection from storms. She is also the patroness of wives whose men are at war.

9 -Saint Bartholomew, A
After the Ascension of Our Lord and the coming of the Holy Ghost, St. Bartholomew preached the Gospel in the East. A constant tradition tells that he was beaten to death in Armenia where he had converted large numbers to the faith, including the sister of the king.
Feast: August 24
Liturgical Color: Red
Devotional Color: Red
Symbol: Butcher Knife
Invoke to reveal the truth to you if you feel like something is being hidden or concealed from you. You can also ask him for protection from violence, violent death and protection and healing while undergoing surgery.

10 -Saint Benedict, Ab
St. Benedict, the patriarch of Western monasticism, was born at Nuncia and after being educated in Rome, retired to the solitude of Subiaco where he founded twelve monasteries for the disciples who carne to join him in the religious life. After three years, he went to Monte Cassino where he founded the great monastery and wrote his Rule. His order gave innumerable Saints to the Church, among them five who have been honored as Doctors of the Church. It was instrumental in propagating the faith through the barbarian nations of Europe and was the great civilizing force in the early Middle Ages.
Feast: March 21
Liturgical Color: White
Devotional Color: White
Symbol: Raven, Broken Cup

Invoke to ask for protection against a variety of evil influences: against poisons, evil temptations, contagious diseases, safety during storms, and assistance during times of healing and death. Saint Benedict also helps heal animals and increase prosperity.

11 -St. Blaise, BM
St. Blaise was bishop of Sebaste in Armenia in the fourth century. In his lifetime he was famed for many miracles, including the healing of sick animals. He suffered death by beheading for the faith. During the Middle Ages, devotion to him became widespread and he is invoked in particular for the healing of all throat ailments. In the Roman Ritual there is a blessing of throats in his honor on this day.
Feast: February 3
Liturgical Color: Red
Devotional Color: Blue
Symbol: Comb, Two Unlit Crossed Candles
Invoke to increase positive communication and self-expression. He also helps with diseases of the throat.

12 -St. Brigid of Kildare, V
St. Brigid was born about the middle of the fifth century of Christian parents, at Faughard in the county of Louth. It is said that St. Patrick baptized her parents. They were careful to give their children sound religious training, and St. Brigid consecrated herself to God from her earliest childhood. She is said to have received the veil from St. Mel, a disciple of St. Patrick. She founded the first convent for women in Ireland. Her life was remarkable for its intense love of Our Lord and His Blessed Mother, and for her charity towards the poor. Many miracles showed the power of her intercession with God, and she exercised a great influence for good throughout Ireland. She died in the year 523. Her remains were first buried in Kildare, but

were later enshrined with those of St. Patrick and St. Columba, at Downpatrick in Ulster. She is regarded as the second patron of Ireland.
Feast: February 1
Liturgical Color: White
Devotional Color: Yellow
Symbol: Cow.
Invoke to become fertile, for healing, for happiness and health of pets and farmyard animals, to assist with breeding livestock, for inspiration, for literary gifts (especially poetry) and the gift of prophecy. Her symbol is a cow.

13 -St. Catherine of Alexandria, VM
St. Catherine was a virgin martyr of Alexandra in Egypt. During her trial she confuted pagan philosophers who were brought to dispute with her. After various torments, she suffered death by beheading.
Feast: November 25
Liturgical Color: Red
Devotional Color: Yellow or White
Symbol: Wheel
Invoke to petition her for beauty, fertility, a peaceful death, confidence, seductiveness and confidence when public speaking. Her symbol is the wheel.

14 -St. Cecilia, VM
Cecilia was a Roman patrician maiden who had made a vow of virginity. When given in marriage to a pagan Valerianus, she converted him and his brother Tiburtius to the faith. All three were martyred in the third century. St. Cecilia is the patron saint of musicians.
Feast: November 22
Liturgical Color: Red
Devotional Color: Green
Symbol: Organ

Invoke for success in a career in the arts, particularly if you are a musician, poet or singer.

15 -St. Christopher, M
St. Christopher, whose original name was Reprobus, was a giant who suffered martyrdom in Lycia in Asia Minor under the Emperor Decius, and from the earliest times devotion to him was widespread in the Eastern Church. He received the name Christopher ("Bearer of Christ") from an incident in which he unknowingly carried the infant Jesus on his back across a stream. Although the modern Church "de-canonized" him in 1969, devotion to him remains widespread to this very day.
Feast: July 25
Liturgical Color: Red
Devotional Color: Red
Invoke for protection from accidents, sudden death, and against storms. Christopher protects motorists and travelers so he is the one to pray to for a safe journey.

16 -St. Clare of Assisi, V
St. Claire was inspired by St. Francis to follow a life of perfect poverty and under his guidance founded the Second Order of St. Francis. Her love of God revealed itself in an intense devotion to the Blessed Sacrament.
Feast: August 12
Liturgical Color: White
Devotional Color: White
Symbol: Monstrance
Invoke for protection against astral attack and for help overcoming addiction to drugs and alcohol.

17 -Sts. Cosmas and Damian, MM
Cosmas and Damian were two Christian physicians of Arabia who accepted no pecuniary reward for their

services. They were imprisoned by the governor Cilicia and beheaded for their refusal to abjure the Faith. Ss. Cosmas and Damian are, with St. Luke, the patrons of Catholic medical doctors.
Feast: September 27
Liturgical Color: Red
Devotional Color: Green
Symbol: Herbs and Palm
Invoke for help with doctors and health, to get a correct diagnosis and for general physical protection. He can also clear obstacles from your path.

18 -St. Cyprian of Antioch, BM
Cyprian of Antioch was born in the third century to a pagan family, and showed a great potential for the magic arts. His trained under the great masters, and was famed for his magic skill and power. One day, a client wanted him to seduce Justina, a Christian maiden of unquestionable purity. Every attempt failed, and the demons told him: "She is protected by a power greater than ours." Cyprian immediately converted to Catholicism and eventually became a bishop, and was martyred along with St. Justina in the persecution of Diocletian in 304.
Feast: September 26
Liturgical Color: Red
Devotional Color: Red or Purple
Invoke to be protected against black magic, conversion attempts by satanists, to grow in strength as a Christian magician.

19 -St. Cyprian of Carthage, BM
St. Cyprian of Carthage is one of the Early Fathers of the Church who lived in the third century. In his *De Unitate Ecclesiae*, he built upon St. Iranaeus' formulation of Church unity. He suffered exile for his faith, and on his

return to Carthage was executed for refusing to sacrifice to idols. He is considered the patron of lawyers and orators; some also call him the patron of Christian magicians, but this comes from confusion with St. Cyprian of Antioch.
Feast: September 16
Liturgical Color: Red
Devotional Color: Purple
Invoke to be protected from womanizers, liars, cheaters, and negative attitudes. He helps homeless people and those who have been convicted from getting a heavy sentence.

20 -St. Dymphna, VM

Saint Dymphna was born to a nobleman whose wife died when Dymphna was but fourteen years of age. Her father, stricken with mental infirmity resulting from her death, searched to no avail for a woman to replace his departed wife. When no woman would marry him, he then decided to turn his affections on his daughter, who received the grace of martyrdom while defending her virginity from him in the year 620.
Feast: May 15
Liturgical Color: Red
Devotional Color: Blue
Symbol: Downward-pointing Sword
Invoke for help with nervous disorders, mental afflictions, epilepsy, insanity, obsession and astral attack.

21 -St. Expedite, M

The name Expeditus is found among a group of martyrs, thought to be either in Rome or from Armenia. He is commonly invoked to bring about speedy results, though there is doubt in the modern Church as to whether he even existed.
Feast: none
Liturgical Color: none

Devotional Color: Yellow
Symbol: Cross with the word *hodie* ("today"), Raven
Invoke to settle disputes or to reverse a negative situation around. This is who you petition to if you need things to change quickly or suddenly.

22 -St Florian, M
St. Florian was an officer in the Roman Army who was executed in the persecution of Diocletian. His intercession is attributed to many cases of healing as well as protection from fire and flooding.
Feast: May 4
Liturgical Color: Red
Devotional Color: Red or Orange
Symbol: Burning House
Invoke to protect the home and for help with any kind of emergency that has to do with home such as a flood, fire, bankruptcy, infestation etc.

23 -St. Francis of Assisi, C
St. Francis (1182-1226) was chosen by God to revive by voluntary poverty the spirit of detachment from material things and to inflame men with charity by promoting devotion to the sacred Humanity of Christ. He accomplished this by leaving all things to follow Christ and by founding the Order of Friars Minor (the Franciscans), which order has given more Saints to the Church than any other order. St. Francis accomplished this reform of the Church not by disobedience or revolt but by humility and the example of his life.
Feast: October 4
Liturgical Color: White
Devotional Color: Brown
Invoke to petition for peace, conflict resolution and to gain spiritual wisdom. He helps to reveal and dismantle evil

plots. He is also an environmentalist and is concerned with matters of ecology and conservation.

24 -Saint Francis Xavier Cabrini, C
Francis Xavier (1506-1552), a native of Pampeluna, was a student at the Paris University when he joined St. Ignatius of Loyola and became one of the first members of the Society of Jesus. He rapidly attained great holiness and, in obedience to his superiors, set out to preach the Gospel in the East Indies. His humility, patience, and charity made his missionary work prodigiously successful. He died on the island of Sancian. St. Pius X declared him a the patron of Catholic missionary works and his feast is kept as a feast of the propagation of the faith.
Feast: December 30
Liturgical Color: White
Devotional Color: White
Invoke to help with matters of immigration, with moving to another city or state or for matters pertaining to health, education or insurance.

25 -St. Gabriel, Archangel
Gabriel is one of the Archangels mentioned by name in Holy Scripture. He announced the mystery of the Incarnation to the prophet Daniel and to Zacharias, the father of St. John the Baptist. Finally he made the annunciation to the Blessed Mother and sought and obtained her consent to become the Mother of God. He is also the Patron of communications workers.
Feast: March 24
Liturgical Color: White
Devotional Color: White, Silver, or Purple
Symbol: Trumpet or Lily
Invoke to communicate with a loved one or to interpret dreams.

26 -St. George, M
Little is known about this martyr of the Eastern Church, beyond the fact that he suffered in the persecution of Diocletian. According to tradition, he was a member of one of the Roman legions. Devotion to him has always been widespread in the East, and after the Crusades it extended to the West when he was adopted by the kings of England as their patron.
Feast: April 23
Liturgical Color: Red
Devotional Color: Red
Symbol: Slaying of a Dragon
Invoke to conquer fears, acquire courage and to overcome jealousy.

27 -St. Gerard Majella, C
St. Gerard became entered the Redemptorist Order at the age of 23. He had the abilities of levitation, hi-location, and the reading of consciences, and exhibited a charity and piety by which he received permission to counsel communities of women. He died of tuberculosis in 1755, and is the patron of expectant mothers.
Feast: October 16
Liturgical Color: White
Devotional Color: White
Invoke to petition to become pregnant. He also helps the falsely accused be declared innocent. He also assists mediums, prophets, psychics and clairvoyants in seeing the truth.

28 -Saint Helen of Jerusalem
Mother of the Emperor Constantine, she converted to Catholicism after her son's great victory, and on a pilgrimage to the Holy Land uncovered the True Cross. She

died in 330, and her sarcophagus now rests in the Vatican Museum.
Feast: August 18
Liturgical Color: White
Devotional Color: Pink or Red
Symbol: Cross
Invoke to ask for the return of a strayed lover and to overcome sorrow, obsession and unhappiness. Her emblem is a cross.

29 -St. Ignatius of Loyola, C
At the age of 33 Ignatius abandoned the life of a courtier and a soldier and consecrated himself to the service of Christ and the Church. With some companions, he formed the Society of Jesus to carry out obediently any task which the Roman Pontiff might assign them. In this way St. Ignatius was the pillar of the Counter-Reformation in the sixteenth century. The society founded by him continues to this day and its success can be measured by the hatred and persecution directed against it by the enemies of the Church. The Spiritual Exercises of St. Ignatius have been for many the path to holiness and he is the patron of retreats.
Feast: July 31
Liturgical Color: White
Devotional Color: White
Symbol: Book and a Plum
Invoke to protect the house from burglary and evil spirits, to combat the enemies of the Church, for conversion of those who have strayed from the Catholic Faith, and for help against slander or proselytizing attempts from Protestants of whatever stripe.

30 -St. James the Greater, A

St. James, with his brother St. John, left all to follow Jesus and with his brother and St. Peter, was a witness of the raising to life of the child Jairus, of the Transfiguration and the Agony in the Garden. He was first of the Apostles to suffer martyrdom, being beheaded by Herod in Jerusalem in
42. For over 1,000 years his relics have been venerated at Compostella in Spain, one of the great shrines of Christendom.

Feast: July 25
Liturgical Color: Red
Devotional Color: Red
Symbol: Cockleshell

Invoke to clear obstacles from your path, conquer or remove enemies and for justice to prevail.

31 -Saint Joan of Arc, VM

The patroness of soldiers and of France, St. Joan of Arc was a peasant girl from Lorraine. Disguised as a boy, she went to the King of France and assisted him in achieving success after military success, restoring him to his kingdom. However, the French did little to thank her, as they did nothing to save her from the Burgundians, who sold her to the English, at which point she was tried as a heretic and burned at the stake. She was canonized by Benedict XV in 1920.

Feast: May 30
Liturgical Color: Red
Devotional Color: Gray
Symbol: Suit of Armor

Invoke to petition her for spiritual strength, freedom from prisons of all kinds (emotional and otherwise) and for ways to overcome rivals and energies.

32 -St. John the Baptist

St. John the Baptist was cleansed of original sin and sanctified from his birth, and fulfilled the prophecy of the angel concerning the holiness of his life. He retired to the desert where he lived most austerely in communion with God while preparing himself for his mission of announcing the coming of Christ our Savior. At the time appointed by God he appeared at the Jordan to preach penitence and to prepare the minds of his hearers for the Gospel of Jesus. In doing so he showed a zealous hatred for wickedness and hypocrisy and a wonderful humility.
Feast: June 24 (Nativity), August 29 (Beheading)
Liturgical Color: White (June), Red (August)
Devotional Color: Green.
Invoke to petition him for good luck, fertility, prosperity and protection from enemies.

33 -St. John Bosco, C

St. John Bosco founded the Salesian order for men and the Daughters of Mary Help of Christians for women. As a humble, poor, apostolic priest he accomplished immense good for the Church in Italy and throughout the world in difficult days in the nineteenth century. In particular, he undertook the care and education of poor and unprovided children and, relying solely on the help of Divine Providence, he raised great institutes to provide homes for them. He died in 1888 and was canonized in 1934.
Feast: January 31
Liturgical Color: White
Devotional Color: Yellow
Invoke to petition him for favors to do with children, students and educational matters.

34 -Saint Joseph, Spouse of the Blessed Virgin, C
Next to the Blessed Virgin Mary, Mother of God, St. Joseph holds the highest dignity among all the Saints. He was true spouse of Our Lady and foster-father of Jesus Christ and exercised true paternal authority over Him as head of the Holy Family of Nazareth. To fit him for this exalted office, he was endowed with great holiness and virtue. Because of the assistance of Jesus and Mary at his deathbed, he is the patron of a happy death.
Feast: March 19 and May 1 (1962 and later Calendars)
Liturgical Color: White
Devotional Color: Yellow
Symbol: Lily, Pitcher with Loaf of Bread
Invoke for help with selling a home, finding job, for protection and a happy marriage.

35 -St. Jude, A
St. Jude, the brother of St. James the Less, is called the "brother of the Lord," because he was a cousin of Jesus according to the flesh. He is the author of one of the Catholic Epistles, and we learn from tradition that he preached the Gospel in Mesopotamia and Persia before ending his life by martyrdom.
Feast: October 28
Liturgical Color: Red
Devotional Color: Green, White, or Red
Symbol: Medal with the Face of Jesus, Staff
Invoke to petition for a miracle: for hopeless causes that seem impossible, to help with addictions or to help someone get out of jail.

36 -St. Laurence, M
Of all the Christian martyrs, St. Laurence is one of the noblest and most lovable. A native of Spain, he was

archdeacon to Pope Sixtus II. After the martyrdom of the Pope, he distributed to the poor all the possessions of the Church. The enraged prefect of the city caused him to be roasted to death on a gridiron. The Saint bore this excruciating torture calmly and prayed constantly for the conversion of Rome. His death took place in 258.
Feast: Augnst 10
Liturgical Color: Red
Devotional Color: Red
Symbol: Gridiron
Invoke to petition for a peaceful, happy home and family, for financial assistance and spiritual strength.

37 -St. Lazarus, M
St. Lazarus is the brother of Mary and Martha, whom Jesus raised back from the dead. In one tradition, he and his sisters went to France, where he became the first bishop of Marseilles before being martyred. Other traditions exist in which he went to Syria or Lamaka, and his relics are in Constantinople today.
Feast: July 29
Liturgical Color: Red
Devotional Color: Yellow
Symbol: Pair of Crutches, Dog
Invoke to ask for help with sickness, disease, addictions, and better health and to obtain prosperity.

38 -St. Louis Bertrand, C
A Dominican priest, St. Louis was a gifted preacher and a missionary to South America where he displayed the gift of tongnes while preaching to the many tribes there (i.e. he spoke in Spanish and they heard in their own languages).
Feast: October 9
Liturgical Color: White
Devotional Color: White

Invoke for help learning languages and protection from evil, accidents, sickness and enemies. He is the one you invoke when children are possessed by spirits.

39 -Saint Lucy, VM
A native of Syracuse, Lucy was reared in the Christian faith by her mother Eutychia. She made a secret vow to consecrate herself to God as a virgin. Because of this, the young pagan who had been chosen as her husband denounced her to the authorities. The governor threatened to expose her to outrage but could not shake her constancy. After many torments, she perished by fire after she had foretold the early ending of the persecution of the Christians. She died in 304.
Feast: December 13
Liturgical Color: Red
Devotional Color: White
Invoke to ask her to help with insoluble or impossible problems, depression, and protection from the evil eye or astral attack, to help you to find the right lawyer and to conquer temptations or addictions.

40 -St. Maria Goretti, VM
St. Maria Goretti (1890-1902) is the youngest of Saints canonized in the Catholic Church. She was born in 1890 in Corinaldo, Italy, and was mortally wounded in 1902 while resisting a sexual assault. She died from that assault, but not before forgiving her assailant, and was canonized in 1950 by Pope Pius XII. She is the patroness of youth, young women, purity, and victims of rape.
Feast: July 6
Liturgical Color: Red
Devotional Color: Pink
Invoke for fidelity in marriage, help with an abusive or battering male partner and a pardon from the death penalty.

41 -Saint Martha, V

St. Martha, the sister of Lazarus and Mary Magdalen, was frequently hostess to our Savior and was especially loved by him. Of her later life no details are known although a tradition says she died in France.

Feast: July 29
Liturgical Color: White
Devotional Color: Green or White
Symbol: Dragon

Invoke to ask for aid with financial problems, the necessities of life, to bring a lover closer, to keep a husband or boyfriend faithful, to subdue or conquer romantic rivals or enemies or bring a new love.

42 -St. Martin Caballero, BC

Born in 315 in the province of Pannonia, St. Martin was the son of a pagan army official who was intolerant of the New Religion. Martin sought out conversion to Catholicism of his own volition, but before he was baptized he was consigned to become a soldier in the Roman army, making him the patron of soldiers. Always remaining constant in his faith, he eventually was baptized and tore down pagan temples everywhere he went, setting up churches in their stead. He eventually became bishop of Tours (he is also known as "St. Martin of Tours"), and lived a life of extraordinary poverty and humility until his death in the late fourth century.

Feast: November 11
Liturgical Color: White
Devotional Color: Red or White
Symbol: Torn Cape and Sword

Invoke to ask for protection from evil, to rescue someone from evil influences and/or to draw customers to your business. Petition him for money, luck prosperity.

43 -St. Martin De Porres, C

St. Martin was born in Lima, Peru, and in 1594 entered the Dominican Order as a lay brother at the age of fifteen, where he worked several jobs (a barber amongst them) and devoted himself to the path of Green Martyrdom. He possessed spiritual wisdom, and in his life of holiness God granted him many gifts, including aerial flight and bilocation. He is the patron Saint of barbers.

Feast: November 3
Liturgical Color: White
Devotional Color: Purple or White
Symbol: Broom and a Crucifix

Invoke to bring harmony to your household. You can also petition him for better health and increased financial security.

44 -St. Michael, Archangel

St. Michael the Archangel is the leader of the hosts of God in their battle with Satan and he is the special protector of the Church. It is he who was responsible for throwing the devil and the renegade angels into the put of hell, and he is commonly called upon as the special protector of Catholic people from any and all dangers. For this reason, many Traditional Catholic churches and oratories are named in his honor.

Feast: September 29
Liturgical Color: White
Devotional Color: Red
Symbol: Sword

Invoke for protection against the enemies of the Church, against danger of all types, for courage, and for victory in battle.

- Chapter Six: Angels and Saints -

45 -St. Monica, W
St. Monica was the mother of St. Augustine. She devoted herself to works of charity and piety after the death of her husband. When St. Augustine fell into the Manichee heresy, she prayed and worked constantly until she secured his reconversion by St. Ambrose at Milan.
Feast: May 4
Liturgical Color: White
Devotional Color: White
Invoke to draw back those who have strayed from the True Faith, especially those being drawn to or proselytized by Greco-Roman Paganism, Manicheeism, Albigensianism, or the New Age Movement.

46 -St. Olaf Haraldsson, KM
The patron of carvers, kings, Norway and Scandinavia, St. Olaf was born a pagan and while a-viking (trading and marauding), and he was baptised in 1013 at the age of 18. He returned to Norway and set about unifying his kingdom and purging paganism from his realm, while the Danes schemed to take the kingdom from him. He was driven into exile, and while trying to reclaim his realm, killed in the Battle of Stiklestad in 1031. The details of the many miracles that led to his canonization are reported in the Heimskringla of Snorri Sturluson.
Feast: July 29
Liturgical Color: Red
Devotional Color: Red or Purple
Symbol: Lion with Battle-Axe in Forepaws
Invoke to become a strong ruler, to combat conversion or slander attempts by followers of Reconstructionist Norse or Germanic Paganism (Asatru, Theodish, etc.), and for help in difficult marriages.

47 -St. Patrick, BC

The loyalty of the Irish people to the Faith and to the Holy See is the great monument to Saint Patrick, their national Apostle. He was sent by Pope Celestine I and his labors in Ireland were accompanied and made fruitful by his extraordinary gifts of prayer and penance. In later years Ireland was known as the Island of Saints and Scholars.

Feast: March 17
Liturgical Color: White
Devotional Color: Green or White
Symbol: Shamrock

Invoke for prosperity, luck, spiritual wisdom, and guidance, and also for assistance against Celtic Paganism.

48 -St. Paul, A

St. Paul, the "Apostle to the Gentiles," was born Saul in Tarsus around 10 A.D. and was received his training from Rabbi Gamaliel I. At first a great persecutor of the Catholic Church, he had a vision of Our Lord while he was on the road to Damascus after which he was instantly converted and received the status of Apostle. He was martyred in Rome on the same day as St. Peter.

Feast: June 30 (Commemoration)
Liturgical Color: Red
Devotional Color: Blue or Red
Symbol: Sword

Invoke for courage, patience, overcome opposition, and to settle disturbed conditions in the home.

49 -St. Peter, APM

Simon bar-Jona, the first of the Apostles, was named by Jesus to be His direct successor. To signify this, Jesus renamed him Peter, "the Rock," upon which He shall build His Church (Matth. 16:18). As the first Pope, St. Peter became known as the "Apostle to the Jews," and wrought

many miracles while guiding the Church in her first decades. He established the two most ancient Patriarchates in the Church, Antioch and Rome, and in 62, Peter was crucified upside down on the Vatican Hill, and his pontificate is still the longest of any Pope in history.
Feast: June 29
Liturgical Color: Red
Devotional Color: Red or White
Symbol: Two Crossed Keys
Invoke to petition him to remove obstacles, business success, strength, courage, forgiveness and good fortune.

50 -St. Peregrine Laziosi, C

St. Peregrine was born to a wealthy family in Firli, Italy, and in his youth was involved in anti-Papal politics. As a result of an incident with St. Phillip Benizi, Peregrine converted to Catholicism and joined the Servite Order, observing silence and solitude as much as possible. He was later afflicted with cancer of the foot, and through prayer was miraculously cured, for which reason he is considered the patron Saint of cancer patients. He died in 1345 and was canonized by Benedict XIII in 1726.
Feast: none
Liturgical Color: none
Devotional Color: White
Symbol: Shepherd's Crook Tied to a Purse
Invoke to petition him for help with cancer.

51 -Saint Philomena, VMT

Nothing is known of St. Philomena's life, save that she was martyred when she was 14 years old. Her tomb was found in the catacomb of St. Priscilla, and she is the only Saint ever to be canonized based solely on the power of her intercession.
Feast: none

Liturgical Color: none
Devotional Color: Pink or Green
Symbol: Anchor
Invoke to help with desperate situations, problems with children, unhappiness in the home, the sick, selling real estate, food for the poor and mental illness. Philomena is a Patroness of the Traditional Catholic Movement and a favorite of single mothers.

52 -St. Pius the Tenth, PC

Born Joseph Sarto, St. Pius X (1835-1914) was the son of the village postman at Riese in northern Italy. After a brilliant and virtuous scholastic career, he was ordained priest and distinguished himself by his zeal both as professor in the seminary and in the care of souls in various parishes. As Bishop of Mantua and later as Patriarch of Venice, he lovingly cared for his flock and was especially active in promoting Catholic social action. In particular, he was noted for his boundless generosity to the poor and afflicted. After his election as Pope he devoted the same vigilant charity to the service and care of the Universal Church. Among his achievements were the suppression of the modernist heresy, the reform of the Breviary and Missal, and the codification of Canon Law. Above all his fame rests on the promotion of frequent and daily Communion, even for the very young. Unquestionably the greatest Pope of the entire twentieth century, he was beatified in 1951 by Pope Pius XII, who also canonized him on May 30, 1954.
Feast: September 3
Liturgical Color: White
Devotional Color: White
Invoke to be granted favors by those in authority (such as a boss or government agency), for help in teaching the Faith

to children, and also for assistance against Modernists and other enemies of the Church.

53 -St. Raphael, Archangel
Raphael, one of the seven spirits that stand before the throne of God, was the heavenly messenger sent to guide young Tobias on his journey and to heal the blindness of his father. He is invoked especially for the healing of mental as well as bodily ailments.
Feast: October 24
Liturgical Color: White
Devotional Color: Pink or Yellow
Symbol: Pilgrim's Staff
Invoke for a safe journey, for protection against ill health and disease, and to heal or cure.

54 -St. Raymond Nonnatus, C
St. Raymond Nonnatus of the Order of Our Lady of Ransom undertook a voyage to Africa to redeem Christian captives. He was imprisoned and mutilated when he surrendered himself as a pledge for the ransom of some prisoners. Later he was created Cardinal but dies at Cardona near Barcelona when on his way to Rome. He received Holy Viaticum from the angels miraculously before his death in 1240.
Feast: August 31
Liturgical Color: White
Devotional Color: Red
Symbol: Monstrance and Palm with Three Crowns
Invoke to prevent gossip, false accusation and for a happy and peaceful home.

55 -Saint Rita of Cascia, W
The patroness of hopeless causes and the impossible, St. Rita suffered for eighteen years as a battered wife until the

day her husband was killed in a brawl. Again, against hopeless odds, she was finally accepted into the Augustinian Order where she lived out her days a nun and received wounds on her forehead resembling a crown of thorns. She died on May 22, 1457.
Feast: May 22
Liturgical Color: White
Devotional Color: White
Symbol: Crown of Thorns
Invoke to assist with an abusive relationship, to relieve loneliness, for deliverance from evil and for spiritual fortitude and strength

56 -St. Rocco, C
Rocco (Roch in France, Roque in Spain) was the son of the governor of Montpellier, France, who went on a pilgrimage to Rome and cared for the victims of a plague afflicting Italy, where he was reputed to have affected a great many cures. When he returned to France, he was imprisoned on suspicion of being a spy in pilgrim's clothing. He died in prison, and after his death it was discovered that he was the governor's son. His intercession is invoked against pestilence and plague, and he is also the patron of invalids.
Feast: August 16
Liturgical Color: White
Devotional Color: White
Symbol: Dog
Invoke to restore health and to be protected from contagious diseases.

57 -St. Sebastian, M
St. Sebastian was an officer in the Imperial Guard in Rome. Because of his assistance to those punished for their faith, he was himself sentenced to death in 288 by shooting with arrows. He was miraculously cured of his wounds and then

Diocletian ordered that he should be beaten to death with clubs.
Feast: January 20
Liturgical Color: Red
Devotional Color: Red
Symbol: Arrows
Invoke to petition for justice, to overcome rivals, remove obstacles from your path, success and good fortune.

58 -Saint Therese of Lisieux, V

St. Therese was born in Alencon and educated in Lisieux. At the age of fifteen she entered the Carmel of Lisieux and nine years later she died there in December, 1897. After her death her holiness inspired such devotion to her that she has become one of the great popular Saints of our time. So abundant were the miracles worked through her intercession that Therese was solemnly canonized in 1925 only 28 years after her death. The characteristic of her holiness was her "little way" of striving by humility and love to obtain that child-like simplicity of heart which Jesus loves, to be a "Little Flower" in the garden of the Lord. Because of her prayers for missionaries in pagan lands, St. Therese was also named by Pope Pius XI as the special patroness of Catholic Missions.
Feast: October 3
Liturgical Color: White
Devotional Color: Yellow
Symbol: Bouquet of Roses
Invoke to be loved by all, for popularity, for help with addiction and alcoholism, for protection from black magic and to restore faith.

59 -St. Thomas Aquinas, CD

Perhaps the greatest theologian and philosopher in the whole of Church history, St. Thomas was born to the family of the counts of Aquino, and was born at Rocca Secca and educated at the abbey of Monte Cassino. He entered the Oder of Preachers (Dominicans) in the face of strong opposition from his family. By vigorous resistance to temptation he attained angelic purity. Although gifted with prodigious power of mind, he was a model of humility. During his lifetime he was renowned as a professor of philosophy and theology in Paris. His writings on the sacred sciences are of such clarity and depth that they have served for the refutation not merely of the errors of his time but of succeeding centuries. They form the basis of all theological teaching in most still-solidly Catholic universities. St. Thomas, who died in 1274, bears the title of "Angelic Doctor," and he was made patron of all Catholic schools by Pope Leo XIII.

Feast: March 7
Liturgical Color: White
Devotional Color: White

Invoke to improve concentration and memory, for understanding, for mental stamina and to help pass exams.

"And as Moses lifted up the serpent in the desert, so must the Son of man be lifted up: That whosoever believeth in him may not perish, but may have life everlasting." – John 3:14-15 (DRV)

CHAPTER SEVEN: TYING IT ALL TOGETHER

In this book, we've endeavored to present a theological framework for the oft-misunderstood topic of magic and how it can be practiced safely by a member of the Catholic religion. Therefore, if the reader is able to walk away from this book having at least a semblance of a foundation of understanding upon which to build one's magical thinking and/or practice, then this book will have more than served its purpose.

Yet, as this book is necessarily more theoretical and theological than practical, we've dealt strictly with those concepts, signs, and symbols which dwell within the context of Catholic theology and ritual. There are a number of signs, gestures, symbols, and methods which are fully outside the realm of Catholicism, though at the same time compatible with the Faith and thus useable by a Catholic mage. In this chapter, I would like to discuss some of these things.

THE PENTAGRAM

> "Unlike what some paranoid alarmists would have folks believe, the pentagram is not a diabolical device, but an abstract sign of the crucifixion."[261]

The above quote gives a perfect summation of everything that could be said on the subject. In and of itself, before we

---

[261] Bilardi, Chris. *The Red Church or the Art of Pennsylvania German Braucherei*. 2009. Pendraig Publishing. *Braucherei*, also called "Pow Wow," is a German-American system of Christian folk magic still practiced in parts of Pennsylvania. Bilardi's book is the authoritative modern work on the subject.

consider it a symbol, we must consider the pentagram is first and foremost a geometric shape. Last time I checked, *nobody* owns the copyright on geometric shapes.

While nobody owns a copyright on geometric shapes, things can be said differently once the shape passes on to the realm of symbol, and the pentagram has been used as a symbol by many cultures, including Catholicism.

The first recorded appearance of the pentagram took place around the 30th century B.C., where it was used in Sumerian cuneiform as a character for the word *ub*, meaning "nook" or "corner." One could say this was no more a symbol than Chinese characters are symbols in the usual sense, or one could say this was symbolic in the sense that all writing is symbolic of the sounds and words it represents. I leave the reader to his or her own conclusions.

The pentagram eventually passed to the Greeks, where during the 5th century B.C., the followers of Pythagoras considered the pentagram a sign of ὑγιεία, "health." In fact it is the word ὑγιεία (*ygeía*) which gives us the English word "hygiene."[262] We now come to the Christian era.

Just as the letters ὑγιεία were attributed to each point by the Pythagoreans (who still existed in the first centuries after Jesus' time), so it was easy enough to do with the five letters of the word *salus* (the Latin translation of ὑγιεία).[263] It is from here that we must pass for about a thousand years

---

[262] For a more detailed description of the pentagram of Pythagoras, see: http://web.eecs.utk.edu/~mclennan/BA/PP/index.html.
(Retrieved December 2, 2014).
[263] Various websites and "dictionaries of symbols" claim the early Christians used the Pentagram as a symbol of health and the five senses, but I've yet to find a primary source documenting this.

in our quest to establish what the pentagram meant for Christians during those ten or so centuries.

By the medieval period, we find the pentagram as a feature of Church architecture, and in the late fourteenth-century poem *Sir Gawain and the Green Knight* we are told that Sir Gawain has the "pentangle" on his shield, and the writer feels prompted to explain:

> "And why the pentangle pertains to that noble prince I mean to tell you, though it should delay me. It is a sign that Solomon set formerly as a token of truth, by its own right, for it is a figure that holds five points, and each line overlaps and locks in another and throughout it is endless; and the English call it everywhere, as I hear, the endless knot. Therefore it suits this knight and his clear arms, forever faithful in five things, and in each of them five ways."[264]

In the next paragraph, Sir Gawain is described as having put all his faith in the five wounds of Christ. It is this – the Five Wounds – which the pentagram came to symbolize in the Middle Ages, while devotion to the Five Wounds was on the upswing, and in heraldry we find both the pentagram, and the five-petaled rose as a sort of stylized pentagram, also representing the Five Wounds.[265] As stated

---

[264] *Sir Gawain and the Green Knight*. Translated by W.A. Neilson. 1999. In Parentheses Publications. Cambridge, Ontario. Chapter ("Fytte") Two, paragraph 6. www.yorku.ca/inpar/sggk_neilson.pdf. (Retrieved December 2, 2014).

[265] This is illustrated clearly in the poem *As a Mydsomer Rose* by John Lydgate (1370-1451), who compares the Five Wounds to a "Rose of the bloody field," and to five wells releasing a red stream to Paradise, "Of whose five wounds print in your heart a rose." The entire poem can be found online at: http://www.poetrynook.com/poem/mydsomer-rose. (Retrieved December 2, 2014).

before, we likewise see pentagrams in church architecture, many which still stand at the present day. Here are some recent examples, all built during the nineteenth century:

Pentagram window at First Methodist Church in Warren, Indiana. This church was built in 1897 and used until 2013.

First Presbyterian Church in Apache, Texas. Built 1873.

- *Chapter Seven: Tying It All Together* -

Saint Margaret and All Saints Catholic Church in Canning Town. London, England. Built 1876.

Saint Barnabas in Bethnal Green Anglican Church. London, England. Built in 1865.

Sometimes "over-kill" is the best way to make a point, and I think we've done exactly that. Even without primary sources, the existence of the pentagram as a Christian symbol is well-attested since at least medieval times, meaning that there is nothing wrong with a Christian making use of it.

Even though other groups have claimed it as their own, especially Neopagans who (following Renaissance Christian magical writers) cite it as a symbol of the five elements – Air, Fire, Water, Earth, and Spirit – or Satanists who invert it thinking it a symbol of rebellion (the "inversion equals evil" idea was invented by Eliphas Levi in the 1850's!), we have to remember that a geometric shape is nothing more than a geometric shape, and the symbols attached to it will come and go with the passage of time. Let others have their symbols and attachments to them, and realize they in no way prevent us from having ours.

One final word about the use of the Pentagram before we move on. It is linked with Jesus' Blood, and has a long history of being used as a protective symbol. For us it is both a symbol of protection through Jesus' Blood, and of the power to cleanse, protect, purify, and conquer that we received through that blood. So even if you don't like traditional Gospel songs, you have to admit that old hymn is right: there is indeed "Power in the Blood."

CIRCUMAMBULATION
The gesture of circumambulation, or of walking about the working area, is very common throughout magical literature as a method of creating a vortex of energy throughout the working-space, which energy is later

- *Chapter Seven: Tying It All Together* -

directed towards one's purpose at the culmination of the rite.

Often this is called "casting the circle" or "forming the circle," or even "creating a cone of power,"[266] in which case the base of the "cone" is the circle around the working space, and the vertex of the cone is right above its center. In these systems, however, the mensa is placed in the center of the working space, and the majority of the operation is performed with the operator in the center of that space, by the mensa.

In the system that I devised and used as a teenager, I would have the mensa in the center of the room and circumambulate for the number of times commensurate with the working in question, while visualizing the circle being filled with an intensifying light of the color appropriate to that working.

In the system given by Gareth Knight in his *Practice of Ritual Magic*, the operator would start in the eastern quarter of the working space, and make three clockwise circumambulations, visualizing a circle of light forming around the space's x, y, and z axes respectively. The end result of this would be a three-dimensional sphere of light surrounding the working area.[267]

In the magical order Aurum Solis, circumambulation is said to be employed for a number of purposes: to create a

---

[266] These are terms found in Wiccan literature, and unrelated to Catholic practice. The practice of using a circle, in spite of its origins in Ceremonial Magic, can be incorporated into a Catholic's practical regimen.
[267] Knight, Gareth. *The Practice of Ritual Magic*. 1996. Sun Chalice Books. ISBN-13: 9780965083980.

simple vortex of energy, to represent a cosmic orbit, or to represent a systematic progress or pilgrimage.[268]

In the connection of pilgrimage, one may also think of the "Patterns" known to Irish folk Catholicism, which existed prior to Cardinal Cullen's "Devotional Revolution" of the 1850's. The Patterns involved a set number of circumambulations around a holy site – usually a well – while saying a set prayer or devotion.[269]

In the Hermetic Order of the Golden Dawn's magical system, the "Mystic Circumambulation" is treated with a great air of complexity, though its bottom-line purpose is stated "to attract and make the connection between the Divine Light and the Temple."[270]

FUN FACT: this process of "completing the circle" is not just limited to Neohermetic or Neopagan groups. It also has a place in the Roman Liturgy. In the traditional Latin Mass, when the priest turns to face the people, he always begins by kissing the altar, then turning "towards the Epistle side" (i.e. to his right) to face the people. As he returns to the Altar, he turns back to his left, so as not to make a circle.

However, at the *Orate fratres*, the Missal is very specific to state that the circle is completed. In *Ritus Servandus in Celebratione Missae* found at the beginning of every Latin Mass Altar Missal, the following instruction is given:

---

[268] Melita Denning and Osbourne Phillips, *Mysteria Magica*, pp. 109-111.

[269] The Patterns deserve a fuller discussion than can be had in this book. As a starting point for more information, the reader is referred to the *Irish Culture and Customs* article on Patterns. (Retrieved July 1, 2015)
http://www.irishcultureandcustoms.com/ACustom/PatternDay.html

[270] Israel Regardie, *The Golden Dawn*, Sixth Edition, p. 347

"...the hands being extended and placed on the Altar, he kisses it in the middle; then, hands joined before the breast, eyes being cast toward the earth, by the left hand towards the right he turns himself toward the people, and facing them, extending and joining his hands, he says in a slightly louder voice, 'Pray, brethren,' and following it silently with 'that my and your sacrifice, etc.' **He completes the circle**, turning back, hands joined before the breast, by the right hand towards the middle of the altar."[271]

In *The Book of Ceremonies*, the Rev. Laurence J. O'Connell gives the following note about turning to face the people:

"Whenever the priest turns to face the people, he turns right, i.e., toward the Epistle side; ordinarily, he then turns left back to the altar, i.e., toward the Epistle side without completing the circle. At the *Orate, fratres,* however, and again after the Blessing, the priest turns right to the altar, thus completing the circle (unless the Blessed Sacrament is exposed, in which case he never completes the turn)."

Before commenting, it should perhaps be noted that at the *Orate, fratres,* the moment comes when the priest enjoins the people to join their prayers and intentions to his, thus this point in the ceremony is the creation of a circuit of power between priest and people, with the circle being completed both figuratively and literally.

---

[271] *Ritus Servandus in Celebratione Missae.* VII, 7. (my translation)

Obviously, the notion of completing the circle has been weakened in the wake of permission for the priest to celebrate Mass facing the people during the 1960's.[272] Yet even here, it can still be said that the priest and people automatically form a circle by their being together for the purpose of worshipping the Divine. So even though we do not have a pure circumambulation in the strict sense of the word, we still have a perfect circle-casting contained in a simplified form.

ALTERNATE SIGNS OF THE CROSS
The average lay Catholic is accustomed to making the sign of the Cross in exactly one way: forehead-breast-left shoulder-right shoulder, to the words *In nómine Patris, et Fílii, et Spíritus Sancti. Amen*, usually said in the vernacular.

What most Catholics may not know is that, in the liturgy of the Roman Rite, the sign of the Cross is also used with other words both in the Mass and the Divine Office. A few examples should suffice to make our point:
1. *Adjutórium – nostrum – in nómine – Dómini.*
   ("Our – help – is in the name – of the Lord.")
2. *Magníficat – anima – mea – Dóminum.*
   ("My – soul – magnifies – the Lord.")
3. *Indulgéntiam – absolutiónem – et remissiónem – peccatórum nostrórum...*
   ("Pardon – absolution – and forgiveness – of our sins...")

---

[272] Mass "facing the people" did not begin with the Novus Ordo. There are recorded examples of it in Germany as early as the 1940's, and it was permitted on an experimental basis during the 1950's. The first time we see it in an official Roman document is the 1967 "Second Instruction" titled *Tres Abhinc Annos*, where it is described under the heading of "Special Circumstances." (n. 17)

- *Chapter Seven: Tying It All Together* -

4. *Nunc – dimíttis – servum tuum – Dómine.*
   ("Now – Lord – you dismiss – your servant.")
5. *Deus – in adjutórium – nostrum – inténde.*
   ("O God – incline – to help – us.")

Some Catholics may also be aware that in the Eastern Churches – both Eastern Catholic and Eastern Orthodox – the sign of the Cross is made "backwards," that is, made from the right shoulder to the left.[273] Actually, the pattern of "right – to – left" is the older method and used in the West prior to the thirteenth century, as attested by Innocent III when he describes the sign of the Cross as being made from right to left, and then goes to describe the left-to-right usage as something already extant when priests make the sign of the Cross over the people:

> "Now the sign of the Cross must be expressed with three fingers, because it imprints the invocation of the Trinity, of which the Prophet speaks: 'Who hangs the bulk of the earth by three fingers?' (Isaiah 40:12) So that which is above descends to that which is below, and the right passes to the left: because Christ descended from heaven to earth, and He passed from the Jews to the gentiles. Yet some make the sign of the Cross from left to right, because we should pass from misery to glory. Even as Christ passed from death unto life and from hell into Paradise, especially that He may consign themselves and others equally to the same path. Moreover, it stands firm that when we imprint the sign of the Cross over others, we sign them from left to right. Verily, pay diligent attention if we were to make the sign of the Cross over

---

[273] Eastern Orthodox will say that it's the Catholics who make the sign backwards!

others from right to left, because we don't sign them as if turned to their back, but as if present to their face."[274]

It seems that Innocent was writing at the moment of transition: the established custom was to make the sign of the Cross from right to left, while the priests made the sign from left to right so as to match the people. Yet others were starting to sign from left to right so they would (in their minds) match the priest!

Fortunately, all we modern Catholics have to do is remember that there are two versions of the sign of the Cross: the Western or Latin, which moves from left to right; and the Eastern or Greek, which moves from right to left. My own opinion is that neither is "better" or more "valid" than the other, and both have served countless Saints over many centuries.

This brings us full circle, to the Eastern formulas for the sign of the Cross. While the Western Church most commonly says the **Invocation** "In the name of the Father," in the Eastern Churches it's common to make the sign of the Cross along with the **Trisagion**:
Ἅγιος ὁ Θεός, – Ἅγιος ἰσχυρός, – Ἅγιος ἀθάνατος, – ἐλέησον ἡμᾶς.
"Holy God – Holy Strong One – Holy Immortal One – Have mercy on us."

In the Russian, East Armenian, Ge'ez, and Old Antiochian Rites, it's common to say the *Jesus Prayer*:
Κύριε – Ἰησοῦ Χριστέ, – Υἱέ τοῦ Θεοῦ, – ἐλέησον ἡμᾶς.
"Lord – Jesus Christ – Son of God – have mercy on us."[275]

---

[274] Innocent III. *De Sacro Altari Mysterio*. Book II, ch. 44. (My translation)

- Chapter Seven: Tying It All Together -

So in essence, what we see before us is a variety of methods for making the sign of the Cross, and we see that different churches are accustomed to different words when making the gesture, though always to the same purpose. This brings us to another form of the sign of the Cross, one that can simultaneously be edifying and problematic.

If the reader were to begin studying "mainstream" modern occultism, he would soon find a version called the "Kabbalistic Cross." It consists of the sign of the Cross made in the Eastern fashion, with words that purport to be the "Protestant ending" of the Our Father in Hebrew.

In and of itself this can be a harmless exercise, because the Protestant ending is actually a doxology giving praise to God from whom all blessings flow. What's problematic is that it's some really bad Hebrew:
Forehead: אַתָּה (*Atah*, "Thou art")
Breast: מַלְכוּת (*Malkus*, "Kingdom")
Right Shoulder: וּגְבוּרָה (*Va-Gevurah*, "and Power")
Left Shoulder: וּגְדֻלָּה (*Va-Gedulah*, "and Glory")
Clasp Hands: לְעוֹלָם אָמֵן (*Le-Olam. Amen.* "forever. Amen.")

As one can see, it reads like somebody started with the English version of the Protestant ending, and then tried translating it back into Hebrew without a strong enough command of the language. This new version, by saying "Thou art kingdom," also shows a bias towards pantheism, as it makes no distinction between Creator and creature.[276]

---

[275] OrthodoxWiki, "Sign of the Cross." (retrieved December 3, 2014). http://orthodoxwiki.org/Sign_of_the_Cross.
[276] While it is a matter of Catholic doctrine that God is present throughout all creation, God is also distinct from His creation. Pantheism rejects the distinction and says God more or less *is* His creation.

On the bright side, there are some very easy fixes. In the first place, I would prefer a left-to-right sign of the Cross (though mileage may vary). The other thing we can do is say the words in Greek, Latin, or English, and we could also fix the Hebrew. I propose to do all these things.

First, I'll start by giving a word of warning. Since we propose to change this exercise so radically, we can no longer call it the "Kabbalistic Cross," and we're probably the better for it. I suggest that we call it the **Doxological Cross**, since the words are a doxology said after the Our Father.

The Greek and Latin texts are easy to learn:
Greek: Ὅτι σοῦ ἐστιν – ἡ βασιλεία – καὶ ἡ δύναμις – καὶ ἡ δόξα – εἰς τοὺς αἰῶνας. Ἀμήν.
Oti sou éstin – e vasileía – kai e dýnamis – kai e doxa – eis tous aiónas. Amén.
"For Thine is – the kingdom – and the power – and the glory – forever. Amen."

Latin: Quia tuum est – regnum – et potéstas – et glória – in sáecula. Amen.
"For Thine is – the kingdom – and the power – and the glory – forever. Amen."[277]

And now for the corrected Hebrew:
Forehead: כִּי לְךָ (*Ki Lekha*, "For Thine is")
Breast: הַמַּלְכוּתה (*Ha'Malkus*, "the Kingdom")
Left Shoulder: וְהַגְּבוּרָה (*Va-Ha'Gevurah*, "and the Power")
Right Shoulder: וְהַגְּדֻלָּה (*Va-Ha'Gedulah*, "and the Glory")

---

[277] The Greek is an interpolation found in Byzantine manuscripts of Matthew 6:13 but not found in older manuscripts. The Latin is a literal translation of the Greek and found in the post-Vatican II order of Mass.

Clasp Hands: לְעוֹלְמֵי עוֹלָמִים אָמֵן(*Le-Olemei Olamim. Amen.* "forever and ever. Amen.")

Now, as always, the reader is free to choose whether to implement this or any other form of the sign of the Cross discussed in this section. As in all things, prayer and experience should be your guides.

TECHNIQUES OF MEDITATION

We have mentioned "meditation" in previous chapters, and its connection with mental prayer. What we haven't done thus far is give practical techniques for meditating; we plan to correct this now.

Within the Christian spiritual tradition, meditation can be considered a form of contemplation, by which one ponders over a given scene from the life of Jesus and/or Mary, or one of the Apostles, or one of the Saints, or one or other doctrine of the Faith. In eastern Christianity, meditation can consist of **Hesychasm**, whereby one seeks to quiet the mind in order to perceive God's uncreated energy and light.[278] If we venture further east, meditation is seen as one of the five forms of Yoga (called *Raja Yoga*), wherein the mind is stilled and union with deity is sought.[279]

---

[278] The term "hesychasm" has a number of meanings in Eastern Orthodox spirituality, and I here use the word in the most general sense. For a starting point to research the subject more thoroughly, see the "Hesychasm" article on OrthodoxWiki: (Retrieved July 3, 2015) http://orthodoxwiki.org/Hesychasm

[279] It may help to explain that the Sanskrit word *yoga* is cognate with the Latin *jugum*, both words meaning "yoke" a "connection." Yoga is that which connects a devotee to deity, such as study (*jnana yoga*) or religious devotion (*bhakti yoga*). The postures which westerners call "yoga" – *hatha yoga* – are merely one part of the whole.

When exploring the meditative traditions of other religions, (particularly Hinduism and the three major types of Buddhism), awe have recourse to a document from the Sacred Congregation for the Doctrine of the Faith titled *Letter to the Bishops of the Catholic Church on Some Aspects of Christian Meditation*, written by then-prefect Joseph Cardinal Ratzinger in 1989:

> "The majority of the 'great religions' which have sought union with God in prayer have also pointed out ways to achieve it. Just as 'the Catholic Church rejects nothing of what is true and holy in these religions' (*Nostra Aetate*, n. 2), neither should these ways be rejected out of hand simply because they are not Christian. On the contrary, one can take from them what is useful so long as the Christian conception of prayer, its logic and requirements are never obscured. It is within the context of all of this that these bits and pieces should be taken up and expressed anew."[280]

While care should be taken to avoid falling into the heresy of **Quietism**,[281] it is possible to bring the mind to stillness and contemplation in seeking union with God. Such a technique could be as simple as sitting and quietly praying the Jesus prayer, or it could involve breathing and visualization of the Divine filling us with His power and His love.[282]

---

[280] The full text can be found here. (Retrieved July 3, 2015) https://www.ewtn.com/library/CURIA/CDFMED.HTM

[281] Quietism was a late-seventeenth century movement associated with Miguel de Molinos, which taught self-annihilation and complete absorption into the Divine. It was condemned as heresy by Pope Innocent XI in 1687, in the bull *Coelestis Pastor*.

[282] The Jesus prayer, "Lord Jesus Christ, Son of the living God, be merciful to me a sinner," is a central element of Hesychast practice.

1. Rhythmic Breathing

The first step in meditation can be called "rhythmic breathing," which is exactly what the name says: breathing in a set rhythm. It's a natural and easy thing to achieve, and a common method to gain rhythm is by counting heartbeats.

In the method I use and teach, we begin by exhaling over a space of four heartbeats, and then hold our breath for a count of two heartbeats. We then breathe in for a count of four, hold for a count of two, and again breathe out for a count of four, repeating the process.

The main thing is to hold the breath for half the number of heartbeats we breathe.[283] Thus, if we breathe for eight heartbeats, we hold for four. If we breathe for six, we hold for three.

Before long, your body will get used to the breathing pattern, and you'll find that you no longer need to count heartbeats. The rhythm comes naturally and unconsciously, leaving the mind free for meditative work.

2. Meditation on the Divine Presence

Breathing, as we discussed above, is religiously neutral; this is self-evident by the fact all people, animals, and even plants practice breathing. Now we take that neutral act of breathing and incorporate it into our religious and spiritual work.

For beginners, I propose the following meditation that I composed many years ago, as an act of spiritual

---

[283] There is another popular system that teaches the student to hold his or her breath for an equal number of heartbeats: breathe for four, hold for four. The reader is free to use whichever system is more appealing.

communion to help become attuned to the power and Love of the Holy Trinity present and increasing in all of us.

1. Sit comfortably, not crossing your arms or legs.

2. Establish the rhythmic breathing.

3. Once you are relaxed, imagine all negativity dissipating from you, helping you relax even further.[284]

4. Now imagine God the Father as a large, brilliant white flame filling and enveloping you.[285] Focus on this image over the next three breaths, while saying mentally:
    1st breath: "God the Father of heaven * fills me with His power and with His love."[286]
    2nd breath: "The Creator of heaven and earth * Who shall judge both on the Last Day."
    3rd breath: "Fills me * with His power and with His love."

5. Afterwards, imagine God the Son in the same manner, as a large, brilliant, golden flame. Hold this image for the next three breaths, while saying mentally:
    1st breath: "Jesus Christ, Redeemer of the world * fills me with His power and with His love."
    2nd breath: "Who died for love of us, * and Whose blood made us free."

---

[284] I once knew a person whose method for doing this was to visualize walking into a church, walking up to the tabernacle, and imagine talking to Jesus in the Blessed Sacrament as taking away one's negative feelings and attachment to this world's problems.
[285] "For the Lord your God is a consuming fire" – Deuteronomy 4:24
[286] Mentally say the part before the asterisk while breathing in, and the part after the asterisk while breathing out.

3rd breath: "Fills me * with His power and with His love."

6. Thirdly, imagine God the Holy Ghost[287] as a large, brilliant, rose-gold flame. Hold this image for the next three breaths, while saying mentally:
1st breath: "God, the Holy Ghost, the Paraclete[288] * fills me with His power and with His love."
2nd breath: "Who descended on the Apostles * and gives power to the Church."
3rd breath: "Fills me * with His power and with His love."

7. Afterwards, concentrate on these three flames as they course through you, and feel them filling your entire being.

8. Continue the rhythmic breathing while the image fades slowly from your consciousness. Afterwards, seal yourself with the Sign of the Cross.

This method is a great daily practice for a budding Christian magician of any stripe, and contains nothing objectionable to Christian theology or moral practice.

THE LESSER RITUAL OF THE PENTAGRAM

For the final exercise featured in this chapter, I'd like to discuss a ritual of completely non-Catholic origin, often known as the "Lesser Banishing Ritual of the Pentagram" and commonly abbreviated as the LBRP.

---

[287] You may say "Holy Spirit" if you prefer. The choice of words is a matter of personal preference.
[288] "Paraclete," one of the titles of the Holy Ghost, means "Advocate" from the Greek παράκλητος by way of the Latin *parácletus*.

The LBRP was originally created by the Hermetic Order of the Golden Dawn and given to new members ("Neophytes") as an exercise with three stated intentions:

1. To help cleanse self, room, and working area.
2. To help banish obsessive thoughts.
3. As an exercise in concentration.[289]

In and of itself, the LBRP can be seen as innocuous and theologically neutral and, with the exception of invoking the Archangel Uriel, contains nothing necessarily of objection to a Catholic.

With this in mind, below I give a version of the LBRP which I use and teach. It will show various concepts we've discussed thus far, and can be used as a daily or bi-daily exercise as part of the reader's regular spiritual practice.

1. The LBRP
1. Stand in the center of the room, facing east. Begin by making the sign of the Cross. As you touch each point, say:
    a. Forehead: כִּי לְךָ (*Ki Lekha*, "For Thine is")
    b. Breast: מַלְכוּתָה (*Ha'Malkus*, "the Kingdom")
    c. Left Shoulder: וַהַגְּבוּרָה (*Va-Ha'Gevurah*, "and the Power")
    d. Right Shoulder: וַהַגְּדֻלָה (*Va-Ha'Gedulah*, "and the Glory")
    e. Clasp Hands: לְעוֹלְמֵי עוֹלָמִים אָמֵן (*Le-Olemei Olamim. Amen.* "forever and ever. Amen.")

The Sign of the Cross may also be said in Latin, Greek, or English if you prefer.

---

[289] The original text and purposes of the LBRP can be is found in Regardie, *The Golden Dawn*, pp. 53-55, and variations can be found all over the internet.

2. Go to the east wall of the room. Hold out your right hand and draw a banishing pentagram,[290] visualizing it in blue flame.

Once the pentagram is drawn, point your hand at the center and vibrate: "Yod Heh Vav Heh."[291]

3. Holding your arm out, walk in a circle toward the south. As you walk, visualize an arc of blue flame being created.

4. At the south wall, draw the pentagram again, this time saying: "Adonai."[292]

5. Repeat the process moving toward the west. "Eheieh."[293]

6. Repeat the process toward the north. "AGLA."[294]

---

[290] In ceremonial magic, the pentagrams are drawn either "invoking" or "banishing," in a prescribed manner for each element. The details are outside the scope of this book, but can be found easily through a perusal of the internet or occult literature.
[291] The Hebrew letters Yod, Heh, Vav, and Heh for the name of God, or Tetragrammaton, which cannot be pronounced but erroneously rendered "Jehovah" in older Bibles. Even the modern Christian pronunciation "Yahveh" is at best speculation.
[292] Hebrew for "Lord."
[293] Hebrew for "I am." (Exodus 3:14)
[294] Pronounced "Ah-Gahl-lah," a Hebrew acronym for "Atah Gavor Le-Olam Adonai," or "Thou art mighty forever, O Lord."

7. Return to the East with your arm outstretched, completing the arc of blue flame. What you should now have visualized is a circle of blue flame studded with a blazing pentagram at each of the cardinal points.

8. Return to the center of the circle, facing east, and stretch your arms out to your sides with palms upward, such that your body is in the shape of a cross.

9. Visualize the Archangel Raphael forming outside the circle at the east, and vibrate:
"Ante me stat Ráphael." (Before me is Raphael.)

10. Visualize the Archangel Gabriel forming outside the circle at the west, and vibrate:
"Post me stat Gábriel." (Behind me is Gabriel.)

11. Visualize the Archangel Michael forming outside the circle at the south, and vibrate:
"Ad déxteram meam stat Míchael."
(At my left hand is Michael.)

12. Visualize the Archangel Uriel forming outside the circle at the north, and vibrate:
"Atque ad sínistram meam stat Uriel."
(At my left hand is Uriel.)

13. Lastly, visualize all this around you, and a brilliant gold-white six-rayed star at your back. Say:
"Circumscríbor cum pentagrammátibus flammántibus, et post me stella radiórum sex lucet!"
(About me flame the pentagrams, and behind me shines the six-rayed star!)[295]

---

[295] The six-rayed star in this rite has many meanings proposed, and newer versions use the wording "in the center shines…" to indicate the

14. Close the ritual with the Sign of the Cross, as given in step 1.

As the reader can see, this rite is clearly non-Catholic in origin, and serves as a bridge-point between Christian Angelology, Jewish Kabbalah, and outright ceremonial magical ritual. Thus I make no claim to this rite's orthodoxy, and only say that it can be used by a Catholic magician so long as he keeps in mind the rite's origins and his or her own purposes when using it.

IN CONCLUSION

So there you have it, the theological framework within which a system of purely Catholic magic may be wrought, a few basic concepts upon which a ritual system can be founded, and finally a basis upon which the techniques of other systems can be reconciled. Now it is for you, gentle reader, to go forth and discover how best to implement these sacramentals into your life that God's glory may better manifest and shine within it. Follow always the path of the Holy Faith, and may God bless you richly in all your endeavors!

---

divine light shining in all of us. The wording here given is that from the original text of the ritual.

EPILOGUE: A MAGICIAN'S SPIRITUAL JOURNEY

As we put this book down, we should lift up our heads and look at the world around us. The sun is shining, even if it is covered by clouds. The rain is falling, even if not in our immediate vicinity. The birds are chirping, the grass is growing, people are dying, and people are being born. All of this is happening on this planet in some or other location, and on some level we are all aware of these things going on around us.

We look at these things, and we observe, and we realize that all of these things are but steps in a process. Then we look inward, and ask ourselves: "What is our process?"

Doubtless, most people who have picked up this book are doing so because they aspire to be magicians. Yet being a magician is not an end to be sought in and of itself, but rather as a side effect resulting from a strong and vibrant spirituality.

As we put this book down, those of us who aspire to be magicians should first and foremost aspire to work on our spiritual life, to submit ourselves to the will of God, and strive to keep ourselves clean physically and spiritually. We should avoid sin and impurity, not because we are afraid of God or hell, but because we know and believe it to be the best thing for us.

To be a magician is to become a current which channels Divine Power, and that power cannot fully reside in a place where the Divine Will does not. This is the reason why the magus seeks always to submit the lower will to the higher will, and the higher will to the Divine Will.

In our spiritual life, we seek always to remain in communication with God through the many means He makes available to us: prayer, meditation, right living, frequent reception of the sacraments, taking care of our bodies and minds, the things we say and do in our day-to-day lives, and especially the way we treat our neighbor. Everything in our lives is a form of communication with God, because everything we think, say, and do sends Him a message about us.

But most importantly of all, we must keep in mind the quest to be a magician is a double quest, for it is empowerment through servitude, or as St. Louis de Montfort once called it, "The Holy Slavery." We must not commit ourselves to this servitude out of guilt or fear of punishment, for the actions of a guilt-ridden and fearful man are the actions of a weakling. Instead, we should serve out of love of God and a realization that this servitude is truly the road to freedom. Meditation on the Third Joyful Mystery of the Rosary would be fruitful in understanding the things of which we speak.

THE ROSARY AS AN ANALOGY

Speaking of the Third Joyful Mystery, the cycle of the Rosary itself is a perfect analogy for the pattern of spiritual progress. Through the three groups of Mysteries we see the progression of the soul through each of the stages of the Mystical Life, call the Illuminative, the Purgative, and the Unitive respectively.[296]

---

[296] In the Illuminative Life, the soul is made aware that there is a goal towards which to strive, and then acquires the basic skills to approach that goal. In the Purgative Life, the soul is tested and purified of its imperfections. In the Unitive Life, the soul, now having been purged of its imperfections, strives forward and completes the process.

As we follow the path of the Rosary and the progression of the Mysteries, we place ourselves not only in the shoes of Christ but especially in the shoes of Mary, recalling and following her progress from her beginnings as a 15-year-old Jewish girl in an obscure backwater of the Roman Empire, to her triumph as Mother of God, Queen of Heaven, and Empress of the Universe. Her joys, her sorrows, and her glories – which culminate in the life, death, and resurrection of her Son – are the pattern followed by our soul as it progresses in the Mystical Life, sometimes forward and sometimes back. It is with Mary that we ourselves must identify in order to perceive the progression of the Mysteries most accurately.

1) The Joyous Mysteries
i. The Annunciation

In the First Joyous Mystery, the Annunciation, we are brought to the spiritual fruit of humility. We also begin our journey here, fixing our eyes upon the form of a 15-year old girl in ancient Judea, who was first made aware of her mission when the Angel startled her. Yet when she gave her fiat and announced herself "the handmaid of the Lord," she displayed the humility to recognize that there was one greater than she, and began her journey in becoming what she was yet destined to become. This is the same virtue that the proud Saul of Tarsus was forced to learn on the road to Damascus (Acts 9:3-11), and which virtue was the beginning of a process for him, by which this proud student of Gamaliel was made to put away his perceptions of self, of God, and of others, and was then able to more quietly and open-mindedly perceive others as they truly were, and discern the good from the bad. It is also firstly through humility that we, like Mary, may become truly impregnated with the Word, that the Word may bear fruit in our minds, in our hearts, in our deeds, and in our words. This impregnation is something I call the "Holy Pregnancy," which is something which all mystics and mages seek in their quest for the realization of God dwelling within them.

ii. The Visitation

The Second Joyous Mystery, the Visitation, is associated with selflessness and charity. In spite of her own discomfort as a pregnant mother, she learned of her cousin Elizabeth's condition, and set out across the desert to go and assist her. When contemplating this Mystery, we must remember that selfishness is the hallmark of immaturity, and that in order to progress spiritually as well as emotionally, we must develop the maturity to lay down our selfish desires and reach out to those in need. Just is a genuine virtue of humility is required for us to truly begin our journey of spiritual growth, so is a genuine charity necessary for us to begin bearing the fruit of being impregnated with the Word. For it may be great to have all gifts, all knowledge, and all power, which is the one thing exclusively sought by most would-be magicians. But if we have not charity, we are as sounding brass and a tinkling symbol. For to have such knowledge, but not to have charity, is an undoing of humility, which automatically condemns us to begin the process anew.

iii. The Nativity

After Mary had helped Elizabeth through her own pregnancy, and Elizabeth had come to term (bearing John the Baptist), the Blessed Mother then went home. Yet when she herself was about to come to term, Caesar called a census of all provinces and required all to register within their city of birth. Even though this was but a small distance, we should make no mistake, for it was still a great deal of work and traveling for a woman who was nine months' pregnant. But to top off her hardships, when it was time for her to deliver, there was no room at the inn, and so her Son had to be born in the stable amongst the beasts, their filth, and the smell of their manure. These crowded and unsanitary conditions, to be sure, certainly paint a disgusting picture in our minds – and I'm certain that the average pregnant teenager today wouldn't even consider giving birth in a stable – but this is how Our Lord was born into the world. The spiritual fruit of this Mystery, therefore, is indifference to the physical world and its conditions, indifference to our own wealth or poverty, indifference to our own comfort or hardship. When we obsess about these things, we allow them to control us and become slaves to them. Yet when we just "let it go," it is then that we no longer allow these things to control us, and instead we begin to take control of them. This indifference also reinforces the virtues of humility and charity, as we here see the relationship between pregnancy and delivery. We become impregnated with the Word through humility, and nurture its growth within us through charity. Yet in our good works and our interaction with the physical world, we bear the children of that pregnancy. However, if we allow any praise, recognition, or condemnation over those works to go to our heads, the soul again becomes puffed up with pride and a lack of charity.

iv. The Presentation

In the first three Mysteries, we encountered the concept of the Holy Pregnancy and how it is nurtured and bears fruit. However, the virtues associated with these Mysteries pertain mostly to us within ourselves. But in the next several Mysteries, we will see the development of spiritual fruits which pertain to our relationship to ourselves and to God. In the Fourth Joyous Mystery, for example, the spiritual fruit is obedience to divine Law. Through humility and charity, we have come to the point of realizing that we need not be obsessed with our wealth, our status, or other things (we should care, yes, but not to where it dictates everything else in our lives!). Having come thus far and nurtured the first seeds of our pregnancy, we find that in order to continue nurturing it, we must gain and maintain a connection to Divinity, and that connection is best maintained through obedience to the laws which God has given us. We do not come to this realization out of guilt or fear anymore, as so many of us were taught in childhood, but instead we come to it out of knowledge and love. All true Catholics are raised on a Catechism that starts out by telling us that we were created to "know Him, to love Him, and to serve Him," and at this stage in our spiritual development, we begin to become aware of exactly what that means.

v. The Finding in the Temple

We were created "To know Him, to love Him, and to serve Him." Let us pause and think of what that means. To Mary and Joseph, as they were seeking her Son in the Jerusalem, they were only thinking that they had lost their Precious Boy and must find Him at all costs! This brings us to the Fifth Joyous Mystery, in which we are told the spiritual fruit is that of true conversion, or of turning ever "to Christ-ward." For us, it means that just obeying divine Law is not enough to form and nurture a connection with Divinity, but that we must also know and love that which we serve and obey, and we must endeavor never to lose sight of Him. In the process of spiritual development, it has been said that the process never stands still, but is always moving either forward or back. Our desire is to continue forward, and to continue forward in the hope of being with Christ and of nurturing our own spiritual pregnancy by His Word, then we must always endeavor to keep our eyes on Christ, and to always turn Christ-ward for help and strength in conquering the temptations that assails us here below.

2) The Sorrowful Mysteries
vi. The Agony in the Garden

In the progression of the Five Joyous Mysteries, we become acquainted with the soul's experience of the Illuminative Life, in which the soul is first made aware of the presence of a power greater than itself, and it is moved to grow in some sort of unity with that power, acquiring the necessary skills and virtues as it progresses. Yet in the process of the Sorrowful Mysteries, we embark through that part of spiritual development known as the Purgative Life, and the mood becomes somewhat darker. For instead of gathering new skills and virtues, we find existing virtues being put to the test, while old vices are being stripped away. In the First Sorrowful Mystery, we meet Jesus on the night before His death, agonizing and questioning the necessity of His impending crucifixion. Yet for all His agonizing, the ultimate answer is "Not my will, but Thy will be done." This builds upon the obedience to Divine Law described n the Fourth Joyful Mystery, where by humility, charity (love), and conversion, this obedience is transformed into a commitment and submission to Divine Will. Before we can truly be filled with Divine Power, we must gain self-control, and then subordinate ourselves to the power we wish to channel through us. This is not a theme unique to Catholicism, but it is in Catholicism that it achieves this level of expression.

vii. The Scourging at the Pillar

As the Agony in the Garden built upon and extended the spiritual fruit of the Fourth Joyous Mystery, so does the Scourging build upon the spiritual fruits of the Nativity. For as in the Nativity we learned the virtue of being indifferent to the physical world and its circumstances, it is here, in the Second Sorrowful Mystery, that the soul undergoes the process of being stripped of the desire for worldly or fleshly things. The traditional description of the spiritual fruit of this Mystery is "mortification of the flesh," and by this we could consider it to mean bringing our lower will under control, so that we no longer unduly desire the things of the world. As stated before, this indifference to the world – in fact, "detachment" might be a better word – is necessary so that we do not become indifferent to or detached from the things of the spirit, thus it is here that the lessons of the Nativity are even more firmly impressed upon the soul, that its pregnancy with the Word may become an even more pure product and bear an even more pure fruit than it did previously.

viii. The Crowning with Thorns

At this point, we find ourselves halfway through the Rosary, and we also find ourselves staring back upon the lessons of its first Mystery. Traditionally, we are told that Jesus underwent the crowning with thorns and the mockery of the soldiers in expiation for our sins of thought and pride, and the spiritual fruit of this Mystery is that we may transcend above those sins. Thus I would call it a purging of pride, which thus reinforces the soul's humility, which in turn reinforces all the other virtues and purgations which the soul has undergone thus far. Another fruit of this mystery ties it into the Mystery which has come before it, in that it is an effort to gain control over one's thoughts and emotions. Thus by control we find that the lower (physical) will is made subordinate to the higher (mental) will, while by the purgation of pride and the subsequent reinforcement of humility, the higher will becomes subordinate to the Divine Will.

ix. The Carrying of the Cross

As the Sorrowful Mysteries progress, we see that each Mystery contains a culmination of those which have come before it, and this is driven home even more so in the Fourth Sorrowful Mystery. Older prayer books refer to this Mystery as signifying "perseverance" or "patience under crosses," and nothing could be more accurate. It is also a reinforcement of the Second Joyful Mystery, because we know all too well that charity is something preached all too often, until it suddenly becomes inconvenient for those preaching to act on it. This Mystery teaches us that the soul must be perseverant in all its works, in all its virtues, in all its strivings for perfection, and must persevere in celebration or in persecution, in good times or bad. This Mystery also takes on a separate meaning, too, in the sense that during the Rosary we are not only Christ, but we are also Mary observing the life of Christ unfolding before us. As Mary, who sees her son buffeted, persecuted, and ultimately slain, so too does the soul see the child of its

Holy Pregnancy being ridiculed, derided, and trod underfoot by the cruel and less spiritual people around it. Yet the soul must continue its work if it is to advance to a state of perfection, and this period is a test which is intended to show whether the soul is ready to shoulder up its cross and continue with the work, or if it needs to re-learn some of its previous lessons before it is truly able to carry on with its journey.

x. The Crucifixion

In the Fifth Sorrowful Mystery, we now witness the climax to all the Mysteries which have come before it, and the gateway to all those which will come after it. For here the soul has learned its lessons and persevered in the work of perfection, but in its submission to God and pursuit of the spirit, at some point the soul must die to the world. It must die to the world so that it may transcend the world. It must die to the world so that it may forgive the offenses, real or perceived, which have been heaped upon it by the world. As the soul has gained virtues and had the corresponding vices purged, so must the soul eventually die to those vices, that it may transcend them. This is what St. John of the Cross called "The Dark Night of the Soul," and the defining point in the soul's journey. This is also a reinforcement of the Fifth Joyous Mystery, for the ultimate way to turn to Christ-ward is to die with Christ, which is exactly what the soul must do at this point in its development. We die to all things which separate us from Divinity, so that we may make of ourselves a stronger channel whereby that Divinity may operate through us. Having become purged of those vices, of pride, of avarice, of lust, and of disobedience, we die to them, that we may emerge from the tomb in glory.

3) The Glorious Mysteries
xi. The Resurrection

We are told that the spiritual fruit of this Mystery is the strengthening of our faith, and this sets the tone for the Glorious Mysteries as a whole. From the youthful optimism that characterizes the beginning of the process represented by the Joyous Mysteries, and from the darker, more somber notes sounded by the soul's purgation in the Sorrowful, we now move on to the lighter, airier, and more sublime strains of the Glorious Mysteries, in which the Dark Night has passed, and the process now works its way to completion. In the Resurrection, we see the Word come back from the dead, and He is now immortal and impassible. From the standpoint of His Mother, we have seen the fruit of the Holy Pregnancy being ridiculed, mocked, beaten, and destroyed, and have seen that fruit come back indestructible. The soul now has passed through the furnace of probation and knows that its work has not been in vain, and as such its faith is quickly edified to the point of becoming concrete, absolute knowledge. This is also the completion of the Fifth Joyous and the Fifth Sorrowful Mysteries, because now the soul is turned to Christ-ward so strongly that it is unconscious and effortless at this point. The soul has conquered the Dark Night, and now the Bright Dawn shines through it and within it, illuminating all those with whom the soul comes into contact. The process of completion has now begun.

xii. The Ascension

Viri Galilaei, quid statis aspicientes in caelum? These are the words the men in white said to the Apostles immediately after Jesus Ascended into heaven, and I think that's a good place to start: *"O Men of Galilee, why do ye look up into heaven?"* We look up to heaven, because by meditating upon the Second Glorious Mystery, we seek to gain the fruit of "longing to be in heaven, our true home." This is where we have found the completion of the Third Joyful and Second Sorrowful Mysteries, in that the soul has now become detached from the things of the world and has gained control over physical desires and the lower will; the soul, in its conversion, now looks up to heaven. It is not oblivious of the world, nor does the soul seek to escape the world, nor does the soul hate the world; rather the soul has simply come to view its true home as being heaven, because the creature now longs to dwell in the same house as its Creator. Through this detachment and love, the power of Divinity flows through the soul even more so, and the soul is prepared for the next stage in its transformation.

xiii. The Descent of the Holy Ghost

In the Third Glorious Mystery, the soul's disposition is transformed. They say that the spiritual fruit of this Mystery is either "the fire of charity" or "the gifts of the Holy Ghost," and I would add that this is an extension and completion of the Second Joyful and Fourth Sorrowful Mysteries. I say this because where first charity had moved the soul to be a force for good on behalf other people in the Second Joyous Mystery, and had moved the soul to withstand persecution and persevere in the Fourth Sorrowful Mystery, so now the soul is filled with the greatest gifts and the rewards to come from that Love. This is because Charity is a two-way street; God loves us so much that He will not give us more than what we're ready to handle, and will definitely not give us something if we're not ready to use it responsibly. Yet it is now through humility, love, obedience, and perseverance that the soul has become ready and worthy of such an influx of divine power, so much so that the soul no longer seeks to hide away from the world (as the Apostles did in the Upper

Room), but instead goes out into the world in love and power, ready to share that power with the world and help heal its wrongs and ills, the way the Apostles did after the Holy Ghost came upon them and the Blessed Mother. Yet for us, in our own role walking in the Blessed Mother's shoes, we see that the Holy Pregnancy has come to fruition, and that the soul has become a channel of unlimited divine power and knowledge. Yet we should always do well to remember that without that fire of charity, all knowledge and all power are as sounding brass, and a tinkling cymbal.

xiv. The Assumption

The journey of the soul is now reaching completion, and the fruit of this Mystery is often described as "a happy death, the reward of a life well-lived." Such a happy death is the reward of obedience to Divine Law, as we have been taught ever since we were little children, and that obedience is not just a literal, blind, or fanatical obedience to the letter of the law, but is instead the co-operation of all the virtues and purgations the soul has received, and a faithfulness to the Law's spirit. The soul has this lived in obedience, in love, and in humility, and now the time has come to receive its reward. The soul's longing for heaven, combined with doing the right things to get it into heaven, have paid off, and now it is time for the soul to be received into the mansion which God has prepared for it. The race has been run, the finish line has been crossed, and the foundations laid in the Fourth Joyful and First Sorrowful Mysteries have now been perfected.

xv. The Coronation

"Receiving the crown that awaits us in heaven," that's always been the way they've described the spiritual fruit of this Mystery. Yet we should realize that at the first stage and the middle stage of the process – the First Joyous and Fifth Sorrowful Mysteries, respectively – the virtue emphasized has been that of humility. And here, just as the soul's humility enabled it to begin this journey and the purgation of pride enabled the soul to continue it, here does the perfection of humility allow the soul to complete and perfect it. Mary was never a proud woman, she was never widely known during her lifetime, and she was so obscure that almost nothing is known about her with any sort of accuracy. But in death, she became the most famous woman ever to walk the earth, and she likewise became the Queen of Heaven, crowned by her Son with a crown of twelve stars. At all stages, the soul is defined by its fruits, and the works that it produces; in this case we have it exemplified that the Holy Pregnancy is only as good (or as worthless) as the fruits that it produces in the soul of the impregnated. After death, we will all be known by our fruits, and during life, the same is equally true. However, here we see the reward we stand to receive, of which the Catechism of the Council of Trent says that "we become, as it were, gods." The soul has attained that state, the baby of the Holy Pregnancy has finally been fully delivered, and the reward has been conferred. Now the soul exists at the right hand of God, the creature at the right hand of the Creator, looking down upon the earth and watching, interceding on behalf of those others who are still in the process of making the journey.

These are the Fifteen Mysteries of the Most Holy Rosary, and the illustration which they paint of the spiritual life. There is a great deal of power in these Mysteries, more than most self-proclaimed Catholics will ever know or comprehend. And that's a sad thing, because the only reason that they will not comprehend is that they *choose* not to comprehend. But for those of us who desire to learn, these Mysteries also contain the complete pattern of spiritual development and unfoldment, and in order to learn more, in order to grow, we need only to be serious and to listen to what the Blessed Mother has to teach us.

THE FIVE KEYS AND SPIRITUALITY

Within the Rosary is illustrated the grand pattern and big picture for spiritual development, which is the reason why it has been the one of the most remarked-upon and popular devotions in the Church over the past 800 years. Yet spirituality can be described in other ways, and even from the Rosary we can discern that there are five keys: Knowledge, Faith, Piety, Obedience, and Perseverance.

They Keys are given in this order, and one must realize that we list knowledge before faith, for without knowing there is a God in whom to believe (or at least hearing there is a God in which to believe), how can you believe?

While faith follows knowledge, for with knowledge, one must believe.

Piety follows after faith, because to truly know and believe in God is to know and believe in goodness; and to know and believe in goodness is to love God.

After these three Keys, obedience to God is next, because Jesus hath said: If you love me, keep my commandments. Therefore, to love God is to obey Him.

And finally, the fifth Key, perseverance: to become perfect, we must persevere in the commandments of our Lord Jesus Christ, and we must be faithful members of His Church, for perseverance without end shall bring us to sanctification in God most high.

The Keys can be explained like the compass-points on a circle, beginning in the East with the inspiration ("in-breathing") of knowledge, while the soul travels through the faith, piety, and obedience in the South, West, and North, respectively, only to come to the East again by perseverance. The soul then perseveres through the four quarters of the circle again and again, and in each pass it gains a greater degree of proficiency in its understanding and application of each of the Keys, which in turn results in an ever increasing closeness to God and a side-effect of spiritual power. In fact, there are some sources which describe magic as being merely "the side-effect of a strong spirituality."

However, the Keys are not only part of a system of spiritual and magical development, since they have definite effects on how we interact with the "real world," too. A true understanding and application of the Keys must also include work to overcome any and all psychological or emotional imbalances, to overcome any vices and replace them with the opposite virtues, and must also be understood to include the way we treat our fellow man. For a magician to be a magician, some sort of all-inclusive[297] path of spirituality must be pursued, or else the magician himself is an empty shell, becoming as sounding brass and a tinkling cymbal.

It is with these words that I shall close this book, in the hope that the student will take up a sincere meditation of the material contained herein.

---

[297] By "all-inclusive," I mean it must include every aspect of how he lives his life.

APPENDIX A: Long Quotes from the Endnotes

These quotes were endnotes found in chapters One and Two of the original edition of this book. However, since they were too long to include as footnotes, I decided to move them to this Appendix. Their original endnote numbering has also been retained.

Chapter One:
8. *Malleus Maleficarum.* Part II, Quest. 2, Chap. 6, my emphasis; p. 180 in Fr. Montague Summers' translation:

> But to return to our point, when a work is done by virtue of the Christian religion, as when someone wishes to heal the sick by means of prayer and benediction and sacred words, which is the matter we are considering), such a person must observe seven conditions by which such benedictions are rendered lawful. And even if he uses adjurations, through the virtue of the Divine Name, and by the virtue of the works of Christ, His Birth, Passion and Precious Death, by which the devil was conquered and cast out; such benedictions and charms and exorcisms shall be called lawful, and they who practise them are exorcists or lawful enchanters. See S. Isidore, *Etym.* VIII, Enchanters are they whose art and skill lies in the use of words.*
>
> And the first of these conditions, as we learn from S. Thomas, is that there must be nothing in the words which hints at any expressed or tacit invocation of devils. If such were expressed, it would be obviously unlawful. If it were tacit, it might be considered in the light of intention, or in that of fact: in that of intention, when the operator has no care whether it is God or the devil who is helping him, so long as he attains his desired result; in that of fact, when a person has no natural aptitude for such work, but creates some artificial means. And of such not only must

physicians and astronomers be the judges, but especially Theologians. For in this way do necromancers work, making images and rings and stones by artificial means; which have no natural virtue to effect the results which they very often expect: therefore the devil must be concerned in their works.

Secondly, the benedictions or charms must contain no unknown names; for according to S. John Chrysostom such are to be regarded with fear, lest they should conceal some matter of superstition.

Thirdly, there must be nothing in the words that is untrue; for if there is, the effect of them cannot be from God, Who is not a witness to a lie. But some old women in their incantations use some such jingling doggerel as the following:

Blessed MARY went a-walking
Over Jordan river.
Stephen met her, and fell a-talking, etc.

Fourthly, there must be no vanities, or written characters beyond the sign of the Cross. Therefore the charms which soldiers are wont to carry are condemned.

Fifthly, no faith must be placed in the method of writing or reading or binding the charm about a person, or in any such vanity, which has nothing to do with the reverence of God, without which a charm is altogether superstitious.

Sixthly, in the citing and uttering of Divine words and of Holy Scripture attention must only be paid to the sacred words themselves and their meaning, and to the reverence of God; whether the effect be looked for from the Divine virtue, or from the relics of Saints, which are a secondary power, since their virtue springs originally from God.

Seventhly, the looked-for effect must be left to the Divine Will; for He knows whether it is best for a man to be healed or to be plagued, or to die. This condition was set down by S. Thomas.

So we may conclude that if none of these conditions be broken, the incantation will be lawful. And S. Thomas writes in this connexion on the last chapter of S. Mark: And these signs shall follow them that believe; in my name shall they cast out devils; they shall take up serpents. From this it is clear that, provided the above conditions are observed, it is lawful by means of sacred words to keep serpents away.

* Isodore, *Etymologiae*, VIII, 9, 15: «Incantatores dicti sunt, qui artem verbis peragunt.»

Chapter Two:
9. St. Augustine, *Contra Epistolam Parmeniani Lbri Tres*, ii, 29: At si forte illum militiae characterem in corpore suo non militans pavidus exhorruerit et ad clementiam imperatoris confugerit ac prece fusa et impetrata venia militare iam coeperit, numquid homine liberato atque correcto character ille repetitur ac non potius agnitus approbatur? An forte minus haerent sacramenta christiana quam corporalis haec nota...

"But if strong be the character on his body that the panicked [soldier], trembled, not performing his duty; and he flew to the Emperor's mercy and by fusive prayer and impetrated favor again started to take up military service, whether the mark be again repeated [re-impressed] upon the man now freed and corrected, or is not the mark more ably recognized and approved? And do the Christian sacraments adhere any less strongly than these bodily things?"

10. St. Augustine, *De Baptismo, contra Donatistas libri septem*, i, cap. 1: Sicut autem baptizatus, si ab unitate recesserit, sacramentum Baptismi non amittit; sic etiam ordinatus, si ab unitate recesserit, Sacramentum dandi

Baptismi non amittit. Nulli enim Sacramento iniuria facienda est: si discedit a malis, utrumque discedit; si permanet in malis, utrumque permanet. Sicut ergo acceptatur Baptismus, quem non potuit amittere qui ab unitate discesserat; sic acceptandus est Baptismus, quem dedit ille qui Sacramentum dandi cum discederet non amiserat. Nam sicut redeuntes, qui priusquam recederent baptizati sunt, non rebaptizantur: ita redeuntes, qui priusquam recederent ordinati sunt, non utique rursus ordinantur; sed aut administrant quod administrabant, si hoc Ecclesiae utilitas postulat; aut si non administrant, Sacramentum ordinationis suae tamen gerunt; et ideo eis manus inter laicos non imponitur.

"And as the baptized person, if he depart from the unity of the Church, does not thereby lose the sacrament of baptism, so also he who is ordained, if he depart from the unity of the Church, does not lose the sacrament of conferring baptism. For neither sacrament may be wronged. If a sacrament necessarily becomes void in the case of the wicked, both must become void; if it remain valid with the wicked, this must be so with both. If, therefore, the baptism be acknowledged which he could not lose who severed himself from the unity of the Church, that baptism must also be acknowledged which was administered by one who by his secession had not lost the sacrament of conferring baptism. For as those who return to the Church, if they had been baptized before their secession, are not rebaptized, so those who return, having been ordained before their secession, are certainly not ordained again; but either they again exercise their former ministry, if the interests of the Church require it, or if they do not exercise it, at any rate they retain the sacrament of their ordination; and hence it is, that when hands are laid on them, they are not ranked with the laity."

St. Thomas Aquinas, in his *Summa Theologica*, III, Q. 82, vii and viii, clearly states that a heretical, schismatic, excommunicate, or degraded priest retains the power to offer the Sacrifice of the Mass.

Treating of heretical, schismatic, and excommunicated priests, article vii: *Et quia consecratio Eucharistiae est actus consequens ordinis potestatem, illi qui sunt ab Ecclesia separati per haeresim aut schisma vel excommunicationem, possunt quidem consecrare Eucharistiam, quae ab eis consecrata verum corpus Christi et sanguinem continet, non tamen recte hoc faciunt, sed peccant facientes.*

"And since the consecration of the Eucharist is an act which follows the power of order, such persons as are separated from the Church by heresy, schism, or excommunication, can indeed consecrate the Eucharist, which on being consecrated by them contains Christ's true body and blood; but they act wrongly, and sin by doing so."

And about priests who have been degraded from the clerical state (i.e. laicization), article viii: *Respondeo dicendum quod potestas consecrandi Eucharistiam pertinet ad characterem sacerdotalis ordinis.* Character autem quilibet, quia cum quadam consecratione datur, indelebilis est, ut supra dictum est, sicut et quarumcumque rerum consecrationes perpetuae sunt, nec amitti nec reiterari possunt. Unde manifestum est quod potestas consecrandi non amittitur per degradationem. Dicit enim Augustinus, in II contra Parmen., utrumque, scilicet Baptismus et ordo, sacramentum est, *et quadam consecratione utrumque homini datur, et illud cum baptizatur, et illud cum ordinatur. Ideo non licet a Catholicis utrumque iterari. Et sic patet quod sacerdos degradatus potest conficere hoc sacramentum.*

"I answer that, The power of consecrating the Eucharist belongs to the character of the priestly order. But every character is indelible, because it is given with a kind of consecration, as was said above, just as the consecrations of all other things are perpetual, and cannot be lost or repeated. Hence it is clear that the power of consecrating is not lost by degradation. For, again, Augustine says (Contra Parmen. ii): 'Both are sacraments,' namely Baptism and order, 'and both are given to a man with a kind of consecration; the former, when he is baptized; the latter when he is ordained; and therefore it is not lawful for Catholics to repeat either of them.' And thus it is evident that the degraded priest can perform this sacrament."

And finally, the Council of Trent defined the sacramental character as a matter of divine and catholic faith, Session XXIII, Canon 4: Si quis dixerit, per sacram ordinationem non dari Spiritum sanctum, ac proinde frustra episcopos dicere: Accipe Spiritum Sanctum; aut per eam non imprimi characterem; vel eum, qui sacerdos semel fuit, laicum rursus fieri posse, anathema sit.

"If any one saith, that, by sacred ordination, the Holy Ghost is not given; and that vainly therefore do the bishops say, Receive ye the Holy Ghost; or, that a character is not imprinted by that ordination; or, that he who has once been a priest, can again become a layman; let him be anathema."

In more recent times, the 1917 Code of Canon Law mentions this while speaking on the penalty of degradation from the clerical state. Canon 211 begins with: Etsi sacra ordinatio, semel valide recepta, nunquam irrita fiat…

"Although sacred ordination, once validly received, never becomes invalid…"

And the 1983 Code of Canon Law uses identical language in Canon 290, which discusses the same subject. Later, in Canon 1338, s. 2, the same Code even goes a little further in explaining: Potestatis ordinis privatio dari nequit, sed tantum prohibitio eam vel aliquos ejus actus exercendi;

"The deprivation of the power of orders cannot be given, but only the prohibition of exercising it or some acts of it." (litteral translation)

The official English translation gives this as: "There is no such penalty as deprivation of the power of orders, but only the prohibition against exercising it or some acts of orders."

Appendix B: Invoking and Banishing Pentagrams

These are the forms I use when drawing invoking and banishing pentagrams for each element. The foundational idea is "counterclockwise toward the element to invoke, clockwise away from the element to banish."

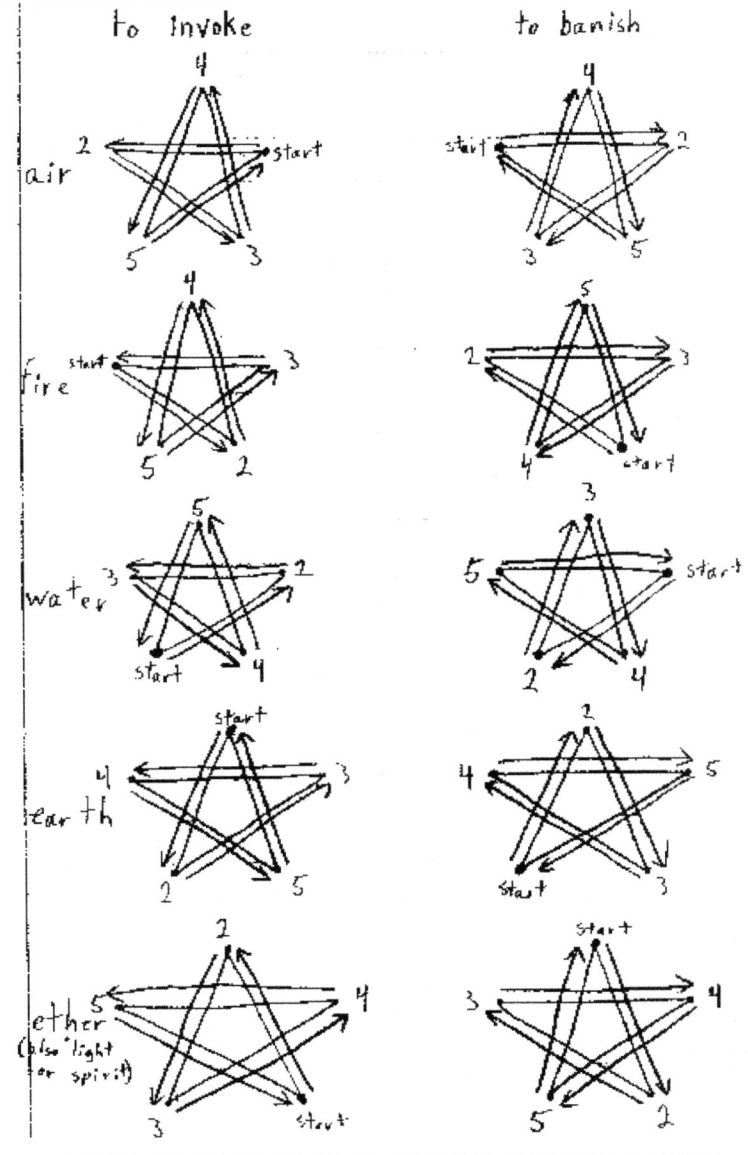

to Invoke   to banish

air

fire

water

earth

ether (also light or spirit)

ALPHABETICAL INDEX

Altar: 61, 63, 72, 75, 78, 79, 124, 135-137, 139, 142, 178, 216, 217

Angels (also Archangels): 30, 97, 101, 110, 135, 153, 156, 158-177, 191, 195, 200, 205, 208, 228, 230, 231, 234

Aquinas, St. Thomas: 13, 22, 162, 164, 167, 183, 207, 256

Augustine, St. Aurelius: 7, 21, 23, 53, 57, 65, 183, 201, 254, 257

Aurum Solis: 215

Avila, St. Teresa of: 7, 107

Baptism: 30, 35-37, 39-53, 55-60, 65, 70, 71, 72, 78, 82, 88, 91, 97, 99, 129, 132, 145, 146, 254-257

Bible: 17, 168

Bishop: 33, 37, 48-50, 55, 62, 67, 68, 91, 103, 151, 180, 185, 188, 197, 199, 204, 224, 257

Blessing: 30, 77, 90-100, 103, 104, 110, 118, 124, 132, 133, 136-141, 185, 217, 221

Candle(s): 109, 124, 133, 139, 141-143, 145, 150-153, 174, 178, 180, 182, 185

Cherubim: 161, 162, 164, 171, 172

Circumambulation: 214-216, 218

- Alphabetical Index -

Color(s): 134, 142-150, 165, 178, 180, 215

Communion: 31, 49, 50, 52, 56, 73, 80, 85, 88, 109, 116, 119, 155, 157, 179, 195, 204, 226

Confirmation: 35, 41-53, 57, 58, 59, 60, 64, 70, 71, 72, 78, 88, 145

Crowley, Aliester: 26

Dominions (Angelic Order): 161, 162, 165, 166, 172

Energy: 28, 51, 59, 70, 87, 96, 100, 103, 117, 118, 145, 148, 214, 216, 223

Eucharist: 41, 61, 66, 71-79, 88, 98, 135, 256, 257

Exorcism: 25, 80, 90, 91, 97-103, 113, 125, 146, 252

Extreme Unction: 71, 72, 88, 146

Gnostic(ism), also Neognostic(ism): 104

Golden Dawn: 216, 228

Grace (Sanctifying or Actual): 33, 34, 35, 38, 39, 46, 51, 52, 55, 56, 59, 60, 63, 70, 71, 76, 80, 90, 109, 129, 130, 141, 142, 151, 152, 189

Hesychasm: 223

Holy Orders: 35, 52-70, 71, 72, 103

Initiation: 34, 35, 36, 39, 40, 41, 42, 50, 59, 61, 63, 64, 70, 71, 78, 79, 86, 87, 88, 90

Kabbalah: 24, 221, 222, 231

Laity: 34, 81, 86, 91, 98, 103, 255

Lay (layman or layperson): 66, 98, 104, 120, 200, 218, 257

Leo XIII: 67, 97, 98, 100, 208

Levi, Eliphas: 26, 214

Malleus Maleficarum: 25, 27, 91, 252

Marriage (Matrimony): 64, 71, 72, 88, 145, 186, 196, 198, 201

Mass: 13, 14, 22, 31, 34, 55, 72, 79, 80, 109, 112, 116, 117, 118, 123, 136, 145, 147, 159, 160, 173, 177, 180, 216, 218, 256

Meditation: 7, 106, 108, 110, 114, 115, 122, 123, 174, 178, 179, 223-227, 233, 251

Mensa: 124, 133-139, 141, 150, 151, 152, 174, 178, 215

Mirandola, Pico: 24

Missal: 13, 14, 112, 144, 159, 173, 204, 216

Ordination (see also Holy Orders): 42, 52, 63, 65, 68, 145, 255, 257

Pagan(ism), also Neopagan(ism): 17, 18, 19, 62, 86, 151, 154, 158, 183, 186, 188, 198, 199, 201, 202, 207, 214, 216

- Alphabetical Index -

Penance: 71, 72, 80-85, 88, 98, 123, 146, 147, 202

Pentagram: 8, 209-214, 227-231, 259

Powers (Angelic Order): 161, 162, 166, 171, 172

Prayer: 24, 29, 74, 79, 92, 93, 94, 96, 98, 99, 100, 103, 105, 106-120, 121, 122, 123, 132, 135, 142, 144, 152, 157, 158, 160, 169, 173, 174, 175, 176, 177, 181, 183, 202, 203, 207, 216, 217, 223, 224, 233, 242, 252, 254

Priest(hood): 15, 26, 31, 33, 45, 48, 49, 61, 62, 64, 66, 80, 90, 91, 92, 103, 104, 116, 118, 120, 151, 160, 177, 181, 195, 197, 204, 216-220, 256, 257

Principalities (Angelic Order): 161, 162, 167, 171, 172

Protestant(ism): 13, 37, 43, 50, 76, 81, 86, 154, 155, 158, 193, 221

Ritual: 7, 30, 92, 93, 94, 96, 97, 99, 102, 103, 114, 115, 116, 117, 119, 121, 123, 124, 133, 136, 139, 142, 147, 173, 174, 185, 209, 215, 227, 231

Saint(s): 14, 34, 85, 98, 109, 110, 112, 136, 142, 143, 146, 150, 151, 154-159, 177-208, 213, 220, 223, 253

Seraphim (Angelic Order): 161, 162, 164, 171, 172

Thrones (Angelic Order): 161, 162, 164, 165, 171, 172

Trent (Council of): 6, 12, 50, 58, 63, 66, 77, 249, 257

Vatican II: 5, 12, 13, 41, 42, 58, 61, 62, 63, 71, 103, 135

Virtues (Angelic Order): 161, 162, 166, 171, 172, 176, 177

Witch(craft): 16, 20, 25, 26